GW01459318

A CONSTANT ALIEN

A CONSTANT ALIEN

Catherine Schell

First published in 2016 by Fantom Films
fantomfilms.co.uk

ISBN 978-1-78196-161-2

A catalogue record for this book is available from the British Library.

Editor: Paul W.T. Ballard

Typeset by Xanna Eve Chown
Cover design by Will Brooks

Printed and bound in the UK by CPI Group (UK) Ltd
Croydon, CR0 4YY

CONTENTS

FOREWORD
by Catherine Schell

Some time ago I received a letter from a certain William Gallagher who professed an admiration for the series, *Space: 1999* and the character I portrayed, Maya, the resident alien. It was not the usual fan letter and did not ask for a signed photograph. He was an acquaintance of some friends of ours – the respected novel, TV and play writer Alan Plater, and his wife Shirley Rubenstein. Dear Alan had passed away and William was in contact with Shirley to research a book which was planned on the making of Alan's popular TV series, *The Beiderbecke Affair*.

During their many meetings, my name was mentioned. Shirley admitted to having a book I had written with the title, *When God Was Out to Lunch*, about my husband, Bill, and my French adventure, for safekeeping on her computer. William was interested in reading it.

I rang the number given in his letter and we spoke. He told me he had enjoyed what I had written and was considering finding a way to having it published, except, he thought, there was not enough about my personal life and career. He was convinced the book would sell better if it spoke more of my entire life and mentioned the films and series I was known for.

I answered, 'That book is about a different part of my life… a new, post-glamour adventure. If you want to read about my history, I'll write an autobiography.'

There was a pause on the other end of the line.

'Okay, why not? Good idea,' he said.

And so, that is how I came to write the story of my life and, even though William had nothing to do with the actual publication, I am very grateful to him for his encouragement.

Until my first concrete memories, I have had to rely on my parents' or older brothers' description of events. I write them as they were told to me. My mother could be prone to exaggeration. If she related a story that my father also witnessed and was present during the telling, he would discreetly correct some of the hyperbole which spiced up her narration. Therefore, I cannot swear to the stark nakedness of the gentleman in Manhattan who opened the door to my mother when she arrived on his threshold in order to retrieve a parakeet.

I was fortunate to have a life which took me to varying countries and let me experience diverse cultures. I had become accustomed to being an alien in my surroundings from a very young age. Ironically, even though I had become an actress, I never sought to stand out from a crowd but donned, instead, a chameleon-like attitude, which helped in the metamorphosis to become as near a native of the new world I was living in.

Did that make me perfect casting as Maya in the second series of *Space: 1999*? I don't think so. In the first series, I appeared as a robot. The business was not aware of my multicultural past. They just knew I was foreign.

William Gallagher advised me to write about my career; to mention the screen credits I would be recognized for.

'I can't do that,' I told him. 'First of all, I've forgotten most of them and, secondly, writing, "and then I did this film and then I did that television" would bore me to tears, not to mention the reader.'

Therefore, I mention certain highlights and, even then, only if there was an interesting story attached to it. But if I'd known when making *Space* that it would attract such a faithful following, I'd have kept a diary and recorded what happened on the set while filming it episode by episode. As it is, I write about those particular occurrences during the making of the series which affected me emotionally and which I still think about today.

1976, the year we filmed *Space*, was one year in my life for which I was very grateful. In that summer I had my 32nd birthday. There were years before and years after whose events were worthy of sharing with a readership. After all, even the circumstances of my birth were precarious and unusual.

A CONSTANT ALIEN

Catherine Schell

CHAPTER I

July 17th, 1944. It was a few minutes before noon. The war from the air had begun. Sirens were howling but this did not hinder my father from drinking a cocktail in his gentleman's club in the centre of Budapest, not far from the Catholic clinic where my mother was screaming in agony and cursing in the foulest language her vocabulary could afford. She was in labour and, although it was her third time round, she was still not prepared for the pain. The good nuns tried to keep her quiet, reminding her that this was not the way a countess from a very noble Hungarian family should behave. The cursing continued becoming even more blue.

My father, anxious for the events happening in obstetrics down the road, was given a message by the club's butler. He was to hurry to the clinic. The birth was imminent. He downed his drink and rushed out into the street. It was exactly noon now. For days, the Americans had begun bombing Budapest as the clocks struck twelve. The British dropped their lethal loads at night. Hungary was being punished for choosing the wrong side to fight on.

He ducked into doorways as he ran, avoiding the falling debris from shattering windows and broken masonry caused by explosions nearby. The journey took about five minutes. Upon arriving at the clinic the last of this formation of grumbling airplanes was flying overhead, on their way to the edge of the city and beyond.

I had arrived while the bombing was taking place. Without ceremony, my mother was ordered to get up and go down the stairs into the basement that was being used as a bomb shelter. With a blanket around her shoulders and bare feet she staggered down the stone steps. I had been taken from her and wrapped in a cloth before she could even glance at me. Another birth had taken place at the same time. That child, too, had been taken from its mother and swathed in a similar cloth.

My father was directed into the makeshift shelter where, to his surprise, he found my mother childless. When the silence returned outside a sister appeared and bade my mother to follow her. On the way she spoke to another woman who then also joined them. They were led to a table in a far corner of the basement. Underneath it was a basket. The sister picked it up and gently placed it on the table. The contents were completely covered in cloth and there was a slight squirming and little whimpers emitting from under the cover. For a bizarre moment, my mother thought the sister was going to show her some puppies. Slowly she lifted the cloth to reveal two crumpled little faces. Neither of the mothers had ever seen their child. Due to the panic of the bombing, the clinic had had no time to tag their wrists. Now the mothers were expected to choose which one was theirs. One child was quite dark, almost gypsy looking. The other had beet red hair curling in wisps to her shoulders. Both had blue eyes. My mother had auburn hair and blue eyes. The other woman was darker in complexion and had black eyes. They made the most logical choice. But it was only after the beet red hair fell out and was replaced by platinum blonde that my mother was truly convinced she had picked the correct baby. I looked too much like my two brothers before me for there to have been a mistake.

Our homecoming was to a cellar in the basement of the Art Nouveau apartment block where my parents lived. It was situated in Petöfi Utca. In the hierarchy of Budapest's districts it compared to London's Mayfair. The move underground was due to the bombing. Carpets and some furniture were cannibalized from the flat above to make the space as comfortable as possible. The living-in maid also sheltered with us there. There may have been a war on but aristocratic families stuck to their customs and a maid was obligatory. Cooking, washing, etc. were done upstairs between the air raids.

The bombings became more frequent which increased the time we spent in this cellar, to the point that after six months and with pneumonia, I was turning blue. The maid, with whom my mother did not have the best of relationships, insisted I needed fresh air, a good dose of oxygen. Mommy was terrified to leave the safety of the cellar. She had, after all, two other children, my brothers Paul (age four) and Peter (age three) to cope with. My father was absent making his way to the Russian front. The only way of saving my life, argued the maid, was to place me on the roof of the building.

'Are you mad?' my mother screamed. 'What about the bombs?'

'She will die anyway if she stays here. Give her to me. At least there is a chance outside.'

They found a box, wrapped me up and placed me in it. This brave woman whose name Mommy could not remember when she, many years later, related the story to me, carried the box, opened the roof door and placed it in such a way it could not slide over the edge. We never saw the woman again. She simply disappeared. A few hours later Mommy steeled herself to climb the stairs to the roof. She found me safe, no longer blue. Even the fever seemed to have abated. I have a nameless maid to thank for my deliverance and I do so profoundly.

Back to the cellar. Some time later, a rocking chair had been added to the furnishings and rolling back and forth in it was my father, dressed as an old woman. He wore a babushka scarf over a borrowed wig, an oversized colourful blouse stuffed with material to form hanging bosoms and a long peasant skirt. Thick socks and woolly slippers finished off the costume. Daddy was hiding from the Gestapo. He had deserted his post.

Due to a treacherous decision made by a certain General Herth who was a German sympathizer in the Hungarian General Staff, and without the sanction of the elected Government and totally against the wishes of the Minister President at that time, Count Paul Teleki, the Hungarians opened their borders to the Germans allowing them to march through the country in order to attack Yugoslavia. Teleki had signed a non-aggression pact and could not assent to co-operate with the Nazi's intentions of an invasion of that country. As an anglophile and realizing the impossibility, due to its geography, of Hungary ever joining on the side of the allies, Paul Teleki fought for a non-belligerent status, harbouring an enduring desire to keep Hungary non-aligned. This act of treason, as he called it, and his responsibility as the head of his Government, shamed him to despair. He committed, in the early hours of the morning, the ultimate act to preserve Hungary's honour, suicide. Winston Churchill lamented his death by announcing in Parliament that England had lost a valued friend. Even the Vatican pardoned his suicide and allowed him a Catholic burial. My mother was born into this branch of the Teleki family and walked proudly near the front of his funeral cortège. She had called him uncle.

When the Hungarians chose the wrong side to fight on, Daddy was already in his forties. At the beginning, he was deemed too old to be of use to the army but as time elapsed and more cannon fodder was required, he was eventually drafted, made a lieutenant and given a disparate assortment of men who formed his platoon. The war was nearing its end. German armies were losing ground. Prisons were being emptied and able-bodied men of all ages, amongst them, intellectuals, who had opposed the Nazis, even Jews awaiting deportation were sent to him to be taken to the Russian lines. He was ordered to give them half rations, just enough to get them there and, although, it was winter, on no account were they to sleep under a roof. Food and shelter were reserved for the regular army. He was also ordered not to bring them back.

My father was not a cruel man. When he could, and for the good of his platoon, he ignored those orders. One night, he requisitioned a farmer's barn so that his men could finally sleep comfortably on piles of hay. To heat water and benefit from a warm glow, they made a fire in the interior. Unfortunately, as they were all exhausted, including him, they fell asleep and the unguarded fire crept into the hay. The barn burnt down killing two of his men. He still felt guilt for this accident when he told me the story many years later.

It was just as well he'd been commanded to engage against the Russians. Had it been the western allies, he couldn't have brought himself to point a gun against them. Daddy had been a diplomat before the war, serving in Paris, London and Washington DC, making close friendships in all of those capitals. As it was, nearing the battlefront, he laid down his weapon and spoke to his men, many of whom had become companions. He told them he was deserting, returning to Budapest and anyone who wanted could accompany him. Others, if they so wished, could surrender to the Russians and hope for leniency from them. Those who went across the line were never heard from again. It was some of those who made their way back with him who would later help us to escape.

He took refuge in the cellar and when the Gestapo arrived, asking my mother if she had heard from him, if she knew where he was, she replied tearfully that she had no idea. When they pointed to the old woman in the corner, rocking slowly back and forth, Mommy told them it was the old nurse who helped with the children. She played her part magnificently, as did my father.

I was never told how long my father was dressed in his 'granny' outfit. In June 1945 the war was officially over. It was safe again to live in the flat above. But not very safe in the streets below. The thud on pavements of Russian army boots brought fear into the hearts of Budapest's people.

Once again, able-bodied men were being gathered at gunpoint and stuffed into cattle cars. What the Nazis had done to the Jews, the Russians were doing to the vanquished. Their destination was labour camps, salt, coal or uranium mines in the motherland.

Towards the end of the war, in February 1945, a conference was held in the Crimean resort of Yalta on the Black Sea. Stalin, Churchill and a weakened Roosevelt, due to his terminal stage of what was thought to be Poliomyelitis, attended. The meeting was to determine post-war strategy and political spheres of influence. Each of the participants had a personal agenda. Churchill demanded free and democratic elections in post-war Eastern and Central Europe. Roosevelt wanted Russia to take part with its troops in the Pacific war against Japan and to participate in the United Nations. Stalin demanded a political sphere of influence in what would become Russian satellite states: Poland, Czechoslovakia, Hungary, Romania, Bulgaria, Albania and Yugoslavia. Also, as reparation for war damage caused by the enemy he wanted the right to forced labour in those countries. Roosevelt, believing Stalin's promises for help against Japan and free elections gave in to his demands.

My father was one of those unfortunates who suffered the consequence of this decision. He had left the apartment to try to find food for us when he was rounded up and taken to the station. A locomotive pulling several wagons was waiting. A crowd of men were being pushed from the platform into the darkness of their interiors. When they were packed so tightly they could hardly breathe, the heavy sliding doors were brutally shut and thus the journey towards Russia began. After several hours the train bumped to a stop. The doors were opened and some who had been pressed against them tumbled down to the platform. In Daddy's wagon, many had fainted from exhaustion or lack of air. They were helped by their comrades back on their feet and gently lowered to the floor outside. The other wagons had also emptied and now 200 men were standing with confused and dazed expressions. They had arrived on the frontier of Ukraine. Two very young soldiers with rifles began giving orders in Russian. They seemed to intimate that the men must walk towards what was another train in the distance. Perhaps the wheel gauge of the rolling stock was different. All that was clear was they were being made to board the other train. As they moved forward, my father had a look around him. He was amazed to discover that there were only these two baby soldiers herding them and began to whisper to his neighbours making them aware of this fact. The word went up and down the body of men. Daddy stopped and with a few others, turned and walked in the opposite direction. He gathered more men as he moved against the flow until they made a considerable number. The boy soldiers shouted frantically for them to stop. Some men, too frightened to risk their chances, remained behind. My father had reckoned they would not have enough ammunition to kill everyone. On the other hand, he would rather have had a bullet in his back than to die a tortured death in a labour camp. As it was, the soldiers didn't fire a single shot. Perhaps, as Russian supplies were exhausted, their rifles were empty. In the future, I would ask why I had never met my godfather. I was told he was one of those unfortunates who disappeared during these round-ups.

When he did not come home, my mother was frantic with fear. She had no way of knowing whether he was alive or dead or, even, why he was missing. But such were the times and Budapest's people learned to cope with this insecurity.

Life was not exactly safe for women, either. Soldiers ruled the streets, parks and alleyways. Many women who walked alone were raped. Yet, immediately after the war, amongst the destruction of the city, food had to be found. There were families starving. Women roamed the streets in search of whatever could appease their children's hunger pains. Not a lot of cats or rats survived the war, according to my mother. Some food entered the city from the countryside. Farmer's wagons drawn by horses and carrying their vegetable produce was quickly surrounded. On occasion, Mommy did manage to come home with some potatoes, peppers or carrots for supper. On one sortie, she pulled a little cart (God knows where she found it). My brother, Paul, was walking beside her. Peter was inside the little wagon holding me. A military lorry appeared from the opposite direction. As it passed, she saw the dreaded red star on its door and noticed soldiers peering out from the back. She hurried on but the lorry stopped behind her and she could hear the clatter of boots hitting the street as a soldier jumped down and then even worse, the sound of running feet coming closer to her. Terrified she grabbed Paul's hand and speeded up, pulling the cart as fast as she could. To her horror, the soldier caught up with us. He put a hand on her shoulder, forcing her to turn round. She looked into a young, broad Slavic face with high cheekbones and bright blue eyes. His other hand was holding a loaf of warm bread. Giving it to her, he gestured towards us, the children, and mimed putting morsels of the bread into his mouth. She almost swooned from the wonderful smell of this freshly baked loaf. He turned and ran back to the waiting lorry. His mates helped him into the back and it continued on its way. Not every Russian soldier was a rapist.

During 1946 life became easier. Food was now generally available. Foreign embassies were reopening. Russian troops were no longer so much in evidence. Our daily existence assumed an aspect of normality. Mommy even found another maid. Her name was Mitzi. She was an Austrian in her forties who had spent the war in Budapest and she spoke Hungarian with a gypsy accent, which I would later imitate when I began to talk. It was rumoured that she had followed a lover many years previously to Hungary. He had then left her.

She was not a beauty by any means but there was attractive warmth to her and her innate generosity was well complemented by a corpulent physique. Mitzi was not only a maid but also our nurse. In this respect, we children had a typical aristocratic upbringing. My mother admitted that she didn't really like the company of small children very much, preferring to give the tasks of changing nappies, cooking kiddy food, bathing and tucking us in at night to someone who seemed to enjoy it. She couldn't be blamed. That was how she had spent her early childhood and we learn from our parents. We did get a kiss goodnight, though, before we were whisked away to our respective beds. When I was able to stand on my own feet without falling over, my training for the obligatory post kiss curtsey began which, when learned, I performed to Mommy's boundless amusement.

Lacking tactile affection from my mother made Mitzi even more important to me. She was large in every way and smothered us with hugs and kisses. In her luxurious embrace, with her amply padded arms, I received all the security I needed.

There is a memory I carry with me still. I am in a room. A curtain is drawn against a window. Just enough daylight steals into the room to keep it from darkness. There is noise coming from the other side of the door. Adult's voices. I can't understand but feel that something important is being discussed. I raise myself from the mattress with the help of the bars that surround my cot. The door opens and Mitzi enters. She lifts me up and holds me in the crook of her arm. I cuddle comfortably against the pillows of her soft bosom. My arms encircle her neck. She smells of milk. I am carried into the living room. My parents and another man are standing, forming a semi-circle around a large black dog. Mitzi brings me to them. From the height of my perch on her bent elbow I look down on the creature. The creature looks up at me and begins to bark. I am not afraid. I know in Mitzi's arms nothing bad can happen to me. The adults begin to speak in concerned voices. I don't recognize the words they are using but I feel I am the centre of attention. Something is expected of me. So, I begin to cry. The dog barks louder and I cry louder, yet feeling not in the least threatened. I am acting the role of what is expected of me. The voices become worried. Mitzi carries me back to my cot with soothing murmurs. The recollection ends there.

I think I was 20 when I mentioned this memory to my father. He could hardly believe it and told me I was barely two years old when this incident happened. He remembered it well. He and Mommy had agreed to look after a friend's black Labrador for a few weeks but on the proviso that the dog and the children got along.

'So, did you accept the dog?' I asked.

'Yes, of course,' he answered.

'Even though I cried.'

'We knew you'd get over it. He was a very nice dog.'

I have no idea how we survived financially during the mid-Forties. My father's family estate, Nagyida, was no longer a haven for the Schell von Bauschlotts. It had been requisitioned by the Slovakian Communist authorities after the war and thus, was not earning any income for us. The property had been a gift by the empress Maria Theresa in the 18th century, who, seeing her vast Austro-Hungarian empire underpopulated, invited hard-working Germans from the region of Schwaben to take up residency. In my family's case, they settled in Slovakia, which was a part of Hungary then. It was lost to the Hungarians after the First World War when Czechoslovakia was created as a unified country by the treaty of Versailles. My mother's family chateau on the banks of the Danube had long been lost. Her father had briefly flirted with a career in banking, using his wife's substantial fortune. He had terrible timing. The venture began shortly before 1929. By 1930 everything was lost and the family chateau was swallowed up in debts. But the banks that claimed the property in lieu of part payment continued to allow the family to live there. Well this was Hungary and you just didn't throw a Teleki on to the street.

At some point, though, my mother worked as a secretary to a journalist called James McCargar. It was to be a fortuitous association. But she was a strange choice, as Mommy had never learned to type, nor take shorthand dictation. She would have translated but her English was poor at that time. I suppose with hindsight, Jimmy, as he was known to my parents, needed someone from their society to get nearer to the people he was sent to Budapest to help.

One of the results of the Yalta Conference between Stalin, Roosevelt and Churchill was the surrender of Eastern Europe to a Soviet sphere of influence. Stalin had promised free elections in all of the countries but when in 1947, all opposition parties to the Communists were disbanded, the writing was on the wall. Journalism was Jimmy's cover. When he arrived in 1946, he was actually chief of the political section of the American legation. Under State Department authorization and orders, he established an escape network in Soviet occupied territories and saved many Democratic Hungarians and Romanian political leaders as well as pro-Western figures and their families in danger of arrest, deportation or death. At some point he would have shared his real motives with my parents.

After sham elections in 1948, the Hungarian government officially became Communist. In appreciation of having saved their lives, my father was warned by some of those who walked back with him to Budapest when he deserted that our family was a target for punishment by the new authorities. Our crime was that we were aristocrats. The children would likely be taken away and brought up in Communist orphanages, and he and his wife could face prison or forced labour. These men, having been dissenters during the old regime were now joining the new political system. They could not help us in the future. Having been warned, Daddy acted accordingly. Undoubtedly with Jimmy's help he began planning our escape.

My mother had to be kept ignorant of his intentions. He was terrified she'd speak to her relatives and friends and the information could reach the wrong ears. She was unaware of the political undercurrents. Cocktail parties and receptions at western embassies were still on the social agenda. Hungary may have gone Communist but it had not yet stopped partying.

It was known that barbed wire was already being stretched across the border between Austria and Hungary to fence in the population. But it had not yet encompassed the entire perimeter. There were still some gaps and it would be through these that the escape had to take place. Who knew where they were? Jimmy's network knew.

We had to flee into Austria. It was the only country on Hungary's borders, which was not exclusively under Soviet control. Having been designated a buffer state between east and west at Yalta, the four allies each occupied their respective zones. After these occupations will have ended and if ever another menacingly right wing government were elected, Russian armies could be sanctioned to invade to protect their satellite states. Whether for good or ill, this meant that for decades Austria had very left-wing governments.

The frontier we had to cross was constantly guarded. A moment of opportunity had to be found to evade the patrols. Trustworthy guides who had experience would be invaluable. But where would my father find these? Jimmy's network, of course.

And so, after the logistics had been studied, the date of the escape was decided: January 31st, 1949. Mitzi had already been told. On the actual day of our flight, she was to dress us in several layers of clothing. This was not against the cold but because we were leaving literally with only the clothes on our backs.

The morning of our planned departure, my mother was finally told. She went ballistic. Short of smothering her, he did all he could to keep her voice from reaching the neighbours. Mommy did not want to believe that their lives were in danger, that we children would be taken away, and that they could face prison or labour camps. Those who warned him were lying. She argued that with their connections to the American and other embassies we would be protected. Her uncle had been Paul Teleki, a hero to the anti-Nazis. Surely Jimmy McCargar with his press relations would broadcast to the world if anything untoward were to happen to them. And that was Daddy's trump card. When she learned of his involvement, of the help he would supply and the reasons why, she began to take our situation more seriously. It was just as well we were leaving on the same day. It gave her less time to have second thoughts.

Mommy insisted, though, that we visit her mother so that she could say her farewells. Her sister Chibby was also there. She was not to know this would be the last time she'd ever see her mother again and what a devastating effect our escape would have on poor Chibby. In retaliation for our departure, the authorities imprisoned her. She was treated terribly and after five years, went insane. An incarceration in a mental institute followed where she underwent experimental electro-shock therapy for another five years. When the doctors could do no more for her sanity and she was deemed inconsequential, Chibby was allowed her freedom and went to live with a peasant family who were known to my mother.

She had a room of her own in their simple little house. The floor was earth and they received a cheque in dollars every month to look after her, which they did as best they could.

We saw Chibby again when I was a teenager living in Munich. She was finally allowed a passport and came to visit us. I was amazed at her generosity of spirit. She never blamed us for her misfortune. I spent hours with her in our garden looking up at a shimmering of stars in a night sky and listened to her explaining which of them were used by the Soviets as watching or listening devices. A star traced her movements via her hearing aid. Another sent messages to her dentures. The chattering of her ill-fitting false teeth, she whispered to me in confidence, was actually Morse code. The whistling in her malfunctioning hearing aid was a sort of radar. We watched her confusion grow from these explainable noises into paranoia. It wasn't until we convinced her that the Communists back home would not punish her if she removed both devices that she calmed down. We became used to her toothless smile and managed to communicate regardless of her deaf ears.

CHAPTER II

There was no moon that night and it was very windy. A car with a driver came to collect us. It waited around the corner from where we lived. I had kissed Mitzi goodbye and was bawling my heart out as any four year old child would when being separated from the person she needed most in the world. We piled into the car and our driver, thanks to Jimmy, drove us slowly through Budapest and on towards the Austrian border. He avoided the major roads, sticking mostly to smaller country ones and turned off his lights and engine when having to sneak through villages. The fact that there was snow on the surfaces helped to muffle the sounds of the progressing car. At one point on the journey, the driver lost control and the car skidded around a bend making the door to the passenger seat suddenly open where my mother with me on her lap was sitting. For a second she had loosened her grip around my torso. It only took that second for me to fly out but, luckily, I landed in the snow and no harm was done.

A few kilometres before the border the driver came to a stop. We had reached the appointed rendezvous. A hay wagon drawn by two sturdy horses was waiting. One man held the reins. Another jumped down and came to meet us. They were our guides from Jimmy's trusted network. I don't know what they earned but they took incredible risks. We got out of the car. The driver wished us luck, turned around and drove back from where we came. We were made to burrow into the hay. The guide who jumped down hid himself along with us and the wagon moved slowly on, sticking to a dirt track away from peering eyes. We arrived near the border at the crossing point. The wagon stopped and we slipped out from under the hay. Our guide led us to some trees that we could hide behind. The hay wagon moved off. Absolute silence was required of us as the guide studied the terrain beyond. During the journey in the car I had been coughing, so my mother placed a hand over my mouth to keep me quiet. No barbed wire but two armed soldiers moved towards one another along the unmarked perimeter. When they met there was an exchange of words after which they turned and walked in opposite directions, continuing their patrol. It was at that moment when there was enough space between the two guards that we had to literally run for our lives, for our futures. So that I would not slow down our progress, the guide picked me up and pressed me against his chest. Holding each other's hands tightly, my brothers, my parents and the guide sprinted into no-man's-land and ran and ran, never looking back. Finally, gasping for breath, we reached a rectangular stone, which marked the actual border. On one side it read, in Hungarian, *Magyarország*. On the other, strangely in English, it read Austria instead of *Österreich*.

Paul, in his excitement, leapt over the stone, later boasting he had jumped into Australia. No shots had been fired, even though our traces in the snow would have been discovered. Either the soldiers ignored them or, according to my father after he had become more devout, it was due to divine intervention. But we were far from being safe. Our escape had landed us into Burgenland, the Soviet occupied zone. Any noise from guns would have alerted the authorities and we could all have been captured.

There was a long walk over a ploughed field, the ridges white with snow. A wind helped to muffle any noise our treading feet made. But the guide was uneasy as the landscape was so flat and white our shapes stood proud for any eyes to see. He thanked God for the moonless night. We came to some trees next to a dirt road. I was put on to my feet and the guide told my father which direction to take. He shook his hand, kissed my mother's and vanished into the darkness. I have an image still of poplar trees, tall with their branches pointing to the sky, guarding the path that we walked. The guide's directions led us to a manor house belonging to the Zichy family. They were Hungarian aristocracy, with another property next to Nagyida. My father knew them well and was sure to find shelter there for us that night. Unfortunately, they were away and not having been warned, the servant who was the guardian didn't dare to allow us in without permission. He was afraid that if our escape had been noticed, this property would be the first to be searched. But he did tell us of a farm farther down the track whose people, it was rumoured, accepted refugees. We should try there. And so, our trek continued. Everyone was exhausted. My brothers either pulled me along or I was carried by my father for a while. I remember a warm light glowing from a window a distance up the track. It beckoned us. Even today, I am attracted like a moth in the darkness to light coming from someone's window. The urge is almost irresistible to be inside that place. That glow defines refuge for me. I have managed, though, to desist from knocking on stranger's doors. But only just.

We had arrived at the farm we'd been told about. The couple gave us sanctuary, but I think, with reservations. The parents were allowed to shelter in the hay of an adjoining barn. We children spent what remained of the night under a kitchen table, hidden from view by a large cover, which hung to the floor. The table was next to a wood-burning cooking stove. When the fierce arguing abated from the couple above in their bedroom, we had a warm and cosy sleep.

Whatever had been resolved the night before, we were offered in the morning nourishing cups of cocoa or coffee and thick slices of farm bread. Again, we walked a long way to the nearest bus stop, which would take us 100 kilometres to Vienna. It was the safest way to travel that distance in the hope of not having to show documents. Daddy had decided not to take any identification papers, as these could be incriminating. Our family was Catholic and we were all baptised in a church, our certificates of birth were actually our baptismal certificates and they contained not only names, but titles as well. Baron Schell von Bauschlott travelling with wife, *née* Countess Teleki and three children would have aroused suspicion. We'd have been handed over to the new muscle-flexing Hungarian Communist authorities. My father's worst nightmares: separation, prison, labour camp, orphanage made reality *pour encourager les autres.*

It would not be the last time that we children were ordered to keep our mouths tightly shut. No-one was to hear Hungarian spoken. Both parents were fluent German speakers as was I, thanks to Mitzi but I too had to keep quiet. What is the saying? 'Out of the mouths of babes...' In all innocence, I could have admitted to our escape.

We made it safely to Vienna. Our feet were standing on a comparatively free pavement. My father was 50 years old, mother 34, Paul eight, Peter seven and I, four. Daddy had $50 in his pocket to start a new life for his family. There were some friends, though, in Vienna who were immediately contacted. We stayed that night camping on someone's living room floor.

The next morning my father presented himself at the American embassy. He was sure the years he had spent as second and then first secretary of the Hungarian embassy in Washington DC during the Thirties would help us receive permission to enter the US and until such time was seeking official refugee status. Unfortunately, a very stubborn, officious Hungarian vetted all the applicants wanting access to the immigration department. No amount of name-dropping of friendly acquaintances – Carnegie, Auchincloss, Mellon, Rockefeller – had any effect on this man. The Americans, he said were only accepting farmers. Thinking of Nagyida, my father replied that he had an agricultural background, which was not a complete lie. The estate did farm, after all, even though, he did not personally participate in that activity. It was his fraternal twin brother, Peter, who even before their father's death was charged with the running of the estate, having studied for a degree in agriculture.

'Show me your hands,' ordered the uncooperative Hungarian.

Now, Daddy had sweet, delicate, little hands. The man laughed at them and barred any future interaction between him and those who could have helped us. How ironic that it would be a Hungarian who would make our lives difficult and dangerous.

On a good day, in the correct month it was quite safe to walk Vienna's streets even without papers. It just depended which of the allies was in charge. Stalin's jealousy of his western brethren in arms turned to paranoia. He demanded that Vienna be quartered as Berlin but that these partitions would come under a different authority every month. So, while you walked a particular street in a particular sector during French, American or British mandate, you were not likely to be pressed into showing documents. But when that same street came under Soviet jurisdiction, and lacking legal papers, it was best to stay indoors. The tense atmosphere in the city during that period is powerfully depicted in the film of *The Third Man*.

Ironically, the most threatening experience my mother was subjected to happened via the Americans. When leaving her work place at night to go home, she was pounced upon and bundled into a large black car by two men. They drove her to an address where she was taken down some stairs into a subterranean room. They sat her at one side of a table. A bare light bulb hung from the ceiling casting a harsh light on the grey walls. A third man entered and sat himself opposite her. Until then, she had not heard a single word spoken and had no idea who her abductors were, nor why she had been brought to this damp, cold place. Obviously, she feared the worst, that they were Russians and when her situation would be discovered, she'd be sent to a labour camp somewhere in the depths of Russia, never to be heard of again.

The newcomer opened his mouth and began questioning her in

German. (They were in Vienna, after all) She also answered in German but heard an American accent in her interrogator's speech. He accused her of spying for the Russians, upon which she burst out laughing and explained in her heavily accented voice in English that she was a refugee who had escaped with her husband and three children from Hungary and, if anything, was hiding from the Russians. She mentioned Daddy's diplomatic history in Washington and dropped a few names of important acquaintances that could vouch for him. At the end of the interview, the Americans admitted to a mistaken identity and drove her to her address.

My mother loved risk. She was addicted to gambling, to the point that on their honeymoon in San Marino, she left her husband sleeping in the nuptial bed to go to a casino where she managed to lose every lira my father took with him to Italy to pay hotels etc. at the baccarat table.

My father, on the other hand, also took risks but stayed cool, calculating the odds. The day after Mommy's debacle he borrowed money from the hotel, went to the same casino and retrieved all the money lost, even making a profit. Although he had won, he still punished Mommy shortly after their honeymoon by allowing her to catch him in their marital bed back in Budapest with one of his mistresses. He'd had a series of them, which was not uncommon at that time but had been more discreet. It was the shock of this act which ever so subtly altered her feelings for him. It certainly led my mother to explore her sexuality and become more independent.

In a way, it was that independence which enabled her to stay in Vienna. My father took us to Salzburg, a safer destination in the American zone where we were less likely to be hassled for official papers. Mommy refused to accompany us, arguing that she could earn more in the capital than in a provincial town. She was as resistant in this respect as she had been to our escape but, this time, it was because Vienna was too exciting to leave. She'd stay behind living initially with friends until she was able to earn enough money to afford her own lodgings.

It did not take her long to find an ideal situation. Along with another beautiful Hungarian woman, she ran a bar called the Peterle. It was owned by an Austrian who recognized the advantage of these glamorous gals fronting his establishment. Not before long, the Peterle became the place to be. There was a piano in the middle of the room. The two women decided that if a customer didn't have enough money but could tickle the ivories to entertain the other guests, he'd have earned himself a rewarding glass of something. A microphone was available for anyone who fancied himself as a stand-up comic, poet or a singer. A lot of talent on their uppers crossed the threshold, attracting customers who bought them drinks. The Peterle flourished, thanks to the two innovative beauties. Tony Curtis and Janet Leigh honeymooned during that time in Vienna. They were frequent visitors to the bar.

My father found lodgings for us just outside of Salzburg in a village called Kniegle. He took two rooms in an inn. It was called *Gasthause* Fuchs. Mitzi, who had Austrian papers, was able to leave Hungary legally. She arrived in Kniegle with our birth certificates and two large suitcases packed with our clothes and a few small bits of family silver. I shared a large bed with her in one room and my brothers with Daddy in the connecting one. What a paradox, that as refugees with very little money we still had a maid, cook, nanny – all in the person of Mitzi. We were her family. She shared whatever bounty or poverty that befell our lives.

Daddy found work as a librarian during the day and sometimes acted in a little Salzburg theatre at night. He gave Mitzi whatever money he could to shop for our food. She managed to eke out the sums to great advantage, coming home on occasion with treats she had simply asked someone for, using us poor unfortunate children to gain sympathy. She never paid for fish. She just walked along the riverbank until she found an angler with a reasonable catch, told the sob story and he invariably would hand over half of his catch.

The adjoining room where the males slept was bigger. It had a beautiful example of the middle-European tiled stove in the corner, which reached up to the ceiling. At the bottom was an iron door, the recipient of the coal, which Mitzi carried up in a bucket every day. In the middle was a rectangular, metal lined recess. This is where she cooked. *Goulash* was left here to simmer in a casserole. Eggs were fried. The surface was hot enough to make *palacsinta* (pancakes). Noodles were boiled and later doused with honey and a generous sprinkling of either ground walnuts or poppy seed (*deos, makos nudli)*. We were warned of the danger of poppy seed. It contained opium, Mitzi whispered conspiratorially. We had no idea what that meant but I have an addiction to any sweet containing poppy seed still today. Mitzi was a great cook. Even the braised lung in sour cream and chives she served with *knoedels* (dumplings) were delicious. We lived the saying 'beggars can't be choosers'. Everything that was put in front of us was devoured and enjoyed. I have many memories of that room and the stove. All of our ablutions took place there. We bathed in a metal tub with water brought up in buckets by Mitzi. She poured most of them in the tub but kept some behind to be heated in the rectangle of the stove so that we didn't wash in a freezing bath.

Not many people can say today that they peed and pooped into a porcelain pot. We had no toilets. Mitzi diligently examined our droppings. She went berserk when she found worms. They were as big as those that gardener's appreciate which help to aerate the soil. Other than the amazed interest when we were shown them, we children weren't bothered. It was all part of our life. I cannot picture my father using a chamber pot, so perhaps there were facilities elsewhere in the building and we children were not aware of them. But we *were* aware of the stick that Mitzi kept in the corner of the room. It was rarely used. She needed only to glance at it and we stopped whatever annoying behaviour we were up to.

One afternoon my brothers got into a stone throwing fight with some of the local boys who held parochial attitudes towards immigrant refugees. Peter and Paul defended themselves. The skirmish happened in the neighbourhood cemetery, which was favoured for such affrays as the gravestones were convenient to hide behind and the gravel paths between the graves afforded the ammunition. The aggressors had slingshots. My brothers had to return fire by casting their stones with superior strength from their throwing arms and better aim. This required standing up from behind the gravestones. Peter mistimed one of these manoeuvres and was hit squarely on his forehead, just below the hairline. The blood from the wound flowed profusely. Paul screamed for the battle to stop. The enemy withdrew their slingshots and looked in horror when they perceived his injury, allowing Paul to help Peter get home to Mitzi's nursing attentions.

I was in the room when they entered. Seeing so much blood flowing down Peter's face started me crying hysterically. Mitzi took charge. The abundance of blood made it look worse than it was. She washed his face and dabbed the wound with iodine, which was now congealing. Satisfied that he did not need to see a doctor, she, then, concentrated her attention on Paul. Blaming him, as the elder brother, she retrieved the seldom-used stick and gave him a bloody good hiding. He yelped loudly. Now, I had two brothers who were suffering which brought on another hysterical fit of crying.

The stick came out once more that I remember. My brothers had an argument, which was not unusual for siblings. They fought, shoving each other around. At that time Paul was slightly bigger than Peter. He had the advantage and pushed Peter up against the stove. He was naked from the waist up with his arm above his head. Even just the slightest moment of the left side of his chest and ribcage meeting the extreme heat of the tiles was enough to give him a dangerous burn. The area turned a violent red and soon began to blister. When Mitzi came back upstairs and saw his condition, she once again administered to his wound and, certainly, to Paul, punishment with the stick. She was not a cruel woman. In those days that was how bad behaviour was discouraged. We all understood.

I think the time spent in Kniegle made me. I have such vivid memories: bathing in a shaded pool of a river with Peter and Paul looking after my safety, climbing the hill behind the inn in summer while picking and munching on wild sorrel, sledding down that same hill in winter, seeing the farmer next door through our window chopping the head off a chicken and yes, they can run headless, American GIs handing out Hershey bars and giving us lifts in the back of their jeeps, looking forward to my first year of school. I was so jealous of my brothers who walked off every morning to what I was convinced was an adventure which I was being denied. While waiting for my turn, Mitzi taught me to count to 100 in German and Daddy taught me in English. He talked about America often and was preparing us for school there. I made mental images of this vast country. It was across an ocean. After my father explained what an ocean was, I pictured a long beach all the way down, from top to bottom with a forest of pine growing on the sand which touched the water. I couldn't wait to be there.

Then, in the summer, I became six and that September my brothers walked me to my first day of school. I dipped a feather pen into an ink bottle! What bliss. How adult. No more pencils or crayons. At the end of that year, I received my first report card. We were graded from one to five: one being best, five the worst. I received all ones except for music, which was a two. Now, I knew I couldn't sing. I liked to sing but when I did I was quickly told to shut up. The noise I made hurt people's ears. All the way home, I was steeped in disappointment. That two ruined all the ones. It was given to me out of pity because I was a refugee. It should have been a five, I felt, and then all the ones would have been deserved. Already then I was suspicious of false compliments.

My mother was mostly absent from our lives during those two years we spent in the inn. She rarely visited us. The only outstanding memory I have of seeing her was on a trip to Vienna and it's an uneasy one. I shared a room with my brothers. In a hotel? In someone's house? I don't know. There were no curtains drawn across the window. Bright light invaded the room and the boys woke up. At first they only whispered to each other and remained in the bed they were sharing. The whispers became louder and something like an argument broke out between them. I tucked myself even deeper under the duvet in my single bed trying to sleep. The argument developed into a pillow fight and soon they were leaping about making the springs of their bed squeak. They laughed and shouted. They were just behaving like boys.

The door suddenly exploded open. Mommy appeared. She was furious. They had woken her up. She held a leather belt in her hand and began using it as a whip, lashing at my brothers with such violence that they screamed in pain. I tried to disappear, to melt into the mattress but the duvet I was hiding under was ripped off me and with the same fury, she began to beat me. Perhaps, I was five years old. The injustice of this act has never left me. I would be whipped again. In those days, it was the middle European manner of punishment but, at least, perhaps I would have deserved it. My father never touched us in anger. For some strange reason physical punishment was our mother's domain. For a very long time I was terrified of her.

When I was of an age and she began to respect me, I became her confidante and learned about her lovers. Mommy had to be in love. She needed to feel passion for someone but, alas, no longer for my father. The incident with the mistress in Budapest so shortly after their honeymoon ruined something between them. She felt free to experiment.

I later forgave her for that beating and all the others that would happen in the future. Her vicious temper could be aroused from frustration. She had simply spent the night with the wrong person. My father had expected his conjugal rights which she dared not deny him (yet) but her thoughts were with Güsti, her Viennese lover who played the violin under her window. She was also deeply romantic. In actual fact, they were badly matched. Mommy was volatile, passionate, instinctive. Daddy was cool, deliberate, intellectual. If he had not been 'correct', they would never have married. While on holiday in Egypt, he received a telegram from her stating that she was pregnant. He replied that he would stand by her and she should begin to make wedding plans. No roses, no I love you, just the reaction of a gentleman. He may have been naughty but he wasn't a cad. On his return to Budapest, she had to admit that she had been 'mistaken'. He could have cancelled the marriage then but as the arrangements were well under way and she was a very beautiful woman from the sort of family he was destined to marry into, obviously sexy as well, he decided to go ahead. At 41, he thought, it was time to settle down and start a family. He later admitted to me that he had not been fooled by the feigned pregnancy. He realized he'd been tricked. I think this is what assuaged his conscience *vis a vis* extra-marital affairs. He would become more discreet, though, in the future sticking mainly to high-class prostitutes, whereas she became more and more indiscreet, finding her adventures amongst their circle of friends. Daddy could not have been naïve. He accepted her follies. They sometimes brought rewards. Güsti was the only poor lover she ever had.

We were finally allowed entry to America. Daddy contacted friends in the States who could pull strings. They were powerful people but it still took over two years. There was a confusion with immigration and even fraud was suspected. Daddy's twin brother Peter had been freed by the American army from a concentration camp in northern Italy. He was placed there as a political prisoner. It was the practice of the US forces, upon freeing such detainees, to give them a choice as to where they would want to go. Uncle Peter spoke English fluently and had Agricultural degrees, so he chose to go to America and his application was immediately accepted. His wife and three children followed him there shortly after. This meant that the authorities became suspicious when they were processing my father's application. There already was a Schell von Bauschlott – male, born September 5th, 1898 in Nagyida, married with three children – living there. His visa was refused several times until Jack Auchincloss, Jacqueline Kennedy's stepfather, and another of Daddy's acquaintances, Senator Claiborne Pell, investigated the problem that the confusion was discovered. No-one had reckoned on the possibility of twins.

Our visas were issued. I watched Mitzi packing our clothes, weeping. She kissed every item, folded them lovingly and placed them into the trunks. We were deserting her. When we left Hungary, she had the hope of joining us in Austria. That had been the plan. But America. It was so far away.

There was a train ride to Bremerhaven on the German coast. We lived in a real refugee camp, a vast complex, sleeping with hundreds of other displaced people under the same roof. Our vaccinations would happen here. We did not stop on Ellis Island. I remember being with my brothers in what may have been a disused airplane hangar. We were moving in tightly packed lines towards a desk where doctors and nurses would examine us before vaccinating. Children were screaming and crying. My brothers promised me it wouldn't hurt. There was no reason to be frightened. Peter held me tightly from behind. Paul was in front. The acoustics were brash, metallic and the sound of the other children's panic infected me. I was so terrified, I peed in my pants. I know what mass hysteria feels like.

The troop transporter *General Ballou* sailed us and thousands of other immigrants to New York harbour. The only thing I remember of the journey was the all-permeating smell of oatmeal. We arrived in June, one month before my seventh birthday.

CHAPTER III

A black limousine came to meet us. We had just disembarked from a ship carrying refugees but a man with a chauffeur's cap and white gloves ushered us to a shining, expensive car. Our luggage was handled by a porter. What could people have thought? He drove us to an address on the west side of Manhattan with views of the Hudson. We were guests of my father's friends who took us that night to a harbour restaurant. That was where I learned to say the word oyster. Perhaps my parents were showing off at the fact that I could already read because I had been given a menu to peruse. Oyster sprang off the page. I had no idea what it was but its pronunciation was so intriguing.

'Are you sure, Katica?' my mother asked me in Hungarian.

'Yes,' I answered. 'Definitely.'

'Do you know what it is?'

'No, but that's what I want.'

I think she had an ulterior motive for giving in. Daddy and his friends were amused. The dish of six oysters was placed in front of me. I looked down on to these blobs of grey slime captured in a shell, smelling like the underbelly of the ocean and almost vomited. Mommy quickly slipped the plate in front of her and finished them off. She hadn't eaten oysters for years and adored them. I was well into my thirties when finally I enjoyed swallowing this grey slime as long as it was doused with lemon and several twists of a black pepper mill.

We arrived in Kent Village, a little dormitory town outside of Washington DC and were welcomed by a crowd of excited children more or less our age. We three kids had hardly piled out of the car when we were pulled along by our hosts indicating at trees, cars, houses, streets, our shoes, whatever, while uttering the word which depicted the object. They were teaching us a vocabulary.

'Me, Jimmy.' A boy pointed to himself and then to me. 'What's your name?'

I got the message. 'Katica,' I said.

He couldn't pronounce it. Peter and Paul were easy. My father came over and said to Jimmy, 'Her name is Catherine.'

'Oh, Cathy! Great.' He smiled from ear to ear. Our friendship was thus established.

We'd been awaited. The neighbours had been told that a foreign family were coming to live amongst them. The friends who'd made the arrangements were called the Mulfords. They found the two-bedroomed flat in a purpose-built yellow brick apartment house and filled the kitchen cupboards and fridge (we'd never had a refrigerator before and it was taller than me!) with a month's supply of food. They paid a quarter of a year's rent in advance and pressed $300 into my father's palm.

'It's up to you now, Kepi,' they said, using his nickname, and left us to settle in.

My father was known as Kepi by everyone during his diplomatic days, to the degree that when a woman friend from Hungary sent him a telegram addressing it simply to Kepi Schell, Washington DC, it was delivered to him at the Embassy.

Three hundred dollars was not going to go far. Work had to be found. Ex-Hungarian diplomats were not in demand, especially now that the country was allied to the Soviets. For the time being, even selling ties in Woolworths was a welcome occupation. He was not proud. When acquaintances from the old days recognized him, they asked what on Earth he was doing behind the counter. He just answered, 'Earning a living.' Upon finding out about his circumstances, invitations usually followed.

I keep an affection for Americans and will never forget their spontaneous friendliness and generosity. Perhaps it was the world my father moved around in. But the children who made us welcome and were eager to be friends had nothing to do with our 'society'. Integration was made easy.

We were given a Crosley. It was a tiny car. I can't remember by whom. (Again the Mulfords?) It was narrower than a Mini but slightly taller and made of more wood than metal. I think its engine was single horsepower because if we five were crunched together and it had to climb a hill, four of us got out to push. The local kids thought it was a playground ride and begged Mommy to take them around the block, which she happily did even though her eyesight was so poor that she was denied a driver's license. As the car couldn't go faster than 25 mph it was still safer than giving them rides on a motorbike. We were very much a curiosity on the highways. Mommy longed for a proper car, something long and flashy, not to drive but to be seen in. She'd get her wish from a Mr Coolidge. But that would come later. For now she'd have to settle for the Crosley and the brand spanking new vacuum cleaner a visiting salesman managed to sell her.

With Jimmy's companionship, I learned enough English to be able to start second grade at the local public school. I was amazed. They still used pencils! I longed for my quill and inkwell. A desk at the very back of the classroom was allocated to me. I could hardly see the blackboard, not to mention the teacher for all the bobbing heads obstructing my view. We must have been 60 in that room. But it would not last long. I was sent off to be educated by nuns in a convent school shortly after our first Christmas when all of our presents were stolen from the back of the Crosley while it was parked in a Washington street. Those presents were bought for us children by the Mulfords and other friends of Daddy's. They had been beautifully wrapped. He'd gone to collect them, placed them on the back seat, stopped to buy something else, neglected to lock the car and *hey presto* they disappeared. Or perhaps a Crosley didn't have a lock. Who'd want to steal one? So, not everything was wonderful in America. We were not used to crime.

I don't remember the journey to the convent. I just remember kissing my father goodbye on the threshold of its entrance. I know it was late because it was dark and everyone was asleep. The nun who took charge of me told me to be very quiet as I was led up some dimly lit stone stairs. I followed her swaying hips, made wider by a long flowing black skirt which dusted the floor as it passed over. With every step she mounted, the long wooden rosary beads hanging on the side from her waist rattled. This sound would bring me nightmares in the future. The nun who I would later call Sister Agnes carried my little suitcase, which contained changes of underwear and such essentials. I would eventually be fitted with a uniform sewn for me by one of the sisters. She led me to a bed up against a far wall in a dormitory containing seven other sleeping girls.

Sister Agnes helped me to undress, put on my pyjamas, took me to a vast communal washroom where I was made to brush my teeth at one of the several sinks, opened a toilet cubicle for me to have a pee, led me back to the bed, made me say a prayer and told me to sleep. She had not been unkind, just a stranger with little warmth, dressed entirely in black except for the white pleated wimple which surrounded her face. Black was the colour witches wore in Grimm's fairy tales and I was terrified of them, the tales as well as the witches. I sobbed for hours into my pillow. This experience was so intimidating. I was alone, away from my family.

The darkness and silence permeated my very being like the chill, which affects one's bones. I trembled with fear. I had been a child of light and laughter, even noisy when allowed to be. How could this have happened? I was only seven... banished at seven.

One would have thought in the light of day things may have appeared less threatening. A different nun woke us up with a sharp clapping of her hands. The other girls slid out of their beds and made their way to the morning's ablutions. My presence was completely ignored except by the nun who dragged me without ceremony from my sheets and shouted to me to go and wash. This was my first encounter with who would become my Nemesis. She was truly challenged, height-wise, not being much taller than we seven year olds. The nuns chose their names after their favourite saints. She had chosen Christopher, the saintly giant who carried the child Jesus on his shoulders across a turbulent river. I'd later learn how she loved 'butch' girls and used her fists in punishment. Not the slapping of a cheek from Sis Chris (as I'd later call her, but never to her face) no, she preferred a quick right fist to the upper mandible, which made one's ears ring. And they do!

I don't remember how many times a week we were allowed a bath but the rule was: no more than three inches of water in the tub. It was a bit like bathing in a puddle. As we didn't take a measuring tape with us, we may have knelt in an inch above or below the exact amount. The individual tubs were placed in tiled cubicles with a shower curtain drawn for our privacy. Only on Sis Chris's watch were our puddles ever verified. She patrolled bath nights with stealth. Sneaking from one cubicle to another, holding her rosary beads to avoid them from rattling, she'd surprise her prey by brutally pulling the curtain aside and having decided there was too much water, she'd dole out her particular form of punishment. I was once on the receiving end of this retribution. My hair was pulled and my head was bashed several times against the tiled wall. The next day I had a bruise near to my right temple. Nobody noticed. I knew I would never mention this to my mother. Children tend to blame themselves. I didn't want to be told that I probably deserved it. I couldn't tell Daddy either. He'd become religious since our successful escape, having promised God that if we all survived, he would go to church every day for the rest of his life (a promise he kept). He'd not have been able to comprehend that a nun could be cruel. Anyway, they were both long distance calls away and the pay phone was in a corridor, which could be overheard.

I don't know if it was this event that prompted me to run away. I coerced another girl my age to accompany me, being too much of a coward to attempt escaping on my own. I also needed her street *nous*. She knew which bus to take to the ferry.

As my parents were still in Washington, I rarely saw them. They could not afford to travel me back and forth. I only saw them for the summer. Christmas and Easter holidays were spent with a Hungarian family in Manhattan whose daughter, Gabi, much older than me, also attended the convent. The morning of our flight, I asked Gabi to loan me 50 cents. She asked me what for. I didn't tell her anything beyond that it was a matter of life and death. She gave me a silver half dollar piece. I then made this poor eight year old girl promise to leave with me after school threatening her with a special word, '*töltött krumpli*' which meant stuffed potato in Hungarian but she wasn't to know. If she uttered this word and reneged on her promise, she would die the most excruciatingly painful death.

'Say it. Say it!' I commanded her. And so she did... with some difficulty.

'My mother is a witch,' I told her. 'And she's taught me to cast spells.' Thank you, Brothers Grimm.

That afternoon, having finished class we made our way down the path to the convent's gate without a suitcase but wearing the school uniform. The imposing metal portals were open and we walked through. To our left on the pavement was a bus stop. We had to wait for no. 54. I had heard that Grand Central Station was where train tickets were bought. I already saw myself there.

A policeman came strolling by. He smiled, nodded and walked on. But not very far. As if he'd had second thoughts, he turned around and approached us.

'So, little girls,' he said from his grown-up height. 'Are you waiting for the bus?'

My English was not yet refined enough to use the nuances of irony, so I simply answered, 'Yes.'

'And where would you be going to?' he asked with an Irish accent. I recognized this melodious speech as we had lots of Irish girls in the school.

'Washington DC,' I said. 'My parents live there.'

'And you, dear?' he asked, looking down on my accomplice.

She gave an address in New York City.

'Interesting... now, how much money have you got for these journeys?'

I can't remember what she said but I proudly told him of my 50 cent coin.

'Well then, I don't think that will take you very far, so, you'd better give me your little hands and I'll walk you back to the good sisters.' He had recognized our uniforms.

We obeyed like trusting sheep. It had been a short adventure. Perhaps the school called the police. I later learned that Gaby had gone to Mother Superior to tell her of my demand for 50 cents. Our presence must have been missed at the four o'clock collation. Perhaps they deduced we were running away.

The nice policeman walked us all the way to the front door of the mansion, which was the convent. Sister Philomina, our Mother Superior, answered the bell and gathered us to her. The policeman was thanked and after he left, we received our scolding and a punishment which was much more benign than anything Sis Chris would have meted out.

Sister Philomina was every parent's dream of what a head should be for a convent school. She didn't become Mother Superior because she was a wimp. But she didn't use intimidation to dominate. She was strict but also fair. Once a month she chose a child to accompany her on a shopping spree in Manhattan. These outings were highly prized by the pupils. They would be spoiled with candies, sodas, ice creams, real hamburgers with all the relishes, more candy to be shared with friends on their return. Sister Philomina was a very generous soul. My punishment was that for the whole remaining year I was excluded from being her shadow on these trips to town. I was devastated. What happened to my fellow escapee was unknown to me. We never spoke again. She did everything she could to avoid me. I was told that my punishment was comparatively lenient. My behaviour could be understood because I had not seen my parents for months, whereas she could go home on weekends. To this very day while writing this, I blush with guilt. She only ran away because of that word I forced her to pronounce, that witch's curse. She never blamed me to the nuns and I never admitted to my tyrannical influence. It was all my fault. If a woman reading this who went to a convent school on Staten Island and, at the age of eight, remembers being terrorized into running away by another eight year old, I'M SORRY!

For some strange reason my parents decided I should have piano lessons. Did they think this would cure my tone deafness? The religious order boasted a musical nun. We were taught in a large, brightly lit room. In the centre, a grand piano had pride of place. Off both sides of the room there were three cells, each containing an upright. This was where we practiced between lessons. There was some soundproofing but not enough to make you feel entirely cocooned. You could still vaguely hear the other pupils playing. I enjoyed my lessons and what I lacked in musicality, I made up by quickly learning to read notes on paper. But my frustration at listening to a newcomer pick out the notes with all the chords of the newest tune in the hit parade turned me green with envy. I couldn't do that, not even with just one finger.

It was during this time, I discovered I was a charity student. My father was not paying for my place in the school. It had been agreed I would have to maintain above average grades in all of my studies for me to stay.

The order originated in Hungary and had been transplanted to Staten Island. When my parents heard about these sisters via the Hungarian jungle drums they approached them. Being aware of my family's background, they kindly decided to take me on. It was understood with time and Daddy's changing fortunes for the better, he would begin to contribute.

I was already stretching their good will, not for running away – that was forgiven – but I couldn't spell. Read, yes. Write, no. I spelled cat with a 'k'. My brain was phonetically programmed. Every sound that one hears when speaking Magyar has the equivalent in its alphabet. There are so many accents and umlauts that the written work looks as if insects had died on it. You would be forgiven for trying to wipe the page clean but those tiny squiggles are permanent. I didn't go to school in Hungary. My first experience was Kniegle. German is a phonetic language. It is written as spoken. I had no problems. English is a pervert, a deviant when written. Why does the sound of 'ough' change from 'owe' to 'uff'? At whose whim was this decided? Why does 'witch' sound the same as 'which'? And how did the 'h' sneak in there? I had to stay behind school while (and why not 'whyle'?) a very kind nun did her best to teach me to spell. She did not succeed.

The piano lessons had to be dropped. They were a waste of time and effort. My fingers were nimble enough to negotiate a Chopin's etude but I had no feeling for what I was playing.

Then there was the bedwetting. I was able to master my bladder but mastering my fear of the devil who hid under my bed for the specific purpose of grabbing my ankles when I'd lower them from the mattress to the floor so that he could drag me down to hell with him, was not always successful. The rattling of the rosary beads worn by the nun who patrolled the corridor at night also terrified me. Sometimes, I did overcome the fear of the devil. Our dormitories had no doors. Neither did the washroom across the way. Timing was of the essence. Like a commando, I'd sneak from my bed up to the hallway and press myself against the wall, keeping out of sight, hardly daring to breathe. I'd wait for the rattling to turn round and move in the opposite direction. Only then, would I make a barefooted run for it. Once in the washroom, I found the cubicle farthest away from the corridor. Leaving the door open, as the sliding locks always squeaked, I would sit in blissful relief. But peeing makes tinkling noises. I'd not yet learned to fold arm lengths of toilet paper into the bowl to absorb the noise. The nun always found me. They have excellent hearing regardless of all that black material they wear to cover their ears and hair. And then the scolding would begin.

'What are you doing here? You should be asleep. Stop drinking liquids before bedtime. Shame on you! Don't ever let me catch you here again!'

What harm had I done? It wasn't as if I'd woken her up. She was on sentry duty. Why were these women in long black gowns gliding secretly up and down our corridors? To catch us delinquents, running cross-legged to have a pee?

Okay, I'm going to be punished for doing the correct thing. Fine. I won't risk being dragged down to hell by the devil. I don't want a run-in with the Gestapo guarding our hallway. I will just pee in my bed. Did they think I enjoyed that? And the humiliation the next day when a nun, usually Sis Chris, would point out the yellow stain on the sheet and deride me in front of my peers? This horror didn't stop until I was nine, when I no longer believed the devil roamed at night waiting to grab us and went to sleep with a mouth as dry and grooved as a walnut shell.

My parents had been told of this shortcoming by Sister Philomina and it was, oddly, my father who spoke to me about it.

'Do you dream you're having a pee when you're asleep?' he asked me kindly, trying to rationalize my behaviour.

It was easier and less confrontational to say, 'Yes.' I did not wet my bed when at home which was now almost every weekend. My parents had moved to Manhattan. Obviously, fortunes were changing for the better. They were renting a flat in an old, very handsome building on E. 82nd Street between Fifth and Madison Avenues, very near to the imposing neo Greek/Roman temple that housed the Metropolitan Museum of Art.

The flat was small for a family of five, consisting of a double bedroom that connected via a bathroom to the living room. This is where my brothers and I slept when we were home, they on a double convertible sofa and I, still little enough, on a single day bed. There was a kitchen with sliding doors that separated it from the living area. We were not frequently all together. The boys were found a boarding school called St Patrick's, run by nuns, regardless that it was a military academy. They wore miniature West Point uniforms. Whatever money was coming in – Daddy now interpreting written documents for the United Nations and Mommy working in Jolie Gabor's jewellery emporium on Madison Avenue – was going on our education. Jolie was the mother of Zaza, Eva and Magda Gabor, the seductive, glamorous daughters who Jolie launched into the pool of America's unsuspecting wealthy males. Zaza and Eva became actresses and all three made profitable marriages... Zaza, several times. As usual, the Hungarian network with its long tentacles reached my mother. She presented herself to mother Gabor on the off chance of finding work and was hired immediately. I think Jolie liked her class. On one of my visits coming home from school I exited the nearest subway station to the shop. I was picking Mommy up to walk home with her. As a surprise, Jolie had made a necklace for me, small cultured pearls with a silver clasp. It fitted perfectly around my narrow neck. I was only ten but she insisted every girl, no matter how young, should have a taste for jewellery. This was just the beginning, she assured. Later, it would be men who'd shower me with gems. I wasn't sure I knew what she meant. The only gems I'd come across were my marbles, which, admittedly, I had a passion for, not to play with, just to touch and admire their melting colours.

You would think we were rich. But we weren't. Daddy had begun to contribute towards my schooling but couldn't afford one hundred percent. Who was paying for St Patrick's? How did we buy the brand new two toned black and white ford with the elegant continental kit attached to its rear that Mommy loved being driven around in? The rental of that first flat in the best part of town would have cost a fortune.

There was a Mr Coolidge, though, owner of a fruit canning company, one of the biggest in America. The Ford was a gift from him, I later found out. My mother swore it was just a platonic relationship. The Crosley was left behind in Washington. It would have been trampled to death in Manhattan's thoroughfares. Mr Coolidge considered it important that we had a car and so the ford was presented to my father, as he would be driving it. He didn't seem to object.

Mr Coolidge travelled to Central and South America in search for new sources for his fruit. From one of these trips he returned with a splendid golden brooch, which he'd bought for Mommy in Panama. It had the form of a bird with wide flat wings and a curved beak and it weighed near to two ounces. The brooch clasp had been added to it in such a way that it did not disturb the integrity of the primitive sculpture. It was what became known as Columbian Gold, ancient artefacts made in real gold and buried in the soil as a sacrifice to the Gods to insure a good harvest. Much later, I took it to the Museum of Mankind in London where it was certified as an eagle pendant. Because it originated in Panama, I was told that the tribe who had produced it were known as the Tsisiki and it would have dated from before the 16th century. As it was bought in the mid-1950s it was most probably authentic. The counterfeits did not begin circulating until the mid-60s. It was priceless. Mr Coolidge must have loved my mother very much as a friend.

We only stayed in 82nd Street for a little over a year. As well as the translations, Daddy was now travelling seasonally with foreign Philharmonics. Because of his language talents (Hungarian, German, French and English) he was ideal as a tour manager, able to communicate and smooth out the ruffled feathers of his prestigious musicians – von Karayan, and a very young Yehudi Menuhin amongst them.

We kids were getting older and needed more space. Mommy spotted an ad in a New York paper for a flat. The tenant was selling fixtures and fittings with the remainder of a fixed rental lease. She phoned the number for further information and made a date to see it. The payment the tenant wanted was well beyond our means but out of curiosity she kept the appointment. The flat was on the seventh floor of a purpose built art deco apartment house in E. 89th Street between Madison and Park Avenues. She took the lift to the floor and rang the bell to the flat. The door was opened by an elderly gentleman. He welcomed her into a large vestibule with three arches leading to other areas. Straight ahead was a spacious living room with walls of wood containing bookshelves set into the walnut panelling. As she was shown around her feet walked over an expensive carpet, which flowed into all the rooms save the pantry, kitchen and maid's bed and shower room. The place was sumptuous, comfortable and decorated to a high standard, if a little dated. It reminded her of chateau living. She wanted it badly but knew it was impossible. While the tour continued, she made loud appreciative noises. A mural of a fountain and flowers covered one of the dining room walls. It may not have been to everyone's taste but, at least, it was gay and original. The master bedroom offered a bathroom en suite and a mirrored dressing room. Crystal chandeliers hung from ceilings where suitable. Another large bedroom with shower and loo would serve for the boys. But all this was wishful thinking and Mommy knew it.

'I've wasted your time,' she said, preparing to go. 'I did not realize it would be so beautiful. We could never afford this.' My mother spoke English in an accent very akin to Dracula. It seemed to amuse the man.

'How much can you afford?' he asked, simply.

'No. I would be insulting you,' she answered and she meant it.

'Go on. Insult me. You are the only person who has appreciated what we did to this place. Everyone, and there have been many who have come, only found fault to bring the price down.'

He began to explain the circumstances for the sale. They had been the first tenants in this flat. His wife had recently died. Most of the decor was her idea. As an amateur artist it was she who had painted the mural on the dining room wall. They could not have children but had many friends who they entertained here. There were too many memories. He couldn't live here alone. When he'd finished his outpourings, Mommy had tears swelling in her eyes.

'You have an interesting accent,' he told her. 'Where do you come from?'

And so she told him of her circumstances, escaping from Hungary, being a refugee, having three children, she and her husband working very hard to pay for their education. Knowing her, she would have pulled a little on his heartstrings. He let her have the flat for a third of what it had been advertised.

It was a marvellous home and I remember it especially for two welcome events: Mitzi arriving from Austria to be with us and our first parakeet called Chépiké.

Mitzi had saved all of her earnings to be able to join us. She paid for her journey. We were her family and it was only natural for her to follow us. She did have a sister in Vienna but they did not get along. As a matter of fact, Mitzi hated her. No-one asked her why. I didn't mind losing the maid's room to move in with my brothers. I came home many more weekends than they, anyway, and had the large bedroom with the black and white television to myself.

It was only four years since I saw her weeping as she packed our clothes and, yet, much had changed. I no longer spoke German, a fact I only realized at a Halloween party when I was eight years old at the convent. A child was dressed as Grätle from the fairy-tale of 'Hansel and Grätle'. The nuns came to me and explained that the poor little girl with blonde braids could not speak any English. Could I make her feel welcomed in German? I was totally fooled by her appearance. She looked up at me with beseeching eyes. I opened my mouth to say something but my mind went blank. Nothing came. An entire language had been deleted from my memory except for numbers and the word *Kravat*. Did it leak out of my consciousness like liquid from a container? We had not spoken German since our arrival in the US. Our parents conversed in Hungarian and when required to answer we kids did so in English. Unused languages obviously evaporate like alcohol in an uncorked bottle. For the time being, though, it didn't matter. I wasn't to know I'd need it later. Mitzi had made an effort to learn a bit of English and now I could teach her as she had taught me. I still loved her but our relationship had changed. The need for her had diminished. Whereas, once, I longed to be folded into her bosom, I was now no longer as tactile. I was older. The situation had changed for her as well. In Austria she had been our surrogate mother: now she was living with the real mother. Tensions between them could be as taught as the elastic on a slingshot with the possibility of stones being cast. They tempered their feelings, though, in front of me. The most I was aware of were doors slamming. I put it down to nasty draughts. Mommy admitted many years later that they had had from the very beginning, already in Hungary, a difficult relationship. Mitzi did not approve of her. The years in Kniegle had brought her very close to my father. She had enormous respect for him, always calling him Herr Baron. My mother had to have been very generous to even allow Mitzi back into our lives. It would have been my father who instigated her joining us. He loved her and she adored him. I think the problem lay there.

Nevertheless, Mitzi played her part diligently. The flat was spotlessly cleaned, our clothes beautifully ironed and when Mommy came home late from work delicious meals were cooked for us. Her presence also gave my mother more free time.

Mr Coolidge was no longer talked about. Daddy traded the Ford in for a brand new rust and cream coloured Pontiac. They were now moving with the upper echelons of the Hungarian set, all immigrants from the old country who had escaped Communism or the Nazis and were doing very well in their new adopted land. That is how she met Victor *bácsi* (Uncle Victor to me). He was tall, dark, handsome and very rich with a family and a large summer house a bit upstate from Manhattan near to the beach. I spent a week's holiday there and became friendly with his daughter, Elizabeth. We were both 12 when we met and our relationship still lasts. She had two older brothers and all the youngsters guessed what was happening between Kati *néni* (aunt Kati) and their father. They had seen them together on other occasions. But there I was, staying in a house with Sari *néni,* Victor's wife and children, never asking why Victor himself was seldom around. Ostensibly, he and Mommy were working in Manhattan where the family had a flat. The two of them arrived in the morning on the last day of my holiday to take me home. Sari *néni* served up a beautiful lunch and we all sat down together, the adults speaking Hungarian in very civilized tones while we children spoke English with broad Manhattan accents at the other end of the table. I didn't notice the looks my companions gave each other because they were 'in the know' and I a complete innocent, but there were a few muffled sniggers I couldn't account for. When we were middle-aged ladies, Elizabeth told me the 'affair' was common knowledge, even to their mother. The way my mother later spoke to me about Victor, I wonder if he had not really been the true love of her life... but life plays cruel tricks. For now, though, her romantic and passionate nature was being fulfilled. Either my father didn't know or he didn't mind or they were extremely discreet in front of me.

I came home one weekend to find we had a charming brindle Boxer. For a brief time we'd adopted this beautiful tiger-like striped bitch that I adored running around with in Central Park. She was my minder, instinctively protecting me. When we were together no harm could befall me except a scratched knee. Bluffy was a fast dog and loved jumping over park benches. I didn't always succeed in my attempts to keep up with her. To my chagrin, but very wisely, a family friend kidnapped her. Poor Bluffy had been locked in the flat for the greater part of a day. It was not a good life with both parents working and Mitzi had not yet arrived. Doggie things were done only on weekends. She was taken away and given to people on Long Island who had a large garden for her to exercise in.

Daddy decided to be more reasonable as far as our next pet was concerned. Enter Cheppi, a light green parakeet. Birds are easy to look after, they don't need constant company, they're pretty to look at and they can feed themselves. Mommy was delighted. Cheppi had a cage but its door was always open except for night times when it naturally flew in as if to its nest. A towel was placed over this home to keep it in darkness and quiet until Mommy decided to wake up. During the day, it had the liberty of the entire flat. There was bird shit everywhere, which was left to dry and then flicked off whatever surface by a fingernail or sucked up by a vacuum cleaner. Cheppi was incredibly friendly and took a special liking to my father. When he came home the bird flew towards him and perched on his shoulder to nibble his ear. He could perch on his spectacles tapping the lenses with his beak, which was a bit off-putting when reading but Daddy was a very indulgent man. The funniest stunt, though, was when Cheppi shared my father's Bacardi cocktail, gripping the rim of the glass with his little claws and lowering his beak into the pink liquid. I don't know if it's possible to stagger while flying but he did.

One day, when my father was away a window was left open and Cheppi flew out into the great blue yonder. Mommy was desperate. She wrote notes and placed them into the doors of all the apartment buildings within a certain radius of our flat. This was Manhattan! I'd come home the day after the great escape. She had not received a reply and I, now of an age that I could help and sympathize, accompanied her to a local pet shop. She wanted to replace the bird so that Daddy wouldn't miss it and reproach her for a lack of attention. There was no parakeet of the same colour in the shop. We went home empty handed. That evening the telephone rang. Someone living nearby said that he was quite sure her bird had lighted on his windowsill. He explained that he had an aviary in his apartment and that her bird was probably attracted to the chattering of his dozens. Would she like to come to pick it up? He gave her his address. I was left at home.

Arriving at his door, she rang the bell. A very pleasant looking man in his forties answered... stark naked. He was still wet from a shower and had not even bothered to wrap a towel around his waist. He seemed oblivious of his nakedness. Mommy's first reaction was to run away but his demeanour was so unthreatening, she felt quite safe to enter the apartment. Don't look down, she thought, always look at his face. She was a very beautiful woman, a cross between Ava Gardner and Joan Crawford but this had no effect on his behaviour. He's probably gay, she thought and allowed him to lead her to a room, which consisted entirely of the aviary. The door they looked through had a wooden frame with chicken wire. She was amazed to see so many birds and not all of them parakeets. There were pigeons, sparrows, canaries, all perching on branches of whole potted trees he'd managed to bring up the stairs or in the lift. He'd installed birdbaths, feeders and swings of different sizes hanging from the ceiling. Mirrors to amuse the parakeets were placed in likely positions. There was a sheet on the floor to collect the droppings and the noise was deafening.

'How can you find my bird amongst all of yours?' she shouted, noticing none of them were tagged.

'No problem. I recognize all of mine.' He opened the door, walked in, held his finger up to a particular twig and made some clicking noises with his tongue. A light green bird, very like Cheppi, hopped on to it. When they'd spoken on the phone, he'd asked her to bring a shoebox with a few little holes in it. The bird was placed in the box. He walked her to the door, politely said goodbye and Mommy walked home with a bird and an unforgettable memory of the last 15 minutes she'd spent. I was not to say anything to my father.

Whether or not it was *really* Cheppi would depend on if he liked Bacardi cocktails. He did... until Daddy squashed him opening the front door of the flat. Once more, I was at home for this disaster. I heard the desperate squawk shortly followed by some sobs. Running into the vestibule, I saw Daddy with the lifeless bird cupped into his palms and tears streaming down his face.

'I stepped on him,' he said, weeping. What made it even worse was that Cheppi had probably heard the key in the lock and moved to the door to welcome him.

It was my mother's turn to be absent for this incident. We went to the pet shop to find another Cheppi. I was sworn to secrecy. Luck was with us. There was a bird of his colouring. Cheppi Mark Two entered our lives. He, too, became pretty friendly but could not be coaxed to drink Bacardi cocktails. Nevertheless, my mother did not become suspicious.

Why did I always have to be home when something happened to the bird? Mitzi had now joined us and this time it was she who had left a window open and Mark Two flew out. When I'd come home from the convent it was Friday late afternoon. I found the poor woman in a panic. Thank God, both parents were gone. Being experienced now, I calmed her down and rushed her to the pet shop. We came home with another light green bird, Cheppi Mark Three. I promised never to tell, but this bird was not friendly.

Daddy was travelling America with an orchestra but Mommy was coming home the next day. We had less than 24 hours to tame it. I stuck it into the cage where it fluttered about, terrified when I stood near. No amount of cooing noises calmed it down. Yet, we had to get it used to us. There was no question of allowing it to fly about freely, so we moved the cage to wherever we sat. Sometime later after supper, Mitzi and I watched television. The cage was placed near to us. I can't remember which show, maybe Ed Sullivan, but a scantily dressed Harry Belafonte was singing a calypso song: *Hayho... hay ay ay oh... daylight come an' I wanna go home,* and then something to do with bananas. I'd stopped worrying about the bird because I was too involved watching Harry's naked midriff with a view of his lovely belly button gyrating to the calypso rhythm. I think this was the very first time a little hormone woke up inside me and I found the opposite sex extremely attractive in a way I couldn't quite define. Thank you, Mr Belafonte. I have you to blame for all of my future indiscretions.

When the music had stopped, my attention went back to the bird who was on his perch moving from right to left and then back again, strangely in a dancing rhythm. He was making little chirping noises, which sounded almost like speech. I wouldn't say he was tamed but I think he was happier. Perhaps he was a she.

When Mommy came home the bird was in its cage, very quiet and often seen with its head buried under a wing. She worried a little.

'I think he's sad,' I told her.

'Yes, he looks depressed,' she said and then continued, 'I vonder vhy?' in her Dracula accent.

'Maybe he's been alone for too long and needs a friend,' I

suggested timidly, being the only person who was aware of the entire history.

The next time I came home we had two birds. They flew happily about the flat and we could leave the windows open with impunity. Somehow, because they were a couple, they didn't need to explore the outside world. No eggs were ever produced, so we never knew their sex, but they seemed to want to be together. Our home was their home and even though I contracted the bird disease chlamydophilosis (due to inhaling the dust from the droppings of now two birds, but curable with specific antibiotics) we continued our close association with our feathered friends. They came all the way to Germany with us and were eventually eaten by Judy, my pet boxer, who became too tempted by these edible treats on the carpet hopping about for years and pecking at her nose. We were living in a house at that time, keeping windows and patio doors open, as usual. Mommy blamed the disappearance of the first on a stray cat. But with the second disappearance and a very guilty expression plus a light green feather still sticking to her muzzle, we knew who the culprit was. Thus ended our relationship with parakeets.

Convent school was becoming more bearable. The fact that I could go home on holidays and weekends helped sweeten the bitter pill. But sometimes those journeys were disturbing. My parents must have had confidence in my guardian angel because from the age of ten, I was travelling alone so that I learned at a very tender age about the misfits and perverts who shared the subway with me. It depended on the time of day. If I caught the train Sunday afternoon to return to Staten Island, I'd come across a few drunks, usually harmless except those who threw their beer bottles at passing trains. Then there were, in New York's parlance, 'the crazies'. These poor souls usually didn't appear until the evening, waiting for darkness like vampires. On the whole, if you had your nose in a book, they'd leave you alone. Eye contact excited them but sometimes it was unavoidable. The amount of times I had banana peels waved violently in my face makes me wonder today if banana skins had not become a sort of juju for these unfortunates. Until I learned how to cope with them, perverts were the most disturbing. If I had a slight fever Sunday lunchtime, something I managed by placing the tip of the thermometer on a heated radiator, I was allowed to spend another night at home. But this meant I had to travel in the rush hour the next morning. In a crowded carriage when everyone is pressed body to body, it's easy for a man's hands to have 'wanderlust'. The first time this happened I was amazed how adeptly my skirt was raised without my even being aware. I suddenly felt warm fingers brushing against the flesh of my upper thigh. I was sure it was the little man I was facing but I was imprisoned against all these taller chests and bellies and couldn't move away. The only thing I could do was scream but I was shy and too embarrassed to bring attention to myself. My convent education did not include this predicament as part of the curriculum. I can still see this man who was pressed against me, his rat like features, staring beady eyes, a skinny moustache shading his fat upper lip and his bad breath puffing in my face. I managed a quiet 'stop it' before his hands reached more private areas and the one thing I wanted to avoid happened: everyone turned to look at me. My whisper had been heard and my cheeks burned with shame. There again, the child feels guilty. We came to the next stop and the man fought his way to the door. By that time, he had a wagonload of eyes searing into the back of his neck. I saw him through the window scurrying away down the platform like the rat he was. Before another crowd could enter, a woman pulled me towards her. She never spoke to me but I understood she was protecting me. One stop before mine, she left the train, giving me a little smile and a pinch on my shoulder. Needless to say, I never saw her again. It taught me some lessons, though: in a crowded train try to stand with women, if that's not possible, just shout the moment you feel an indiscreet hand and to avoid rush hour, stop doing your thermometer against the radiator trick unless you know you'll get a lift to school.

I don't know why it happened but Sister Philomina invited me to share her room. This was a great honour. Her accommodation was a plain room with three single beds, each with a night stand and a little lamp for reading as well as a corner cell in which she slept made of wooden walls which did not go all the way to the ceiling but gave her enough privacy from her guests and a separate private bathroom off the entrance to her room. Whoever was invited into this hallowed chamber used the washing facilities upstairs.

She was not obese but there was a certain plumpness to her figure, which hinted to a disposition for finding pleasure in food, which she would share. Some people don't like drinking alone. She didn't like eating alone. It was usually between nine thirty and ten that Sister Philomina retired. I could still be awake reading. My life as her guest was less restricted. In the dorms upstairs lights went out at a strict time but being with her meant I could stay up a little later. When she'd make her entrance, she was often carrying a tray upon which could be certain treats: ice creams with hot chocolate sauce, a dish of French fries, ketchup and salt shaker supplied, delicious soups and sandwiches (she made the best tuna fish salad I'd ever tasted – I still imitate it today), and the best of all... steaming hot hamburgers in toasted buns with all the relishes and a large beaker of ice cold Coca-Cola to wash it down with. She'd give me my plate and then disappear behind her wooden walls. For a time, we'd talk. I was asked about my day, my studies, friends and parents. All of these conversations were accompanied by munching noises. When finished I'd put my plate or bowl onto the side table and stay awake to watch the main attraction: Sister Philomina getting undressed. As her walls did not go all the way up, I could see the light in her cell project shadows on the ceiling. Punk had not been invented by 1957, but the sight of dark spikes growing out of her head as she lifted off her bonnet and veil would have impressed those future bands. She seemed to shadow box her way out of the encumbering nun's habit and then I'd see raised arms and something slipped over the spikes which smoothed them down a bit. I heard more than saw the struggle with the nightdress being forced into place. Perhaps she'd not gone on a shopping spree lately to buy a larger size. There followed a silence and the vague form of a rounded shadow, which I presumed was she, on her knees praying. After a few minutes, the shadow moved and a squeak of springs from the bed told me she had climbed onto the mattress and then came a quiet 'good-night' in case I had already fallen asleep.

On one of these wonderful nights, she asked me if I didn't want to invite two friends to keep me company, there being three beds, after all.

And so we, who called ourselves the Three Musketeers all shared in her bounty. My mother had told me that I would eventually enjoy the boarding school, that I would look back on the experience with fond memories. Fond moments was more likely but I was happy in these last few months. Sis Chris seemed to have faded out of our lives. At 13, we'd grown taller than she. As with most bullies our size protected us.

We were an international trio. Susan was of Greek descent, Marlene was Cuban and I, a Hungarian. We were not overly devout. Becoming a nun was far from our aspirations. We were beginning to notice boys. The school had day students and boys were allowed in the elementary grades. All Three Musketeers had a crush on identical Italian twins called Michael and Robert. If things had worked out, one of us was going to be left out in the cold. As it was, the twins completely ignored us. Boys mature later than girls. Beyond this minor disappointment, I was beginning to have more confidence. I discovered I had a sense of humour, loved playing the clown and could make my friends laugh. My genetically inherited passion for horses manifested itself now by riding and drawing them. I was growing up. No longer, the sudden whinnies in corridors making nuns think I'd smuggled a pony into the building. Until my voice deepened I really could whinny and for a long time, I didn't run naturally, I cantered... sometimes with a stick between my teeth and a rope attached to both ends making a bridle. Some foolish friend would hold the rope like reins and follow my cantering around the playground. I was a horse shaking my mane and I could jump. The bit of bar between the seesaws made a perfect obstacle, as did leaping through the chains which held the seat of a swing. My 'rider' could not always negotiate these hurdles and so, either I was abruptly brought to my knees or she was. For years, I carried my ochre-coloured brushstrokes of iodine covering the scratches on my knees with pride.

A wonderful nun who was the art teacher in high school had seen my drawings. I remember her in a white veil, which meant she'd still have been a novice and I see her in my memory as quite young, perhaps in her early twenties. She was beautiful in a natural way and I wondered why she wanted to be a nun and not get married. At this time, I was in the eighth grade – a year before high school.

'I'm looking forward to having you in my art class,' she told me. 'Keep drawing whatever you want to. Just draw. You have a real talent.'

It was the first time someone had encouraged me with such enthusiasm. This is how the building blocks of confidence construct a self-assured person. It only takes a few stimulating words uttered sincerely. I doodled like mad and couldn't wait to become her art student.

Then the carpet was whipped from under my feet. During the Christmas holiday of 1957, my father announced that we were going to Munich, Germany, the following February.

My brothers had stopped being miniature soldiers and became students at a boy's lay Catholic boarding school in Connecticut until they'd run away. Unlike my very young escapade, they really had reason. The headmaster of their school was a sexual sadist.

Whatever brought the punishment on, nothing could have warranted the pain and humiliation Paul suffered. His underpants were ripped off him in a bathroom. The headmaster, a large man, sat on the edge of the tub and forced Paul across his knees. He beat his naked buttocks with a long handled scrubbing brush about 40 times. At the age of 16, one would have thought he'd outgrown such chastisement.

Paul was determined to run away the following day but he had to let Peter know. It was then that Peter begged him to take him along. He was afraid to be left behind and rightly so. The two snuck out of the school's property at night and made it to the train station where they stayed out of sight until the train heading for New York arrived which was near to midnight. As they were boarding the train, Paul felt a hand on his shoulder, turned around and looked into the face of his headmaster who was accompanied by two policemen. Both boys were taken back to his office. It was well past midnight. The headmaster picked up the telephone.

In New York my father woke up and got out of bed to answer the headmaster's call. He was told about the incident. Daddy asked to speak to Paul and when the phone was transferred to him, he began to relate his side of the story in Hungarian. Paul was not especially fluent in the language but had enough vocabulary to explain and accuse the headmaster of being a *buzy*, the Hungarian for a 'queer'.

My father arrived at the school at ten am and picked up his sons. The headmaster threatened to sue for lost fees. Daddy threatened to go public about his mode of punishment. Stalemate.

The fact that we were going to Munich was welcomed by the boys. There was too little time to enrol them into another school so for the time being they found little jobs to earn a bit of spending money.

I returned to the convent for a few weeks after the holidays. It was a sad time knowing the chances of seeing Susan and Marlene ever again were slim, no matter how much we promised each other. Munich was far away and I had no idea for how long I'd be there. Our farewells were loud and tearful. We were the Three Musketeers! We'd spent time at each other's homes and known each other's deepest secrets. I was 13 and despaired of ever having such close friends again.

I had trepidations about the new school. Would the art teacher there be as encouraging? I remember throwing a fit about having, yet again, to learn another language and was afraid I'd lose a grade. The term had already begun which gave me no time to relearn German. Daddy calmed me down. It was an American school, he told me. All lessons were taught in English.

In one way it was an adventure but in another, my roots in New York were beginning to grow. I was too young when we moved from Hungary to Austria and then to America to understand what uprooting meant. It was my family, which had made up my life but now I'd acquired a personal universe, albeit small, but it was expanding. I had friends and interests beyond my familial enclave. I was only 13 and had serious worries about what the future would bring.

In the end, the sense of adventure won out, the opportunity to explore another world began to intrigue me.

Once again we'd kiss Mitzi goodbye. She had been found a position with another family and was staying in New York. I didn't watch her pack the suitcases this time and didn't see if she cried. I felt mature and determined to do my own.

CHAPTER IV

The four turbo-prop engines roared. My whole body felt the vibrations as the TWA Super Constellation taxied its way around La Guardia airport towards the runway from which it would lumber up into the night sky. The adrenalin rush I was feeling was not caused by fear but rather the thrill of it all. In six years' time I would be winging around the world, nonchalantly swallowing air miles along with Champagne. But this experience was unforgettable. As the plane climbed, it banked and the lights from the city twinkled up at us. I was in an upside down world and loving it.

Radio Free Europe generously travelled us in style. We had been given first class tickets and in those days, first class meant exactly that. There were even bunks behind drawn curtains for us to sleep in. A glamorous stewardess served us the dinner on porcelain plates with silver plated cutlery. We had white linen serviettes. Smoked salmon and filet mignon were on the menu. I was allowed a taste of Champagne in a crystal glass. How travelling has gone downhill since then.

We were only my father, Peter and I. It had been explained to me that Mommy would stay behind until matters with the flat had been settled and some arrangements for the shipping of furniture completed. No-one mentioned why Paul remained with her. I presumed it was to keep her company. He was her favourite, after all.

The following morning a simple welcome awaited us at Munich airport. We had flown from the opulent to the meagre. Having left La Guardia with its brilliantly lit, sprawling size and busy traffic, we'd landed on a single strip of runway cutting through fenced off fields in a flat countryside, which, come the spring, would be used for grazing sheep and cattle. No other planes were in sight, no great terminals, just a red brick building, perhaps four stories high with the glass encased uppermost of these serving as the control tower.

The traces of February 6th's Munich disaster, when the BEA plane carrying Manchester United's 'Busby Babes', their supporters and journalists crashed on its slush covered runway on their third attempt to take off were cleared away. Our departure had been delayed for one day for this reason. My father had mentioned an 'incident' at Munich's airport, but for fear of frightening us, he did not go into detail.

We were met by Erik Hazelhoff, the legendary Dutch resistance fighter, RAF pilot and author of *Soldier of Orange*, which in 1977 was made into a successful film starring the actor Rutger Hauer who played Erik on the screen.

He was now in a more discreet role as director of Radio Free Europe and the friendly gesture of him collecting us was appreciated. We would benefit from RFE's family atmosphere towards their employees. Daddy was going to work for the Hungarian desk. It was not yet two full years since Budapest's uprising and important to continue broadcasting the truth and advocating democracy to the countries behind the iron curtain. Rumours abounded that RFE was not innocent in stirring up the passions which led to the demonstration outside the government controlled radio station. It was from there that the secret police fired their guns into, as yet, a peaceful crowd containing women and children. That was the igniting flame which burned into an abortive, violent struggle: Molotov cocktails against Russian tanks. We've all seen the news reels. What was not common knowledge at the time and for some years later, was that RFE was CIA funded. Not until the clumsy plot of arsenic-polluted salt-shakers in its Munich canteen was uncovered in 1960, did the suspicion of 'a front' organization for the CIA come up.

Erik drove us through Munich to the apartment which was allocated for our family. He explained districts and landmarks as we passed them. Daddy was in front with him, Peter and me in the back. Most of the city was intact but there were certain horrifying pockets which we looked out on in disbelief. We had been protected. New York had not suffered any destruction. Neither had Kniegle. We were too young to remember Budapest, so seeing the results of the bombings was shocking. These areas had not yet been cleared away by the bulldozers. We sat in the back in silence digesting the sight. Nineteenth century mansion blocks containing dwellings had imploded in to rubble, their stone balconies with gracefully carved images hung askew across what remained of their facades. A church with a shard like steeple scratched the sky. It had a crater where there should have been a roof.

Our car bumped along cobbled streets crisscrossed by tram tracks. We arrived at our destination, a suburb of Munich called Nymphenburg, seemingly untouched by the war. Ludvig of Bavaria built a palace nearby from which the area received its name. His intention had been to outdo Versailles. He almost succeeded.

The Americans built housing for their troops and those who worked for their companies. In a few days' time, I'd discover an isolated world dedicated to make life bearable for its citizens. The huge military headquarters called McGraw Kaserne was home for unmarried soldiers living in barracks, a large snack bar and the overseas branch of the University of Maryland as well as the military police and their holding cells. There were many other buildings with officers circulating within but I never learned for what purpose they were for. Beyond its gates was a school, hospital, cinema, church and purpose built apartment blocks, little villas for the more important with scheduled buses to carry passengers for free to their chosen addresses. They knew how to look after their own and in these zones, never a word of German needed to be spoken. There was also a shopping centre called the PX where all things American were available to guard against its people going into culture shock. No bratwurst and sauerkraut was forced on its citizens but some came to enjoy such fare, especially the beer. The springs and wide wings of huge American cars foundered on Munich's narrow, cobblestoned streets and yet, they were preferred to the more practical Volkswagen. The goods were paid for with a special paper currency as the dollar was protected. You can imagine all the troops and their dependents exchanging dollars into marks would have depleted the federal reserves. These paper bills reminded me of monopoly money. They were certainly not more substantial.

Erik helped us bring our suitcases up the stairs. He opened the door with a key and then handed it to my father wishing us well and leaving us to make our own explorations. Our three-bedroomed flat was on the third storey of a double fronted building. All of the apartments the house contained were for RFE employees with families. The floor above ours, under the roof, had six bedrooms with washing facilities for the maids. One for every family. We were encouraged to have home help. RFE salaries were generous. Poverty and unemployment were rampant in post-war Munich. By hiring a maid we were helping the economy. I would hear this theory later coined with the expression, 'The trickle down effect'.

The basement consisted of a huge garage, enough space for six cars and a washroom with the newest machines. All necessary furniture was supplied. The kitchen had a reasonable compliment of pots, pans, cutlery, etc. Even sheets and towels made up the inventory. As everything was already there, I wondered what furniture we'd have room for when it arrived from America. We marvelled at the consideration that went behind making a family ready to take up residency.

Then came a gentle knock on the door. Trudi introduced herself. She was small, thin, red haired, in her early forties with deep lines sketched into her face. She began telling my father in broken English that she'd been notified of our coming and was presenting herself in the hope of becoming our maid. They lapsed into German and my father replied that he would be happy to employ her but warned of my mother's impending arrival and, of course, she would have the last word. Trudi accepted this condition and asked if she should do a little shopping for us. She would like to begin immediately and she knew the neighbourhood. Daddy had been given enough Deutschmarks to tide him over so he handed her an amount she thought she'd need. Trudi left and Peter and I looked at him in amazement.

'You've just given a complete stranger some money,' Peter said, aghast. 'Why?'

The rest of that conversation which had taken place in German, we couldn't understand. Daddy explained and we waited with baited breath for her return to see if she merited the trust he had given her. When almost an hour had passed, he began to feel a bit of a fool but then came another light knock on the door and there stood Trudi holding a cloth bag containing our essentials. She handed over the change, put things into the fridge and excused herself until the next morning when she'd prepare our breakfast. Trudi stayed with us. She occupied one of those rooms in the loft and I would learn from her about Munich during the war and what its inhabitants underwent. She had chosen domestic service over prostitution because she wanted to be a good example for her daughter who was living with her mother. Trudi's pittance of a salary went to buy mother and daughter their necessities. She never spoke of a husband or the father to her child. And I didn't wish to pry. Trudi was kind to me and understanding, often comforting me after having witnessed some of Mommy's more violent tempers, which we all would soon enough.

Once again Mommy did not want to follow us. Unbeknownst to Peter and myself, our parents were planning a separation. Divorce was forbidden in the Catholic faith and since our escape, Daddy had become more and more religious. She was desperately in love and wanting to stay on in New York with the hope of a promise from the partner in their affair... Victor. Their situation must have been discussed because we children had been divided amongst the two of them. Peter and I with Daddy and Paul with her. Victor would not commit himself to such a serious undertaking. I'm sure he was in love but not yet ready to separate from his family. He did so later, leaving his wife for a much younger woman, went to live with her in Arizona and became virtually *incommunicado* to his children. It was after this event Elizabeth told me that if ever there had been a question of divorce, she and her brothers would have preferred Kati *neni* as their stepmother.

Maybe the timing had not been right. When he refused to consolidate their relationship, Mommy made the only choice an 'all or nothing' person would: she accepted the first available second class cabin on the luxury liner, *SS Elizabeth*, to join her husband in Munich. Paul came with her but he travelled steerage. Although RFE were generous, travelling on a cruise liner was more expensive than our first class tickets on an airplane. When the ship steamed into the deep Atlantic waters, she sent a telegram to Victor, quoting from their favourite song of the time sung by Julie London, 'Cry me a river. I cried a river over you.' Well, she was a romantic.

Her arrival with Paul at Munich's main station, the *Hauptbahnhof* and the consequent introduction to our flat was disturbing for me. We waited for their train on the platform. Daddy had parked our Opel near the station. When the train pulled in, porters went to meet the opening doors of the wagons. All I saw through the bobbing heads of the crowd approaching us was Paul and Mommy behind a trolley piled high with suitcases being pulled by a porter. We waved our hands over our heads to be noticed. The laden trolley and Mommy passed by, she staring straight ahead, determined to ignore us. Only Paul stopped to give us a hug. We followed the luggage to the entrance, Mommy never turning round. Daddy explained to the porter that he'd fetch our car but it was also necessary to pile some suitcases into a taxi. Not a word between our parents had been spoken nor from Mommy to Peter and me. This feeling of rejection stayed with me for a long time but even longer with Peter who was more sensitive and easily hurt. We piled into our car with the taxi behind. During the entire journey a frigid silence answered any comments and small talk my father may have made. Mommy looked out of the window, still as a marble statue. In the back of the car, Paul tried to lighten the mood for Peter and me but we were too shocked to pay him much attention. When we arrived at the apartment house, each of us carried whatever load we were capable of up the two flights of stairs.

On opening the door and Mommy crossing the threshold we heard the first words she uttered since arriving at the station.

'Where's the bedroom?' The question was not posed out of curiosity. It was loaded with animosity. Whatever Daddy had hoped for with their reconciliation was shattered in the next few moments. She strode into the bedroom and furiously yanked the single beds, which had been placed against each other apart. That was the start to the rest of their lives together. My brothers were adolescents. I was just beginning this confusing state of being. We were not equipped with the understanding that comes with experience, nor with the facts. All we saw was our mother behaving unjustly towards our father. This did not bode well for the future. We were all going to have to live together: no more boarding schools for the children, no more long absences for Daddy travelling with his orchestras which meant no more private time for Mommy to indulge her passions. She was 43, living in a strange country and utterly dependent on her husband. She was going to have to get used to this new situation. Having lost Victor, she'd had too much time to think resentful thoughts on the journey across the ocean.

The separation of the beds had a reason, which she admitted to me when in years to come I was unsuccessfully trying to become pregnant.

'I don't understand. All I had to do was to look at a man and I'd become pregnant,' she told me.

'But you only had three,' I retorted.

There was a pause after which said, 'In my day, we didn't have the pill. Either I had to do everything possible to avoid pregnancy or it was the man. But Kepi was not always so responsible.'

Then she told me about the abortion. Finding herself pregnant at the age of 41, she turned to her closest Hungarian girl friend, who gave her an address of a doctor in Harlem and made an appointment. He did what was necessary and told her to go home to wait for the pain. But before she left he asked, 'Do you drink?'

'Yes.'

'Good. What's your poison?'

'Scotch,' she answered.

'Buy a bottle on your way home. You'll need it,' he said and, 'do you have a friend who can be with you?'

'Yes. I'm going to her place.'

'Good. Any problems, call me. I'll come immediately.'

She paid him. It was virtually a pittance, she said. He told her, he did not practice this act for the money. Living in Harlem, he saw too many unwanted pregnancies and their results. He was on the woman's side to choose. She shook his large black hand when leaving. He gave a little squeeze to her delicate white one and wished her luck.

Other than the excruciating pain and the bleeding, all went as the doctor had told her to expect.

She was positive it was not Victor's child and wrote a letter to my father who was in California at the time, describing in detail what she had gone through. Never, she had written, would she allow him to touch her again. That was the end of their intimate relationship and the cause for the gesture of separating the beds, lest Daddy harbour other ideas.

I glowed in those moments of being her confidante and admired her honesty. I made no judgments on her actions. It was her life. Having missed out on motherhood, though, I often wondered what it would have been like having a sibling almost 12 years younger than me. I think I would have liked that. On the other hand, I may have smothered the brat with a pillow out of pure jealousy.

CHAPTER V

While the cat's away, the mice will play. By the time Mommy joined us, this mouse learned to smoke and to accept drinks bought for her by friendly GIs in shabby little bars. I was only 13, albeit tall for my age, but never was I asked for identification. Either Germany didn't have underage drinking laws, I could pass for 18, or the barkeepers didn't give a damn. I think the latter must have been the case.

Daddy didn't come home until seven. School finished at four. This gave me enough time to misbehave. I always arrived before he did, went straight to my room and pretended to do homework.

Munich American High School belonged to the USAREUR category. It existed to educate the children of the American forces in Europe as well as RFE, Radio Liberty, Voice of America, the Diplomatic Corps. Actually, all Americans whose offspring were of school age had the right to attend for a fee. Army dependents went for free. When compared to the public school system in the States, the standard of teaching and the wide curriculum in these schools was exemplary.

Every morning before lessons began, we gathered as groups into what was known as 'home room'. Each of these had a different teacher who was there to advise and help us organize our day. We could use these 20 minutes to finish off homework, copy a smart friend's homework or just gossip. On my first day at this gathering the teacher introduced me to my classmates. I noticed that, at 5 foot 7, I was a head taller than all the boys. For some strange reason, he chose a girl to show me the ropes who would become the instigator of my vices. It was as if he paired us together thinking we were two of a kind and it was not at all the case. I may have looked sophisticated but was an innocent; she was sophisticated and already well travelled on the road to debauchery. I have forgotten her name but will call her Pat. She was only supposed to take me to the different classrooms, show me where my locker was, the gym, canteen, etc. I don't think the teacher intended for Pat to show me how to smoke, to drink pure vodka without vomiting (not always successful) and how to play 'hooky' from school. We were in the eighth grade! She was 13 going on 30. I was 13 coming from nine. My schooling had been strict and disciplined as was my home life. I had not been prepared yet to think for myself. It was easier to follow, as I wanted to belong and was not confidant enough to assert myself. I was flattered that Pat liked me. Besides which, I was enjoying it.

The most naughty I had been was when we Three Musketeers took a smuggled cigarette and some matches behind a bush in the convent grounds. We lit it, took a puff, coughed copiously, took another puff to prove we weren't sissies, turned green and decided it was something only movie stars and our parents could do with grace. This became known as the burning bush incident as one of the nuns spotted the cloud of smoke hovering over our hiding-place. We were not punished because she did not know who the culprits were and we didn't offer to inform her.

By the time Mommy took over our control, some of the harm where I was concerned had already been done. I was hooked on nicotine but ten cigarettes a week was all I could afford. When the need to feed my habit became stronger, I am ashamed to admit, I resorted to nicking cigarettes from my mother's packet as well as a dollar or two from her wallet, which goes to substantiate the connection between drug taking and crime.

To tell the truth, I completely unravelled in those months between February and the end of term in June. It was as if the tightly fitting jumper, which had been expressly knitted for me with different coloured and textured wool was being unpicked. It had been made as a constraint and now a flabby body was bulging out. It was not a pretty sight.

On some of the days I played hooky. I got off the school bus, met with another delinquent and boarded the free bus, which drove us to a tram station. We'd then travel to the centre of Munich, which was beginning to boast some department stores and indulge in a bit of shoplifting. I'd been given a coat for the previous Christmas, still in Manhattan, but with the anticipation of going to Munich in deep winter. It was a full length brown fake fur made of nylon and I called it 'the bear'. We'd stroll through the aisles of the store where articles of clothing were strewn across counters. They ranged from underwear to pullovers, scarves and blouses. It was before these stores became more organized and displayed their wears more fashionably. I'd get a wink from my companion who'd point to an article. The bear was placed upon it. I'd scrunch it into a fold, pick the coat up, hold it tightly and walk calmly out of the premises followed by my accomplice. Once outside, she'd scream with delight. I had made a true friend. I can honestly say I never stole anything for myself. I was afraid Mommy would not recognize the article and ask pertinent questions. She always knew when I lied. My face turned red as a radish.

One day, during a shoplifting sortie, a woman shadowed us. I felt her presence wherever we stopped to examine the goods on display. The bear remained hanging across the crook of my arm. To the disappointment of the friend I was with, we walked out empty-handed. Outside on the pavement, the enormity of what I was doing and risking suddenly hit me. Instead of the usual addictive thrill I enjoyed whenever I got away with it, this time I suffered a cold warning shiver up my spine. It cured me of this nasty habit.

The fact that I failed the end of term exams, which meant I could be returning to the 8th grade, made me come to my senses. I must admit, my parents were very understanding. Even the school made excuses for me. They had received my records from the convent academy. I'd been a good student there and on arriving to Munich American High, we kids were given an IQ test. I had not failed because I was incapable.

My parents and I sat quietly listening to the school principal, Mr Gleason.

'This has been known to happen,' he began. 'Sometimes the change from a strict environment to a more liberal one can cause a child to disconnect from their former behaviour.'

If he only knew, I thought.

'It takes time to acclimatize to this more relaxed method of education. The stricter the past, the more confusing the present.' He was being so reasonable.

My parents nodded, agreeing with Mr Gleason. Everyone was being utterly sympathetic. I hung my head in shame.

'So,' he continued. 'We're going to give her a chance. We'll pass her up to the Freshman year in high school on the proviso that she maintain a C+ average for the first half of the term.' He looked at me through his thick glasses and said, 'One F and you're back in the 8th grade.'

I didn't need another reminder. Just the thought of being surrounded by 13 year olds when I would have had my 14th birthday, was anathema to me. Surrounded by babies half my size! Ooh, the arrogance of youth.

When the next term started, Peter was in his junior year and Paul, his senior. Over 6 foot tall and of athletic build, Peter discovered football and played on the school's team. He was a popular student, admired by girls and boys alike. When it was discovered that Gregory was his middle name, it became his sobriquet. With only a slight tweak of the imagination, Peter resembled Gregory Peck. But he was shy and I don't remember him ever going out with a girl during his high school years. I do remember, though, an unforgettable sight. A football game had been stopped because he had lost a contact lens during the affray and his hard helmeted, broad, plastic shouldered team mates as well as those of the opposing side were on their hands and knees searching through the muddy mess of the football field... and they found it! He stuck the lens in his mouth to rinse it and once it was popped back in his eye, the game restarted.

His ambivalent nature, though, was beginning to surface. Most of the time he was a gentle giant with poetic leanings but a more aggressive mood could envelope him. During these, he liked to go 'rumbling' with a friend and find unsuspecting Germans to brawl against. After these bouts, he returned with bruised and swollen knuckles but hardly any marks on his face, which could only have meant that he, got the better of his victims. Peter was not a bully. It was as if he had to satisfy a devil within himself, a devil that required causing pain to others, so that afterwards, he could be free to satisfy the angel who suited the temperament he was more comfortable with. At that time the 'bad behaviour' would have been blamed on adolescent testosterone. He was only 17 and still five years away from an eventual diagnosis of paranoid schizophrenia. The relation of that tragedy will have to wait for now.

Paul, on the other hand, was very aloof. He found a best friend called Patrick O'Neil whose father was a writer living in Munich. The two were inseparable, living in a sophisticated world of their own making. They ignored most of the students in their senior class, preferring to seek adult amusements such as getting on a train and spending a weekend in Paris. I don't know about Patrick but I never saw Paul study. It seemed he only had to sit in a class and, by osmosis, he'd absorb the lesson. Their life style was enviable, the epitome of cool, chic and charm. Ergo, nobody liked them.

An American company came to film a television series at the Bavaria studios on the outskirts of Munich. It was to do with the Vikings and starred Jerome Courtland and the ex-boxer, Buddy Baer. When Patrick heard about it, he presented himself for whatever role possible. He was a good-looking lad in an Irish gamin way and was hired. Thereupon, he kissed the school goodbye. Paul, also a good looker, did a bit of extra work for the money but decided he wanted to graduate and go to college. This must have been where Patrick was infected by the 'acting bug'. When in the following year, he returned to the States, he continued to work in the business acting in a popular TV western called the Virginian and then later acquiring fame as Rodney Harrington in *Peyton Place*. There already being a well respected theatrical actor by the name of Patrick O'Neil, he changed his name to Ryan. And the rest is history.

When, in the future, Peter had become a quadriplegic, and had been repatriated from Germany to a hospital in Bethesda, Maryland, by the State Department and upon hearing of his plight from Paul, Ryan, to Peter's astonishment and delight, leapt on a plane to give him a surprise visit. The nursing staff could not believe their luck when he strolled on to the ward. They had never been in such close proximity to a handsome, romantic hero. According to the press and gossip, Ryan could have 'personality problems'. It was said he could resort to violence to settle certain issues. And, yet, he was obviously capable of great kindness. The visit was a source of tremendous happiness for Peter, just to know he had not been forgotten.

Mr Carlini was extremely gay in every sense of the word. He was the speech and drama teacher and it was his responsibility to produce and direct the junior/senior class play. I was in my penultimate year when he was casting for *Ring Around the Moon* and he offered me the role of Lady India. It was a small part with little to say but a show stealer. I had to dance a tango with my husband, which we achieved, to the hilarious amusement of the audience. I loved being on stage and with Mr Carlini's encouragement I realized I could be quite outrageous. But I also learned that making people laugh is a deadly serious business. The stricter and more sober our expressions were while moving through the intricate steps of a classical tango, the more the audience laughed. I think it helped that I was several inches taller than my partner. We were trained for the tango by a professional dance teacher and I have to admit, we did it terribly well, receiving a standing ovation as we glided off the stage. At the end of the performance, Mr Carlini promised me a starring part in his next production. It never happened. Mr Carlini disappeared. He did not return the following year but I joined the speech and drama class nevertheless with a different tutor, and appeared as Gwendolen in *The Importance of Being Earnest*. My mother who had been in the audience the previous year watching me as Lady India decided to invite a well-known Hungarian director called Géza von Radványi to witness my performance. This was done secretly. I had no idea that a proper theatre and film director would be watching me and didn't realize she harboured ambitions for me. It was not as if she had showered me with praise for Lady India. If he deemed I was good, she'd push me. If I was useless, I could forget an acting career. For me, it was just fun. I had no intentions of continuing seriously.

There was a sympathetic art teacher who was very encouraging, like the nun in the convent, as was the creative writing tutor. For a while, I thought of becoming a writer and illustrator but knew there was a shortage of money. I also toyed with the idea of being a reporter but for this, I'd need a university education. I felt ill equipped to comment on world events without the benefit of further education – which Daddy had told me he couldn't afford as he was already sending my two brothers to college in Florida. This was the only argument I ever had with him. Mommy witnessed it but remained quiet throughout. He didn't think girls needed to go through university. We would get married, anyway. It was a waste of money. I couldn't believe my ears that this normally reasonable man could have such antiquated ideas.

I remember the argument well. We had moved to a house in a green suburb of Munich called Bogenhausen. It took place in the spacious living room and, when I heard his refusal and the reasons why, I stomped up the stairs to my bedroom, shouting over my shoulder, 'In that case, I'll become an actress!' – thinking this would shock him into submission.

On the contrary. At this point, Mommy chipped in with, 'That's fine but you will have to go to acting school.' For a moment I saw myself in New York and thrilled at the thought. But how could he afford that? Then she continued, 'Here in Munich, of course, which means you'll have to learn perfect German.'

After the performance as Gwendolen, von Radványi was invited back to our home to discuss my future as an actress. My mother had not told him which part I was playing and according to her, the moment I walked on stage and said my first line, he nudged her and whispered, 'Whoever that girl is, she was born to be an actress.'

During that evening I was lectured about the utter commitment required to becoming an actress. He described what I would have to forsake: the career comes before personal relationships, no partying as I'd need beauty sleep, no alcohol when working because I'd need a good memory to learn my lines, (also because it would give me lines). I'd have to follow a strict diet to retain my figure.

'I assume you want to be a leading lady. When you're much older you can start playing character roles. Eat whatever you like then.' He explained. 'And smoking should be to a minimum. You'll need good lungs to get through long soliloquies without gasping for breath.' He was smoking a big cigar as he spoke.

Every decision I would make for my future as an actress would be with a tenacity to concentrate only on that goal, remaining narrow-minded and blinkered. The further he expounded, the less sure I was of wanting to pursue this profession. It didn't sound much fun. I might as well become a nun. He was painting a picture darker than the reality to determine my resolve. As in the 'black dog' situation from my early childhood, I reacted as was expected of me – I cried. My tears were interpreted as a recognition of the pain I would assume in my engagement to the career I'd dedicate my life to. We talked about acting school. There was an excellent one in Munich called the Falckenberg *Schule*. It was terribly difficult to get into. An audition was held for prospective students out of which very few would be accepted. Of course, the audition would be in German. He presumed I'd be fluent enough by that time.

I was having difficulties with learning languages in the school. I'd failed French and, as a 'punishment' by my father, who considered languages the passport to life, I was sent to a school in Château-d'Oex, Switzerland for the summer in the hope of returning with a bit more use of the language. It was the happiest summer I ever spent, galloping along Alpine tracks, spending time with Elizabeth who had come from New York, meeting sweet Italian boys who were there for the same reasons in their summer schools and French was the only language we had in common. When my parents came at the end of eight weeks to pick me up, I babbled in French to them. But, unfortunately, back in Munich American High, writing it was still difficult. French is not phonetic. I only achieved a C+ even though my accent and fluency were better than our teacher's who took our hour's lesson immediately after lunch as his naptime. He had perfected a technique of sitting straight behind his desk, head lowered to his chest and snoring discreetly while we wrote whatever he decided for us so that we didn't need to disturb him with conversation. Being tested on these dissertations, which concentrated more on spelling and grammar than content, I didn't receive high marks.

German classes were no better, having forgotten everything except to count and the word *kravat*. It is said that language returns because it is never lost but just packed away in the subconscious. Well, my German had been packed into a trunk, locked and the key thrown away. I struggled with the vocabulary and the complicated grammar as if I'd never heard it spoken in my life. It did not help that our teacher, short, stout and very blond was a German herself who taught us with the sensitivity and charm of a Gestapo officer. We spent more time in furtive ridicule than attention to the lesson. I also only received a C. If I was going to do this audition, I'd really have to buckle down.

After graduation it seemed as if all my friends melted away. One by one, they went back to the States leaving me on my own. I was told the audition would take place early September and I'd have to do soliloquies from three different plays of my choosing. During that summer, Daddy gave me an allowance for which I furiously washed and waxed his car. He also paid for lessons at a Berlitz school in the centre of Munich. Having been cocooned for years in an American atmosphere, I was now having to interact with the people of my host country. Once again I felt an alien in another world. But I had done it before, I could do it again. I put myself into integration gear and began mingling with some delightful Germans. We never stopped laughing. When I hear people say that Germans don't have a sense of humour I become very angry. What do they know if they don't speak the language? Although not yet fully fluent, I still understood enough to be highly amused and if I didn't get the joke, it would be explained to me in perfect English, which already then was their second language.

The three plays I'd chosen were Tennessee William's *A Streetcar Named Desire*, Bernard Shaw's *Saint Joan* and Shakespeare's *Macbeth*. Having found the German versions, I began to study. My mother was wonderful. As I didn't have the plays in English, she helped me to understand the texts. I do believe she enjoyed coaching me. All languages have their peculiar rhythms and stresses. Unless you're acquainted with them, you can make nonsense of a sentence. It's all well and good to speak a language one is learning amongst friends but talking text is what actors are trained to do. Making it sound natural is the secret. Having Mommy as an audience was very useful but as she was helping me I realized I was picking up her Dracula accent. For the moment, there was nothing I could do about that. Anyway, it sort of came naturally.

I received the letter from the Falkenberg telling me the day in the beginning of September to present myself and at what time. It was in the middle of the afternoon. I took the bus and then a tram with the pocket-sized plays quivering in my sweaty hands and the buzzing of a beehive in my stomach. On arrival to the school, I was told to wait in an anteroom of the auditorium where the audition would take place. The organizers, with typical German pre-planning had got the timing almost to perfection. I could hear a voice coming from next door from another contender reciting her prose. She came to an end. There were low voices in conversation, which after a moment became silent. She must have used another exit because I never saw her leave. A woman opened the door and popped her head through to usher me in. It turned out this door led directly to a well-lit stage. As the lights were in my eyes, I could barely distinguish the people sitting in the middle seats of the audience.

A brief exchange took place with these dark shapes. They asked which plays I had chosen. I named them and was then directed to start. I began with Saint Joan. There was a bit of humbling on my knees for that one. The next was Blanche accusing Stanley of being a brute. The last was Lady M. walking back and forth in distress while wringing her hands complaining about copious amounts of blood. I finished having remembered all my lines. The shadowy figures huddled together and discussed. I stood peering at their silhouettes. It took quite some time for them to come to a decision. I was convinced I had failed.

And then, one of them said, 'Good. We would like you to do an improvisation, though. Imagine that you need to make a phone call. There is a public booth but there is already someone using the phone. How would you get this person to hang up? If you so desire, feel free to speak in Hungarian.' They'd noticed the accent.

'Actually,' I said in German, 'I hardly speak Hungarian. English is my best language.' After some puzzled murmurings, they told me to start. I exited the stage and walked back on in a hurry, stopping abruptly in front of the imaginary phone box. Finding someone already on the phone, I turned around and walked a few feet away looking at an imaginary watch on my wrist. I waited looking up to the sky with one foot tapping on the floor. I turned my head to see an imaginary other person approach the phone box and rushed forward to stand at its entrance, signalling that I was first in the queue. My eyes followed the person walk away. I grinned stupidly, shrugged my shoulders and whispered, 'Sorry'. I went to the side of the phone box to stare in and mimed knocking on the glass. I lifted my left arm and pointed at my wrist. The imaginary person turned his/her back to me. I rushed to the other side of the box and mimed pounding on the glass with my fists.

There was some chuckling coming from the audience. I hadn't intended to make them laugh but it was an encouraging sound. My movements became more frenetic running from one side of the box to the other interspersed with more pounding on the glass. The chuckling turned into laughter. Until now other than the whispered 'Sorry', I hadn't uttered a word. I stopped, gasping for breath at the front of the box and swung the imaginary door wide open. The word, 'motivation' in an acting sense was unknown to me and yet, there had to be a reason why I needed to make this phone call so urgently. Suddenly some course reading came to mind from my last year's psychology class. I shouted into the interior of the phone box, 'You don't understand! I have to phone my psychiatrist!' and proceeded to pull the person out of the box and push them rudely away.

In between laughter, I heard one of the silhouettes say in English, 'Fine, very good (chuckle, chuckle). You can go now. We will be in touch.'

Also, happily unknown to me was the famous Hollywood studio instruction, 'Don't call us. We'll call you.'

I had no idea if I would be accepted. Receiving the mail became a nail-biting time but it was not the only revelation I was anxiously waiting for. I had had an unfortunate brush in with sex a little over a month after my 18th birthday. In those days, the expression of 'date rape' had not been invented. What I went through was neither a real date nor a real rape. It was more a reluctant coercion. I call it the 'incident' whereby I lost my virginity.

He was five years older than me and a corporal in the Intelligence Corps. We'd gone out together the previous year when I was only 17. I considered myself unready, in the then vernacular, to go 'all the way'. This became a frustration for him so he dropped me for an older college girl who was the daughter of a general.

Our relationship ended for me in complete humiliation. There was a reason one evening that I had to stay behind school and would miss the bus home. S promised to give me a lift in his car. We arranged to meet in our usual bar/café, the Blue Room, at a certain time. I was there and waited almost an hour until he finally walked in holding hands with this college girl. They sat down at a table and began laughing in a conspiratorial way. It was obvious this was not their first date. I wanted to sneak out unseen but there was only one exit and they had chosen the table next to it. I couldn't believe I'd been stood up so callously. Hitherto, he had shown some sensitivity. I liked the way he spoke about his parents and his close relationship with his sister. Although he came from the Deep South, he was, by no means, a bigoted redneck as were many other GIs I'd met from his state. At least, that was the impression he gave at that time.

Forced to pass their table on leaving, I stopped so that he'd notice me. For an asinine moment I imagined what I'd seen was all a terrible mistake. Surely, he could not have forgotten and they hadn't really been holding hands when entering. She was actually his sister on a surprise visit and I'd be introduced. All would be well. He looked up and saw me. If a facial expression can depict 'oh shit', his was a study.

'I thought you were taking me home tonight. Don't you remember?' I asked meekly.

'No,' he answered with a touch of embarrassment.

And then I posed the most ridiculous question of all. 'So, you're not going to drive me home?'

And the obvious answer followed. 'No.'

I gathered whatever pride I was left with and walked out of the door into the night with no idea how I was going to get home, tears streaming down my face. The nearest streetcar was a long walk away and it was too late for the bus that would have taken me there. Luck was with me, though. Someone I vaguely knew, another student from the U. of Maryland, came riding past on his Triumph motorbike and saw me. Realising I was in distress, he stopped and asked what the trouble was. I told him I'd been stood up and didn't know how I'd get home. Those were the days before helmets were obligatory. I was wearing trousers so he beckoned me to straddle the saddle behind him, to hold tight and took me all the way across Munich to where I lived. It was the first time I'd ever been on a motorbike. The cold air blowing through my hair and on my face helped to dry the tears. Like a white knight on his black steed, he dropped me at my door, turned and kicked the bike as if to gallop. I watched mount and rider speed away.

It would have been after nine when I walked in and went straight upstairs to my bedroom. I had started crying again when I heard a gentle tap on my door, accompanied by my mother's voice calling my name.

'Katica,' she whispered. It was almost as if she didn't want my father to be involved. Somehow, her instinct had told her this was going to be woman's talk. I told her what had happened. I may have had a difficult relationship with her but there were some things I knew I could depend on. If I was threatened, she'd fight like a tiger to defend me. If I were ill, she'd nurse me with the devotion of Mother Theresa. And if I had love problems, I could count one hundred percent on her sympathy and advice – the advice not always being what I wanted to hear. So, being told I was better off without him and I'd meet someone else far more deserving of my love was a palliative I was not prepared to swallow. Love is blind and young love, even more so. He was tall. Yes. His fair hair was already receding but for me, it gave him an intellectual forehead with an interesting widow's peak. Only one of his large grey eyes worked. The other he had rubbed with metal grit as a child and was taken too late to the doctor. It resulted in blindness but was hardly visible. I found him devastatingly attractive and so much more mature than the boys in my class.

In the months that followed seeing him close to his new paramour in all of our familiar places was painful but I coped, admittedly still carrying a discreet torch.

Sometime after I had turned 18, I had a date with one of my best girl friends who was still in Munich waiting with her parents to be rotated back to America. We were to meet in the Blue Room, where my alliance with S had ended. I arrived early with a book to entertain me while I'd wait. But before I got there, a car drove slowly beside me and I heard my name called out. It was S, with four of his male friends. My heart beat a little faster at seeing him womanless.

'Hi, Cathy. What are you up to? Where are you going,' he asked from the interior of the car.

'I'm meeting Peggy in the Blue Room,' I told him. He knew her from when we'd gone out together.

'Well, phone her and say you're at a friend's place. She can meet you there.' The friend was the driver of the huge American car.

'Yeah, come on. I can offer you a drink and you can use my phone.'

I looked into the car. They all seemed decent guys.

'I'm going back to the States the day after tomorrow,' S chipped in. 'We're having a little party. Join us for old time's sake.'

So, he was vanishing forever out of my life. My first reaction was sadness for the loss of hope, my second, relief. I could finally forget him. Stupidly, I agreed to go.

The apartment was on the second floor of a building in McGraw Kaserne, which housed unmarried officers. I phoned Peggy and explained where I was. She would arrive in a little over half an hour. We were in the living room sitting on sofas or easy chairs. I was offered a drink. Conversation was easy and I noticed S looking at me in a reminiscently romantic way. There was no doubt that I was pleased. From the time I'd walked in, I needed to have a pee and asked, a little embarrassed, where the bathroom was. It was down a little corridor directly next to the bedroom. Excusing myself, I disappeared. Having finished, I reopened the door to re-join the group. S was standing in the doorway to the bedroom. I acknowledged him, thinking, he too, needed to use the facilities and went to walk past but he stopped me, putting his arm around my shoulder and thus lead me into the bedroom. I pulled back but he held me by my upper arms so that I was facing him. Then came the dialogue.

'Come on, Cathy, I just want to talk to you. You still love me, don't you?' He spoke seductively.

I could think of nothing to say because I did still love him but didn't want him to know. He let go of me with one arm and with the other, he closed the door. I knew what was coming; the bed was an elephant in the room. Struggling silently, knowing there were four men next door, I whispered, 'I don't want to do it.'

The whole situation was intimidating. Do I shout for help? How could I know they would come to my rescue? Or would they hold me down and assist S with his intentions? Would they all take a turn themselves? These were the thoughts rushing in my mind.

I was being pushed onto the bed now. His familiar hands were touching me, pulling at my clothes, uttering the famous line many women in my predicament will recognize, 'You know, you really want it.'

He lay on top of me and I knew I wasn't going anywhere, so I gave in to the inevitable. The penetration was difficult. It hurt a bit but at no time could I swear in a court that he had been rough with me, that he had forced me with threats of violence. When the act was completed and he had zipped up his trousers, he was quite sweet. He brushed the hair out of my face, gently stroked my cheek and talked to me with the sensitivity of a man who appreciated that I had given him the gift of my virginity, albeit not exactly willingly.

Very shortly after returning to the living room there was a knock on the door. I was sure it was Peggy and went to meet her. Before she made her appearance in front of the others I told her to make excuses for us to leave immediately. My embarrassment and shame vis-à-vis the four other men was unbearable. I was certain they knew what had happened a few feet away from them on the other side of the wall. Peggy didn't ask me why, she just said 'hello' to everyone and made up a reasonable story why we had to go. Outside in the street I told her what had happened, mentioning that I was now terrified of becoming pregnant.

'You mean, he wasn't careful?' she asked. 'No rubber? He didn't pull out?'

'No.' I wouldn't have known what a rubber looked like and we hadn't been taught *coitus interruptus* as part of sex education in Biology.

'Did you go to the bathroom afterwards?'

'Yes, but I hardly peed because I'd gone before.'

'Peeing usually helps to wash away the sperm,' she said knowingly.

I had no idea she was so experienced in these affairs. As close as we were, we had never really discussed each other's sex life or the lack of it. I don't think she was aware at that time that she, herself, was pregnant. When the orders came for her family to repatriate, she was carrying a three-month-old embryo in her womb. So much for the peeing advice. We kept in touch for a while and in her last letter she wrote that after the birth, which took place somewhere secretly, her mother pretended it was her child to save Peggy's reputation as far as finding a future husband was concerned. I never heard from her again.

The night after 'the incident' I received a phone call from S. My mother answered and handed me the phone. I heard his voice. It was obvious because of the background noise that he was in a bar celebrating the following morning's departure.

'Cathy, do you still love me?' he asked a little drunkenly.

'Yes,' I said quietly, not knowing if I should hope for something.

'You're a scum sucking pig!' he slurred. Then he laughed and hung up.

I was paralysed with shock. How could he have used such language? Where did he learn such an ugly expression? I had never heard him curse before. Thank God, my parents were watching a programme on the television and ignored me. Eventually, I managed to put the receiver on the cradle, walk up the stairs and reach the bathroom in time to vomit.

CHAPTER VI

Shakespeare wrote the words, 'all's well that ends well.' Perhaps, but it's just another platitude. It does not take into consideration what one suffers on the road to 'well' and how it can affect the future. I went through agonizing nerves waiting for my period, scouring medical books in the library at McGraw learning everything there was to know about conception. The 'incident' occurred 17 days after menstruation. Normally that should have been safe but I was extremely irregular. My cycle could vary from 22 to 32 days. Ovulation may have taken place outside the normal mid-term, as it were. The audition had taken place before my curse. I don't know how I managed it, how I was able to concentrate on the text and hiding from my mother what I was going through. This worry was something I didn't dare share with her. I was terrified of her reaction and, even worse, my father's. It would have hurt him too much. He still thought me innocent. Mitzi, once again had joined us all the way from America. She seemed to feel that all was not well with me, spoiling me atrociously with cookies and cakes she would bake but that I couldn't eat. There was no way I could confide in her either. She had become deaf and the thought of shouting my predicament into her ear was hardly conducive. Then, one day, I suffered a terrible pain in my lower abdomen and began to bleed. I was not pregnant but, perhaps, I had started to be. If so, it would have been the only time in my life.

Later in the week, the letter arrived from the Falkenberg stating I had been accepted as one of eight students from 130 applicants. Everyone around me was thrilled. And I was doubly relieved. The opportunity to be trained for the future I had chosen was being offered to me and I was spared the shame of an illegitimate pregnancy.

It was a wonderful school. Although we were there principally to learn about acting, the fact that a professional theatre was attached to the school meant we were given an insight into the machinations of what went on behind the scenes. There were ateliers dedicated to design and the building of sets, the creation of costumes. It was an independent microcosm for the production of plays. Our teachers were actors, themselves. An understanding on having been accepted was a commitment to join the repertory at the attached theatre for two years after finishing at the school. One couldn't ask for a better apprenticeship.

The curriculum included dance, movement and fencing. We were taught to breathe using our diaphragms in such a way that our words were projected into every far corner of an auditorium seemingly without effort. And then there were the texts to learn. I loved every moment. Some of the disciplines came easily to me, all those to do with movement and improvisations. The words, though, were a problem. I took my texts home and feverishly studied the plays we had to absorb. But, alas, to no avail. After a month and a half, I was invited into the principal's office. He was a well-known classical actor whom we addressed as Herr Bruder and he explained very gently, that I was not going to be able to keep up with the strict tutorial as far as learning the lines was concerned. He was not bothered with the accent, it was more a matter of understanding. Although, it was improving, my German was far from being up to memorizing vast tracts of Goethe and Schiller and he was afraid that I would fail the three monthly exam for which we had to soliloquize mountains of lines from classical works.

'You had us fooled at the audition,' he said. 'You learned your speeches like a parrot.'

I had to nod in admission. He then went on to tell me, if I were to fail, I'd be out of the school for good. Whereas, if I were to leave on my own accord, I'd be reaccepted the following year without the need for another audition. But I would undergo an interview in German to determine my fluency and comprehension of the language.

I opted to leave with the hope of returning. As I exited the Falkenberg's portals, Herr Graevert, actor/teacher said goodbye to me.

'I fought for you,' he kindly said. 'I could tell from your improvisations that you had what it takes. But the language is too difficult. Learn to speak it properly! And please come back.'

They were the words that launched me into complete integration. I had to stop being an alien in a country I was trying to make my home. Via connections, I was offered a job for the Christmas period in an upmarket glove boutique and was grateful for the opportunity to earn some money. Afterwards, again with connections, I worked in a department store known for things Bavarian such as its range of *lederhosen, loden* coats and their matching green felt hats with pheasant feathers sticking out from the band. For the ladies there were colourful and elaborate peasant costumes called *dirndls* consisting of smocks with brocaded aprons, which were worn over white lacy blouses usually with a deep *décolleté* to show off the generous Bavarian bosom. I sold men's socks and ties but didn't last long. I'm not a salesperson and found some of the clients very rude. The deep Bavarian accent is strong and almost impossible to understand so I could be rather slow in showing the clients what they were asking for. They shouted at me and I muttered back curses in English under my breath. It was just as well that I had no intentions of continuing with this profession. Already the fact of knowing what I was going to do every day when I woke up was abhorrent to me. I was not meant for a steady job.

In June, a situation was found for me at a *gasthaus-pension* that was also a sailing school. It was on the side of a large lake called Chiemsee. I could never have guessed how useful this experience would be for me when in the far future, I'd practice everything I learned there. My chores were to be a waitress, chamber maid, cleaner, kitchen help and when required, I was presented after dinner to entertain the sailors, laughing at their jokes, never flirting with the men lest their ladies would be upset, amusing everyone when answering questions in my peculiar accent and accepting drinks when offered which was beneficial for the boss's profit. He was very glad that I had an unusual capacity for alcohol and not the worse for wear the following morning. It must have come from my school days' training. We worked shifts seven days a week, either from seven am to two pm or two pm until the sailors were too drunk and went to sleep. All this for 100 Deutschmarks a month, which was the equivalent to £10 sterling, and everything we could eat. But I did learn German, which was the paramount reason for my being there. Everyone had been told not to speak English with me and after only eight weeks I became totally fluent. Unfortunately the Dracula accent remained but less pronounced. I celebrated my 19th birthday amongst friends there and as in Switzerland, many of them were foreign. German was our language in common. The *gasthaus* had a policy of accepting foreign girls from all over Europe. In exchange for working for a ridiculously small wage, we were given the opportunity to use the language. I'm convinced this is the best way to learn. We were all up against the same challenge and so we couldn't judge each other. What is important is to converse and not be afraid of making mistakes. We sometimes don't speak a language because we're too embarrassed. Once we get over our inhibitions and communicate, grammar and vocabulary is absorbed.

I came back to Munich the very beginning of September. If I was to rejoin the Falkenberg, I'd have to make an appointment. Even though,

I babbled now, I wasn't sure I could speak convincingly the incredibly convoluted texts of classical German, not to mention the Shakespeare translations. He was difficult enough in English, but German!

Sometimes fate intervenes. By chance, my brother, Paul was going out with a young woman in her early twenties called Olga. Her aunt with whom she lived was at that time the most famous agent in Germany. She was a Yugoslavian from the Hungarian pocket of Croatia. Her name was Steffie Jovanovich and she represented such luminaries as Maximilian and his sister Maria Schell, Curd Jürgens, Gert Fröbe, Klaus Kinski and just about every internationally known name from Germany.

On one of his visits, Paul mentioned me to Steffie, relating the Falkenberg story and that I was still intending to become an actress.

'Does she have your good looks?' Steffie asked him.

Paul, being a brother could hardly enthuse. He'd never looked at me that way.

'I guess so. We're both blonde, blue eyed and have high cheekbones. She's pretty presentable.'

'Then let me meet her.' Steffie was also afflicted with Dracula tongue in every language she spoke and she spoke many.

Paul accompanied me for the introduction. She lived in a huge apartment, which took up the entire second floor of a mid-19th century mansion block overlooking the river Isar. Two large rooms, which opened from a wide corridor, made up her offices, one for her and one for her associate, Renata Lazar. Glamorous photographs of her clients dedicated to Steffie adorned the walls of both offices. As our meeting was informal, we arrived in the evening and were welcomed into a spacious salon at the end of the corridor. Steffie offered us a drink. She was already clutching a whiskey tumbler in her hand. Her niece, Olga, was also there and I was grateful for that because from the first moment, she was friendly and put me at ease. Steffie could be intimidating. Short, stoutly built, with a masculine haircut, she had a voice scraped up from the bottom of a gravel pit. But for the flowery scented perfume, she could have been a man. Within a short while and after several more whiskeys, she mellowed. I began to like her. She had a quick sense of humour, which her stern appearance belied, and seemed genuinely interested in me, asking all sorts of questions. I told her of my intentions to continue at the Falkenberg but that it would mean two years of study followed by two years in the rep company.

'Much too long,' she said in her deep, heavy voice. 'I know someone, a private tutor who will teach you everything you need to know.' She gave me the name of this person: Anne-Marie Hanschke.

'You're going to do movies. Your face is made for it. Don't misunderstand me, theatre is important but stage work will come later, when you're famous and can ask to play whatever roles you want.' I wasn't sure if she had turned into a gypsy and was predicting my future or if this was the way she intended to direct my career. So far, not a word had been spoken about signing me on as a new prospect in her illustrious stable.

The conversation changed. She spoke to Paul and Olga asked me questions. What do I do with my time? Do I drive? Do I ski? It was not an interrogation, just a way of getting to know me. We would become the closest of friends: she, guiding me down ski slopes, sitting next to me, being a calming influence after I'd received my driver's license and helping me over those first panicky moments when I was newly in charge of a vehicle. Although, her English was perfect, she determined, for my sake, that German would be our mutual language. But all of that was still to come.

The evening ended. I was given Anne-Marie Hanschke's telephone number but still didn't know if Steffie intended to represent me.

On arriving home I was greeted by my very excited mother.

'Steffie just phoned!' They had conversed in Hungarian.

'What did she say?' I asked, with surprise.

'She is going to make you into the new Grace Kelly!' Mommy said proudly. 'But, of course, with my permission.'

So Steffie was going to take me on, after all. I was daunted by the implications. My father was thrilled for me as well and we stayed up late into the night, discussing, planning, dreaming.

Steffie had spoken at length on the phone. She advised the private tutorage, that way, she could find me bit parts in films to help with the finances and to get experience. I would have to have photographs but she knew a Hungarian photographer who would probably do the session for free. This, too, was important; I had to learn to pose for still photography. It was not only ability, voice and poise which led to success, one had to sell one's looks too.

The matter of name came up. There were already four Schells in the business: Maximillian, Maria and their two younger siblings, Immy and Carl.

I asked my mother, 'What does Katherina Teleki sound like to you? Can you see that in lights?'

She liked the idea. It was her name, after all. 'But we have to ask permission from the head of the Teleki family.'

I have no idea how she found out. There was no Google in those days. It would have taken a more physical search, with phone calls and letters but she discovered his address. He was living in Canada and answered to her request that, yes, I could use the heroic Teleki name but must never bring shame upon it.

If you blink while watching the credits in my first two films you won't have seen the name. You will hardly have seen me.

The very first I appeared in was for an English producer called Harry Alan Towers. He was quite well known in the business for his thrillers. I played a Hungarian radio announcer and was only ever seen through a glass partition behind a microphone. There was no script and I was expected to prepare my own dialogue. The job happened so suddenly, I had no time to ask either of my parents to give me lines to say in Magyar.

Steffie had tracked me down via my mother to a castle in Austria where I was a guest with some of my newly made friends, all from a particular 'clique' made up from the sons and daughters of my parents' aristocratic circle. When my host learned about the phone call and my need for transport he kindly loaned me a car to drive to the little studio just outside of Salzburg and gave me some vague directions. I drove off early the next morning and, on the way, picked up a woman hitchhiker. I told her where I was hoping to go and, by chance, her destination was near to the studio. She knew it well and took me to the exact spot.

The only thing I could think of to do once the camera turned over was to repeat the names of places I heard my parents mention and then put numbers after them as if I was reading out soccer scores but knowing very little about football my numbers were ridiculously high, so: Budapest 35-Debrezen 60, Szob 45-Zebegen 102. For the minutes I would be on screen I had to invent names of cities, ergo: *Kicsii var* (little town) 25, *Nagy var* (big town) 18, *Piros var* (red town) 35, *Fehér var* (white town) 85. Running out of adjectives, I had to think quickly of some nouns I could remember: *Kutya var* (Dog town) 10, *Mocska var* (Cat town) 75. I never saw the film and can't even remember its name. I hope I was dubbed or, at least gave some amusement to Hungarian speakers.

The second was an all-German production. The title tells you of its intellectual content: *Wenn Man Baden Geht auf Teneriffa* (When One Goes Swimming in Tenerife) My part was as an airhostess. I have no idea why we were cavorting on the Canary Islands. There must have been music in the film as the star was Peter Kraus, a well known pop star at the time. I do remember, though, getting the worst sunburn ever while falling asleep on a deserted black sandy beach on this volcanic island. The hotel phoned a doctor who came with unguents and rubbed them on my back and buttocks. It was the first time I'd exposed my other cheeks to the sun and a long time later before I would ever do it again.

Lessons with Anne-Marie Hanschke began in her tiny studio flat. She had been an actress in her earlier years and was now teaching, on the whole, girls my age to augment her meagre pension. Kind and encouraging, she lived vicariously through her students, loving whatever little successes we incurred. As I was always alone in her flat, she would have to speak the lines of the other characters in the plays I studied. I became quite adept at talking to lampshades or flirting with houseplants, kneeling on the floor and weeping over a dying cushion. She was a marvellous audience, laughing on cue or eyes misting up when listening to a particularly emotional speech. I would later find paying audiences much more difficult to please and actors not at all behaving like lampshades or houseplants.

The Hungarian photographer phoned me and we made a date to meet at his studio. He told me he would take some glamorous pin-up shots. I should bring a bikini and whatever other sexy outfits I might have. Never thinking of myself as sexy, I avoided dressing with that look in mind but I did have tight riding breeches, high leather boots and a whip. 'Would that do?' I asked.

'Excellent!' he replied in Dracula speak.

The session was torture for me. I was told the camera loved me. It was not reciprocated. The only photography I'd done until then was for Daddy, who loved taking pictures. These were hardly posed. They were a journal of our lives and their only importance was to be stuck into an album where no-one but the family would see them.

I had no idea how to be sexy. The bikini I'd brought was quite chaste. My breasts never enlarged beyond adolescence and to show the cleavage required, my upper arms had to squeeze my bosom together. I loathed the process. The camera was my enemy, demanding ridiculous positions while a forced smile was smeared on my face. I never blamed the photographer. He began to concentrate more on my legs, which were, at least, long with thin ankles. The puppy fat that filled out my upper thighs was obscured by clever lighting.

The riding outfit suited me better. Somehow, being fully dressed relaxed me. I played with the whip, stuck out my bum, never realizing these were the sort of photos those who practice s/m were likely to pin up on their walls. As far as I was concerned, I was riding a horse.

Fear of the still camera has always remained. Very few photographers could coax out the exhibitionist within me. Charlie Waite, better known for his landscapes, nevertheless managed to take some sublime portraits. I think a few totes on a joint also helped to relax me. They appeared in *Spotlight*, the actor's photographic directory, and to the amazement of immigration personnel, my passport.

There is a huge difference between the images of a moving camera, which are liquid, and the single shot frozen in time. In the 'movies', as the word depicts, one hides in a role and is photographed during the flow of a scene. I have never been confident enough with the persona I project to pose without playing a part. The publicity stills from a film are shot during rehearsals when one is in character. They have never bothered me. There are a few decent pictures in circulation today. With time I learned to overcome some of my inhibitions and managed to react professionally to the click of a camera. If people only knew what complexes I had to swallow in order to produce those.

Steffie had her glamour shots to begin to promote me. I was introduced to directors and producers not necessarily because they had a role for me but to become acquainted with the process of interviews, another immensely important discipline for furthering one's career. Having been rubbish at selling gloves, men's socks, ties and underwear to those who had entered the premises for the specific reason to buy, it was even more impossible selling myself. I don't know what dichotomy ruled my personality at that time. My brain was conscious that I was a perfectly reasonable looking 19 year old with enough character to hold interesting, amusing conversations with my peers. I could make them laugh... and yet, another part of my brain saw myself as boring, inadequate, unworthy of attention. Perhaps the slapping around when I began to dare to hold opinions and, certainly, the 'incident' didn't help my fragile confidence. Steffie and Anne-Marie helped me through this period. They were the horse whisperers to my uncertain, shy filly. I would later learn when acting opposite brilliantly talented people I was in awe of, that our profession, on the whole, is not made of extroverts. Most actors are shy. They need roles to hide behind. The person you see on stage or in the cinema is rarely the same in their dressing room. There they are, sometimes, full of complexes and doubts.

One way of concealing my inhibitions during interviews was to say as little as possible and listen attentively, eyes looking with intense interest at the person speaking and laughing whenever expected. Sometimes the laughing bit was embarrassing because the producer or director had not meant to be funny. I didn't work with those but I did with Blake Edwards who was genuinely hilarious during our interview for *The Return of the Pink Panther*. All poise left me. I could not control my giggling and later learned when he offered me the part opposite Peter Sellers, it was that which decided him. I should sue him for the crow's feet that became etched into the outer corners of my eyes because of the laughter we experienced during the filming.

Life was good. I was enjoying acting with inert objects at Hanschke's. Steffie took me very much under her wings. She had a reputation for being a notorious lesbian but I never felt a hint of this within our relationship. I continued socializing, being invited to grand mansions and schlosses owned by the ridiculously wealthy or the high aristocracy usually in the company of my parents. All was well. No clouds on the horizon. And then, real life crashed into this unreal world.

I'd returned from a weekend at the Underberg's, the brewers of the well known miniature bottle of the digestive carrying that name. The family made their fortune during America's prohibition period. Although alcoholic, Underberg was classified as a medicament, an aid to digestion, and thus, available over the counter.

Daddy came to fetch me at the *Hauptbahnhof*. He was in the company of a friend I'd made from my Chiemsee experience who had been hired by us as an *au pair*. She came from Hannover and spoke the most beautiful German. It was hoped this would have an influence on my accent. I was full of myself, wanting to relate every amusing incident I'd experienced at the Underberg's estate. Christiane cut me short.

'Your father has terrible news. Be calm and listen to him,' she said under her breath. As I approached him, I could see he had been crying. I put my arms on his shoulders and looked into his face. Our eyes met and he broke down. In between sobs, he kept repeating the word, 'Pétiké.' My brother, Peter, was known as *Pétiké,* as I was *Katica* and Paul was *Palika.* These were the diminutives in Hungarian.

'What's happened to him?' I asked a little hysterically, fearing the worst.

Again through sobs, he said, 'I'll tell you when we get home.'

'Is he dead?' My hysteria was growing.

'No,' he answered, 'but it's bad.'

His driving on the way home was erratic. I hadn't yet passed my license and so couldn't take the wheel. All I could do was to warn him of oncoming traffic when he strayed into the opposite lane, to turn the blinkers off and to stop at red lights, all the while imagining what horrible thing could have happened to my darling brother Peter.

Mommy was home and she, too, had been crying. We sat down together and I listened to the incredible news. Peter had been found in a park at night in Washington DC, completely naked, screaming to the dark sky, 'Oh, God! Let me be like my brother!'

The police had been called and taken him into custody. He was put into a cell but had banged his head against the steel bars and concrete walls to such an extent that he had to be restrained in a straight jacket and transferred into a padded cell. There must have been some identification in his clothes because the police contacted my father's twin brother, Peter, in New York. It was he who broke the news to us and accepted, for the moment, to take responsibility for decisions made on his behalf. Daddy would have to make arrangements to travel to America which could take a little time even though, Radio Free Europe would accommodate as much as possible.

It was at such a moment that we were grateful for the connections my father had kept from his diplomatic days. In a dire necessity, he was not embarrassed to use them. It was thought Peter had suffered a nervous breakdown and was in need of treatment. He didn't have health insurance. Jack Auchincloss was called. Could he help in any way?

There is a US Government funded scientific research establishment called the National Institute of Health. By a fortunate coincidence its headquarters were in Bethesda, Maryland, very near to Washington DC. Jack promised to pull every string possible for Peter's acceptance into its mental health care and he succeeded. As its main existence was for experimental research, no payment was required. Peter was admitted into their psychiatric department. It was 1963. Our knowledge of the brain and the hormones and chemicals it naturally produces for normal functioning behaviour was, perhaps, not in its infancy but certainly in its adolescence. He was diagnosed as paranoid schizophrenic and underwent experimental drug therapy.

My mother and I visited him in August 1964. Daddy had been a few months earlier. Although it was not mentioned, I couldn't help but think of my aunt Chibby, or the time Mommy answered my question, 'But where were your parents?' when a certain calamity had happened.

'In a sanatorium.'

'Why?' Thinking they were being treated for tuberculosis.

'They suffered from nervous disorders.'

She had spoken to me of her other older sister who, I was told, I resembled astonishingly. She died from a train accident while walking across the track supposedly to reach a lake. My aunt was partially deaf and it was determined that she didn't hear the oncoming train. Mommy doubted this conclusion. She suspected suicide. They had spoken often and intimately. She was aware that her sister was unhappy. My aunt would have known exactly what time the train passed. Steam engines make a great deal of noise and although, there was a bend in the track, it would have been visible even for that split second to get out of its way. And then there was Paul Teleki. His suicide was honoured as an heroic act but it must take a massive imbalance of chemicals and hormones in the brain to overcome what must be, after all, our greatest instinct, that to survive. The Catholic church deems suicide to be a grievous mortal sin instead of recognizing that it may be the result of a serious mental illness, depression.

Peter seemed fine when we saw him. The psycho drugs were obviously having the required effect. I found nothing unusual or abnormal in his behaviour. He did in mine, though.

'Why are you talking so strangely?' he asked, as if a little disappointed in me.

'What do you mean?'

'You're putting on a phoney accent. What's that about?'

It had been three years since we last saw each other. I had to explain that learning to speak another language and concentrating on diction, which was part of my work, had affected my speaking voice. I no longer had the strong Manhattan accent. He didn't like it. I was alien to him.

We made an appointment with the psychiatrist in charge of the mental health department to speak about Peter's progress. During the meeting, he asked Mommy if there had ever been mental illness in the family, to which she brazenly replied, 'No. Never'.

I couldn't believe my ears but decided, it was best to keep quiet. Afterwards, I asked how she could deny Chibby's condition. She seemed to think our family's history had nothing to do with the psychiatrist. In a way, she was right. If it were determined that Peter's problem was genetic there may not have been the same hopeful treatment for him. As it was, they were even talking of allowing him to leave and have outpatient treatment. And that is exactly what happened with tragic results.

During his incarceration, Peter had made a friend, a boy, 17 years of age, called Arthur. The lad hero-worshipped Peter who was at that time 23. Arthur's father visited him frequently and so, became acquainted with Peter. There was an incident in which Arthur needed instant specialist attention and it was Peter who alerted the doctors thus saving the boy's life. Thereafter, the father was forever grateful. The lad was allowed to go home before Peter, so that the day it was decided that he, too, could leave the hospital, Arthur's father invited him to live with them. It was an ideal situation. Peter would do some casual work, gardening, mow the lawn, general little repairs for which he would receive room and board with some pocket money. He was there, primarily to keep an eye on Arthur, to be like a big brother to him.

We were in contact with him. He seemed happy and we were relieved. Then came another phone call, again from my father's brother in New York. Peter had stabbed the young lad several times with a kitchen knife and ran away. Arthur managed to crawl to a neighbour who rang an ambulance and the police. A huge manhunt was underway. Back in Munich, we were beside ourselves with worry and frustration. There was nothing we could do but imagine the horrific situation he found himself in. He was a fugitive, alone, hiding, frightened and hungry. The American police were not known for their moderation in using arms. For three days, we lived in sympathy with him, not eating, not sleeping, and jumping every time the phone rang. Finally the news reached us: Peter was alive. He was found hiding in a garage by a child. The police took him away and he was readmitted immediately into the NIH.

Peter had listened to the voices in his head commanding him to punish Arthur for his disrespectful behaviour towards his father. Six months without the medication, the voices became more and more insistent, to the point he could no longer ignore them.

The pattern repeated itself. At the NIH, he was treated with the drugs, which enabled him to function. After several months of seeming sanity, he was once again allowed to leave its protection. This time, though, into his family's care.

Peter arrived in Munich in spring 1965. We were still in the house, so there was plenty of room. He had been told that if there was the slightest inkling of hearing voices again, he should see a psychiatrist immediately. My parents contacted one who came on a social visit to meet him. He had not been given any medication nor a prescription. The doctor assured him of treatment but it was up to Peter to contact him when needed.

I accompanied him to translate for job interviews. He was offered a position with a company who packed and transported the belongings of US personnel who were being rotated back to the States. As an American, he would have been the head of the team. Peter turned it down.

'Why? It's perfect for you!' I argued.

'A guy like me can't be put in charge of a bunch of normal guys,' was his reply.

'But you're okay now. Nothing's wrong with you,' I insisted.

He didn't answer. Were the voices already beginning? He had made a girlfriend, a sweet young German woman who adored him. We were thrilled. Even Mommy, who was not easy to please in such matters approved of her. Then, Paul found him a job at the snack bar in McGraw Kaserne where he washed dishes and was happy with that. He was popular amongst the staff. Eventually, Peter moved out of the house to live nearer to his work. In the American enclave attached to McGraw were the apartment blocks where the married personnel lived with their families. Under the roofs of these buildings were the maids' rooms. As they were not all occupied, Peter rented one of these.

I was in Czechoslovakia filming when I received the phone call from Mommy telling me that Peter had attempted suicide by leaping out of his dormer window four floors above the ground. He had been laughing hysterically with some of the maids he shared the space with, holding a tin of shaving cream and squirting its contents all over his face and in his mouth. At first they were bemused with his behaviour but then they watched him climb on his narrow windowsill and to their horror, saw him disappear. It was a woman on the second floor who had called the ambulance after seeing his body drop across her French window. Upon landing, he had snapped the fourth vertebrae in his neck. As he was at McGraw, Paul was the first to have been alerted and it was his unpleasant task to relay the news to my parents.

When they arrived at the US Forces hospital where he had been taken, Peter was paralysed but conscious and lucid. It was too difficult for my father to remain any time with him. He had broken down with uncontrollable crying and was ushered out of the intensive care unit. Mommy found the strength to stay.

'Why?' she pleaded. 'We thought everything was so good for you.'

Then he told her about the voices. Once again, they were telling him to kill. They had been hovering for some time already, at first whispering for him to kill someone at work. He desisted. Then, they ordered him to kill a priest. He refused. When the voices began to scream their commands to kill someone from his family, to silence them, it was best to kill himself.

By the time I returned, Peter had been transferred to another US hospital farther north in Frankfurt. We were told that he could not be kept indefinitely in Germany in American care. We would have to make other arrangements.

It was at this time I really learned to drive. We wanted to keep Peter in Germany but that meant searching for an institution, which accepted to treat a quadriplegic, who also had mental problems. Because we couldn't afford to stay in hotels overnight, I had to drive to the destination and return home the same day. This meant leaving Munich at six in the morning, driving to Hamburg, Hannover or any such city and back again. I was with Mommy and we did almost all of West Germany this way day after day, until in my sleep I dreamed of speeding traffic, flashing headlights, horns blasting and the wipers thudding rhythmically from one side of the windscreen to the other. I drove my father's car, a sporty little Opel Kadet coupé. She did us proud, clocking up the kilometres with remarkable stamina and speed.

It was out of the question that we would be able to pay for Peter's care in a private establishment. He had no insurance. The wealthy circle of friends who surrounded my parents generously offered to pay towards his hospitalization. But even so, the cost at all of the places we visited, was well beyond being able to accept their kindness.

The last time I saw him was when Mommy and I visited him in

Frankfurt. Daddy was already in contact with the State Department discussing his repatriation. Ironically, he would be flown back to Bethesda where his incarceration began.

Peter was in a ward with several other patients. He had a strap across his chest circling the back of his wheelchair to keep him sitting upright. Under medication the deliriums had parted. He spoke normally and was happy to see us. I remarked on the gadget the nurses had devised to enable him to smoke. It was fashioned from a wire coat hanger and attached to his right wrist. The cigarette was lodged into the enlarged coil at its neck. The little movement still remaining in that arm was just enough to lift the cigarette to his lips and satisfy his nicotine craving. The nurses joked that they had become sick and tired of holding his cigarettes while he dragged on them. Remember, in those days, smoking was considered almost good for you.

When we were alone with the nurses, we asked for his prognosis. Normally, we were told, patients in his condition, due to lack of movement and the hours trapped in a horizontal position, were threatened with a pulmonary embolism. The average life expectancy was two years. By sitting him in a wheelchair, his breathing was momentarily alleviated but it was not enough to make a difference.

Mommy and I said our goodbyes. She traced a sign of the cross with her thumb on his forehead and kissed him stoically with surprisingly dry eyes, completely in control... outwardly. I blubbered as is my wont, tears streaming down my cheeks.

'Don't cry,' he whispered. Those were the last words I ever heard him say.

CHAPTER VII

I only wore a garland of plastic flowers above my waist. It hung down from my neck to just below my stomach. For the sake of modesty, I had glued the flowers strategically to my breasts. They were unceremoniously and really rather painfully ripped away by the director of the film, Géza von Cziffra.

'Why are you hiding your tits? It's the only reason people will want to see this film!' he, being another Hungarian, said in Draculese. 'You're not a nun in the jungle! Get naked!' he shouted. If there were such beings as poison dwarves... he was their leader.

Steffie had suggested me for the title role of a film called *Lana: Queen of the Amazons*. It was in the spring of 1964 and I had flown to west Berlin through the bone shaking corridor western airplanes were limited to. The altitude was such that it presented the most turbulence for the pilots. I'm sure the height was expressly chosen by the East Germans to make the experience uncomfortable. It was best not to drink on those flights. When bringing the glass to one's lips you could risk breaking a front tooth or else the contents would spill, usually on the lap of the passenger sitting directly behind you.

West Berlin was a strange place in those days. In between screen tests and meetings, I took the time to discover its streets and boulevards, admiring what I thought were linden trees which guarded its most famous thoroughfare, *Kurfürstendamm*. The trees, planted long ago, represented the past for me and contrasted with the unnatural modernity of the ubiquitous, brash billboards which sprouted in front of all manner of crumbling edifices. I had the impression there was nothing lasting to the city. Either the giant advertising of western goods were there to hide the fact that there was very little renovation happening, no investment because of an uncertain future or it was the exuberant and brazen face of Capitalism shouting down the grey and sober Communist east. There was something flimsy in its atmosphere, as if a wind could blow it all away but not the wall, which divided the city, it seemed the most solid and permanent structure at that time.

The producer, Gero Wecker, steel-blue eyed, silver haired and distinguished looking, talked in a low, mild voice. I was in his office and he was offering me the part. There was only one problem... my name. In a gentle way, he explained that Teleki had unfortunate connotations for the Germans.

'You are aware of the history?' he asked me.

I responded, 'Of course, he was a close relation to my mother.'

'Then you will understand. There are many Germans still today who are uncomfortable with that name.'

In this statement, he apparently included himself. It was some time later, in the same gentle voice, that he related a wartime experience. He was an officer serving in Czechoslovakia. A number of his men were blown up by the local resistance. Such an outrage could not be allowed. He went to the village where the suspected 'terrorists' came from and asked for them to be handed over. A time limit was set. The village elders were warned if they did not comply with his request, he would be forced to come back with his men and kill a proportion of the male inhabitants. The village refused to submit and he was true to his word. All the men who had not escaped or gone into hiding and found themselves there when the soldiers arrived were stood against a wall and with his orders, shot to death. He was inferring by this story that he had been (perhaps still was) a Nazi sympathizer and there were many still left in the country. The name, Teleki, of a man who had shot himself so famously while at the head of a government in defiance of Nazism, would be an unfortunate reminder.

The chilling revelation was spoken in his mild voice, almost like a bedtime story to me, a virtual stranger, not yet 20 years old.

'If I ever went to Czechoslovakia today, I would be arrested and put to death as a war criminal.' He looked at me with his icy blue eyes asking for pity... or understanding? The events would have taken place 20 years before and must still have weighed on his conscience. I was speechless but did change my name.

He liked the name Schell. It sounded Arian, so it was Steffie's idea, in order to differentiate me from the other Schells in the business, that I use the V from my middle name, Virginia, and place it between Catherina and Schell thus becoming Catherina v Schell. The 'v' would be translated as 'von' which a born baroness had the right to carry. I didn't argue with her and Herr Wecker was satisfied.

Thus Catherina von Schell appeared on the screen in her first starring part playing the only survivor of an airplane crash in the deepest Amazonian jungle. She had been found as a small child by a primitive, native tribe and because of her white skin, was raised to be their queen. Then, other Caucasians arrived, some with good intentions, some with bad. It was rumoured there was wealth to be found in the jungle. The 'goodies' came to study the natives and their surroundings. They meet the tribe's incongruous queen. A love story develops, blah, blah, blah, and the lovers canoe down the Amazon River into the setting sun.

The filming took place on location in Brazil, some outside of Rio de Janeiro and also near the port of Belém, which is on the mouth of the Amazon. I was treated horrendously. Still too inexperienced and insecure to assert myself, I was dealt with contempt.

Before boarding the flight from Berlin, the production manager handed me a suitcase. It contained my costume: plastic orchid garlands, a chamois-leather thong which would hang from a chain encircling my hips to cover crotch and bum, various gaudy trinkets to be hung from my neck and if glued properly, cover my boobs and a genuine jaguar pelt which would be thrown as a shawl across a shoulder with a clasp to hold it in place.

The suitcase was put in my charge with strict orders not to lose it or I would have to pay for its contents. I was too ignorant to know that an actor, not to say the star, is not responsible for their costume. There is a department for that and the people who travel with you are called 'dressers'. They are charged with the welfare of one's wardrobe.

We filmed on a snake-infested island, an hour's ferry ride from Rio. It was inhabited by people who lived in round mud huts with straw roofs. One of these was purloined for me as a dressing room. I carried my suitcase with me and changed costume when required. Some time, in the middle of the afternoon, I'd finished my scenes and retired back to my hut and changed into my 'civvies'. The crew went to other parts of the island to continue their filming. There was a blanket on the earth floor that I could lie down on. I dozed off. When I woke up I was confronted with an eerie silence. Even though the crew were not in the settlement, I could always hear some faint noise in the distance coming from the process of filming. All was unusually quiet. Suddenly, I realized there was only one ferry in the morning that returned to Rio. It came back in the afternoon and departed at five thirty. There was no transport until the following morning. I looked out of my hut. A few smiling faces greeted me but not a single member of the crew or actors was to be seen. I had no idea of the time and none of the locals had watches.

Grabbing the suitcase, I ran to the port. The little ferry sounded its horn. Water bubbled furiously from under its propeller. I raced down the pier. The aft of the boat was just releasing itself, pushing into deeper water. Adrenalin can make you do the impossible. I leapt from the pier across almost two metres of water to land on the back deck of the ferry, still holding the valuable suitcase. I often wonder what would have happened had I missed the landing. I'd have been chopped to pieces by the propeller blades and made a good meal for the sharks.

The director, crew and cast were sitting on wooden benches inside the little ferry. They saw me arrive, sweaty and gasping for breath.

'What happened to you?' Géza von Cziffra asked looking at me as if I was some jetsam floating too near to him.

In my fury, I found a voice. 'You left me! You didn't even tell me you were finished! I could have missed the ferry and had to stay the night on this island with poisonous snakes!' I screamed with rage.

It had little effect. He just shrugged his shoulders. There was no place left for me on the benches. Not an actor, nor crewmember stood up to offer me a seat. I went to stand outside on the stern where I had jumped on to the deck, keeping the precious suitcase between my legs and held on to a railing. My eyes stung with tears but I didn't allow them to overflow. I still had make-up on and there would have been telltale rivulets running down my cheeks, confirming my humiliation.

Up to then, I'd never heard of a stand-in or a stunt-double. When it came to crossing crocodile or piranha-infested waters, I was expected to do it myself. Thoughtfully, stones were strategically placed to insure a safe passage, but one slip... and there goes a leg. On one occasion, a goat was slaughtered to attract the piranhas and any stray crocodiles up-river – but that was when the entire crew were having to cross.

In Belém I got into a motorboat, which took me and a disposable native crewmember doubling as my lover into the middle of what was at that point a wide Amazon River. We dropped a canoe into the water at a designated spot when ordered to do so via a walkie-talkie, which was mistakenly returned to the shore with the driver of the boat. My partner and I began to paddle. No-one had asked me if I could row a canoe. They were not to know that years at a summer camp in the Adirondacks of upstate New York taught me to behave like a Native American. We had to wait for a helicopter, which would film us floating happily into the sunset.

We remained, paddling furiously against the strong current. I saw in the distance, arriving from the other side, a solid curtain of tropical rain and gestured to my fellow canoe occupant. The Brazilian looked worried. As we were without the walkie-talkie, we were out of contact with the crew and couldn't know exactly when the helicopter would be flying overhead to photograph this romantic scene. The menacing curtain was quickly approaching, as opposed to the film camera. The setting sun had become obliterated by dark, angry clouds. White froth from the torrential downpour on the surface of the water was only a few metres away. We were not going to wait any longer and literally paddled for our lives towards the shore. The rain came over us and was quickly filling the canoe. First, it covered our feet, then our ankles and began to creep up our shins. By the time we reached the pier, our knees and bums were soaking and the canoe began to sink. We managed to climb some wooden steps to bring us up to the pier. The canoe landed on the bottom of the river. We separated. My lover's double headed off in another direction having pointed out to me approximately where I would find the unit hotel.

I was in my costume: thongs hanging from my hips, chains with large golden discs strung from my neck barely covering my breasts and the jaguar pelt flung across my shoulder. My bleached (for the film) long platinum blonde hair hung wet and matted like fettuccini around my face and down my back. On the expressions of those poor souls who were also caught out in the rain, I must have looked quite a sight. Having found the hotel, I dripped through its entrance. Loud conversation and laughter was emitting from the bar. There they were: director, production manager, lighting cameraman, operator and co-star, all having a wonderful time. It was only the look of the bartender when he saw my soaked self that turned the heads of my colleagues around to me.

The first words spoken at my sorry appearance were from Géza v. Cziffra. 'You haff vetted the skin of the jaguar. It better be dry tomorrow!'

I had not really ever learned to curse in German. The worst I could say was *scheise* (shit). It was not enough to express the anger I was feeling. As when having been left on the snake-infested island, there was no remorse. The fact that I'd been in the middle of the Amazon in a canoe during a rainstorm did not bother anyone. The possibility of my drowning as a result was not even considered. I screamed how such a thing could have been overlooked. Did they forget where I was? Their star was put into extreme danger and nobody cared!

It's difficult to make a dignified exit, dripping wet and in full exotic costume but I tried. At least there was silence as I disappeared. Years later, when I was more familiar with film making procedure and thought back on the nightmare experience of *Lana* I became convinced they didn't really care if anything happened to me. I was expendable. The publicity bonanza that a misfortune would have generated could have more than financed a new ending to the film. It's not that difficult to match the original with a double. Clever revisions to the script and photography could have realized that. Thank God, these thoughts had not entered my head at the time. I'd have become completely paranoid.

There was another incident that provoked animosity between the production and myself. A certain scene I was expected to film had me appearing completely nude. This was not as I had understood it in the script. I put my foot down, relying on the fact that in German law, I was still a minor. The producer would have to get permission from my parents to allow the scene to proceed. As in English, there is bathing and bathing. It is the same in German. Bathing can be washing as it can mean swimming. I presumed in the script it meant swimming and I could easily have worn something. It was a matter of semantics.

In 1964, getting on the telephone from Rio to speak to the European continent was not an everyday event. I needed to get in touch with Steffie, my parents and even Herr Wecker who was controlling the film from his Berlin office. I wrote letters. The ones in German were kindly translated from English by a fellow actor in his forties, the only one who was sympathetic towards me in the whole cast. His name was Anton Diffring, a well-known actor, mainly for playing Nazi characters in American or British war movies and very recognizable for his chiselled features in a Germanic, blue eyed, handsome face and speaking English with an elegant German accent. I would meet him later when living in London where he told me he was gay. Thank God, there was one person on the filming who had the sensitivity to take pity on a confused and naïve young woman.

Anton helped me to compose my letters. Obviously, to my parents I could cope on my own, begging them not to allow the nudity. Why had I been educated in a Catholic convent, to now have to cavort completely naked for the titillation of an audience... not to mention the crew and on-lookers? In my letter to Steffie, I mentioned the other disasters which, had I been in constant contact, could have been avoided by stern words to the production on her part. This was what I needed her to do now. Did she really think Grace Kelly would be photographed in the nude? Where was my future career going to?

There was no reply except for a telegram from the producer telling the director to go ahead with the scene. He had received consent from my parents, a fact I later berated them for.

The scene, in itself, was innocuous. When I saw it later, I couldn't imagine why I had been so upset. I am a tiny figure, running out of the waves towards an outcrop of rocks. The next moment on the screen, I'm discreetly covered from the waist in my thongs which I would have put on out of picture. I go to my lover who is waiting on the beach with only my breasts exposed. We speak and exchange a chaste kiss. Some of the Brazilian crew must have told their buddies about what was going to be filmed. A lot of men were standing out of the camera's viewpoint on the raised dunes staring in my direction. It was that which bothered me the most.

When I returned to Munich, I was determined to quit the profession. I'd had enough of cruelty, of my fellow actors behaving rudely, of their filthy language and vulgar jokes. It was a disgusting world and I wanted nothing more to do with it. Yet... the Brazilian experience was valuable. Not only did it strengthen my resolve to defend myself against tyrannical behaviour in the future but, most importantly, I discovered a social conscience there. My hotel room did not have a view of the Copacabana. Those were reserved for the production's big shots. My window overlooked a *favela,* a steaming shantytown of narrow alleyways and corrugated roofs with garbage and exposed sewage attracting flies. The stench that emitted from there made it impossible for me to open my window. There were street children who slept in doorways or on the beaches. They wrapped themselves in discarded newspapers against the cold. We sometimes came across a few rummaging for food in rubbish bins from the expensive restaurants some Brazilian acquaintances had taken me to. That poverty existed, in what was a third world country at that time, was not unusual. It was the blatant wealth of the few and their determined disregard for the plight of the huge underclass which shocked me. I felt shame for the cosseted life I'd had, how well protected I'd been from an unattractive reality.

A body lay on the side of a road we were being driven on early in the morning to get to a film location. A police car was parked nearby and two patrolmen casually smoking cigarettes stood guard over it. Our driver slowed down to have a better look. It was not the first time that I'd seen a corpse. When I was nine, the nuns paraded us past a sister who was lying in state in an elaborately carved four-poster bed. Her hair was hidden inside her wimple and her hands were crossed on her chest, holding a rosary with black beads, which contrasted to the white lace linen sheet her hands, beads and crucifix were resting on. Freshly cut flowers and lit candelabras with their scent and glow gave an ambiance of peace and beauty to the room, which was directly next door to the chapel. She looked asleep and we children were not at all frightened. The body in the road was in a tortured position, obviously a victim of a hit and run accident. After two hours of filming, it was still there on our return. If there is little respect for the living, there will be even less for the dead.

Back in Munich, Steffie was sympathetic when hearing of my filming experience but had no intention of supporting my decision to give up the profession.

'Every film is different and so are all the people who work on them. You had a bad time but you will have learned from it.'

She always insisted that I remain contactable wherever I was travelling to with a phone number or an address. So, it was not a miracle that, when I was with Mommy visiting Peter in 1964 at the NIH outside of Washington DC, I received the following telegram from her: *Signed you for film STOP Good role in thriller STOP Starting immediately in London STOP Production will cable you plane ticket STOP Steffie.*

There wasn't a question of whether or not I would accept. I left my mother to travel back to Munich on her own and flew to Heathrow. The film was called *Traitor's Gate*, an Edgar Wallace thriller. It was a German-British co-production directed by Freddie Francis. Amongst the leading players, Gary Raymond starred for the Brits and Albert Lieven, Margot Trooger, Klaus Kinski and yours truly represented the German side. I had survived the ridiculous and was now living the sublime. The difference in treatment, the politeness of the British crew, actors and production personnel was in exact contrast to what I experienced in Brazil. For the first time, I was allocated a 'stand-in'. I didn't know such a person could exist. If I remember correctly, her name was Fiona. She brought me tea or coffee on the set and suffered the harsh lights on her face when the cameraman was setting up for my close-ups while I, sitting in a canvas chair with my name on its back, was fussed over by make-up and hair artists trying their best to make me look presentable. She'd slip quietly into the shadows when I was called to take my position in the limelight in front of the camera. We became great friends. It was via her advice and connections that I left the hotel and rented a little flat in Earl's Court. The production agreed to give me a living allowance in cash and thus, for the first time, I became completely responsible for myself. I shopped in the little local stores, cooked my own meals and tidied the place. I loved being an adult. The studio sent a car to pick me up for work. Perhaps mine was not 'top' billing but I felt like a star.

While in London, I was represented by the agency ICM, in the person of Dennis Selinger. Agents have agreements to look after each other's clients in one country to another. Steffie looked after ICM actors in Germany and it was reciprocated in Britain. Dennis asked to take me out to dinner. He had a plan, he said. The first James Bond movie had been filmed and was a huge success in the cinemas. The production company was near to casting the next. He knew that Harry Saltzman was going to eat at the popular show-biz restaurant, the Pickwick Club, that night and was convinced that Mr Saltzman would show an interest in me. I, still only 20, was cautious about going out with someone from our notorious profession who I didn't really know and asked if Fiona could accompany me. He sweetly agreed. To make up a foursome he invited Michael Caine. I had never heard of him. Dennis had ordered the table diagonally opposite Harry Saltzman's and placed me in full view of him. During dinner, we all spoke politely. Michael, wearing horn-rimmed glasses, looked very pleasant and made cockney witticisms that, unfortunately, I couldn't understand. I'd never heard that accent before. By the end of the evening he must have thought I was either very stupid or extremely deaf from the amount of times I asked him to repeat what he had said. He did not stay for dessert and through some sort of unnoticed collusion left the restaurant with Fiona on his arm. I remained with Dennis who explained how important Michael was after filming *Zulu* in the new hierarchy of up and coming actors. I had neither seen nor heard of it.

'What? Even though, he wears glasses?' Ooh, was I dumb.

Harry did notice me. When Dennis and I were left alone he signalled for us to join him at his table. I was sat down next to him. He studied my face. At that time, in private, I wore my hair parted to one side. It was long and straight falling across my cheek and covering one eye. Harry lifted his hands and swept the hair back from my face and forehead.

'There!' he said. 'That's better! Why are you hiding behind all of that hair? Your face should be seen.' He then turned to Dennis and said, 'Bring her to our office next week. I want her to meet Cubby.'

Now, that's good work from an agent. I did go the following week to meet them both but was suffering from a dislocated disc, walking as stiff as a broomstick and didn't appear in that particular James Bond. Cubby Broccoli spoke to Dennis after the interview. He said I looked and seemed far too innocent for the usual Bond girls. They were not looking for angels. He would change his mind about me in the future when I had grown up and lost the puppy fat.

Fiona introduced me to some of her friends, amongst whom was a writer. When Harold Wilson was elected Prime Minister in 1964, I witnessed the jubilation late at night in Trafalgar Square with him. We were standing amidst a crowd of thousands who went crazy with joy when the results were finally authenticated that Britain would have a Labour government. It was important for Derek that he win, as he wrote many of the speeches Wilson had uttered. He felt a little responsible for this success. How naïve I had been to think politicians spoke their own words.

Although, our relationship, as far as I was concerned, was platonic and he never pressed for it to become romantic, I did have an unforgettable experience due to him. After dinner at an exclusive London Club, instead of driving me home, Derek suggested we visit some friends of his in Hampstead, a north London district. I mentioned the lateness of the hour but he insisted these people did not retire early and, anyway, they were expecting for us to drop in. We arrived at an expensive looking property surrounded by a garden. There were a few cars parked in the driveway. We rang the bell and a diminutive woman with a pointed little nose and a pouting small mouth answered the door. She was our hostess. Her welcome was genuinely warm and enthusiastic. We were led through a large square lobby with doors leading off it. One of them was partially open and a soft red glow emitted from its interior. She walked us to a little cosy sitting room and closed the door behind her. A bottle of Champagne was already cooling in a bucket of iced water. So, we really had been expected, I thought. Derek and I sat on a sofa while she hovered over us, pouring the Champagne in our glasses, making conversation and every now and again, admiring my long, thick hair which she would fondle lovingly.

'You have hair like a pony,' she enthused. 'Do you mind if I call you Pony?'

'Not at all,' I answered. 'You call me Pony and I'll call you Mouse.' But I added quickly, 'You don't mind if I call you Mouse? I mean it well.'

She went into paroxysms of joy, clapping her hands together, excitedly shouting, 'Oh, I shall be your mouse and you are my pony!'

Weird, but quite sweet, I thought. No threat. We continued to talk, drink and laugh together. All was normal but I did begin to wonder where all the other drivers of the cars parked outside were. Never mind, maybe they were hosting a bridge competition in one of the rooms off the lobby. My parents were champion bridge players and often invited guests to play. These sessions could last until well past midnight. I didn't wish to seem nosy. We finished our second glass of Champagne and Mouse opened our door. It was a gesture I hardly noticed and we continued to speak but then, certain noises began to intrude on our animated conversations. They were sounds I'd not heard before. Derek glanced at me. Mouse studied my expression when filling my glass. I felt they were expecting a reaction but I could give them none. I was high on Champagne, babbling and giggling like a teenager. Admittedly, the noises were completely different to those I was used to when my parents friends were playing at tables in our living room, the shuffling of cards, bidding, arguing. Eventually, Mouse asked us both if we wanted to meet the other guests.

'Yes, of course,' I said, getting to my feet.

She led us across the lobby to the gently glowing room and opened wider the door. Against all rules of etiquette, I was still holding my glass of Champagne. We entered. There was no furniture, just a carpet, what I could see of it, poured wall to wall on the floor. There were couples, threesomes, foursomes, all writhing upon it in a study of sexual acts and positions. I had stepped into an orgy. Now, what to do? Do not drop the glass of Champagne. Keep it clutched between your fingers. You may need it. Don't look down. Remain indifferent to what is happening on the floor. Pretend there is nothing extraordinary about all of this and couldn't your hostess come up with something more interesting. We stood for a few minutes on the threshold. I, sipping my Champagne, studying the nudes and semi-pornographic paintings on the walls as if I were an art critic.

A hysterically funny thought came to my head. We were standing here to be introduced. Will people in mid-orgasm stretch out a hand for us to shake and say, 'How do you do?' Will I want to touch that hand? Or, perhaps, Mouse will clap her hands together to stop the proceedings. 'Will you all stand up, please? I'd like you to meet some new guests.'

I was about to faint from suppressed laughter when Mouse took us back to the original room. A few minutes later, her husband joined us. I didn't recognize him from the mêlée on the floor, but then, I was trying very hard not to look. Another bottle of Champagne was opened and another conversation ensued.

It began with, 'We're Satanists.' And this, to a convent-bred girl!

'Really?' I replied, politely. What else could I say?

They then explained how worshipping the devil had helped them achieve all of their goals. 'This splendid house was bought from an enormous salary earned as Director General of (and he mentioned the European airline) which has never had a disastrous incident. Other people pray to God. But Satan is more powerful.' He paused for affect. 'And more appreciative.'

The begged question I wished to ask but didn't, was, 'What do you do in return? Have orgies? Is Satan a voyeur?'

It was a long, long time ago and as far as I know that particular airline has really never had a fatal accident. Did they draw up a contract offering their souls into perpetuity? Is hell their home now? I wonder what happened to their house in Hampstead.

Derek drove me back to my flat. The journey took at least three quarters of an hour. We spent the entire time talking about everything but what we had just experienced. Very British.

CHAPTER VIII

'You poor girl, you have such an ugly mouth,' the famous French actress, Martine Carol, said to me in her melodious accent as I was applying lipstick in preparation for my close-up. We were making a film together called *Hell is Empty* in which I played the *ingénue* role to her wicked stepmother. Her part was not wicked, as such, but she managed to infuse it into our off-screen relationship. The filming took place at locations outside of Prague and we were staying at a no frills, Communist conversion of an aristocratic hunting lodge turned hotel. It was here that I received the devastating news of Peter's attempted suicide.

Ms Carol was somewhere in her forties when starring in the picture. She was tiny with all the petiteness that went with such a small structure, child-like hands and feet that would have slipped into no larger than a size 4 shoe. I, a giant compared to her, felt gauche and clumsy in her presence. My admiration for her was not so much as a person but for her elegance and perfection. She had the most extraordinarily beautiful eyes. Black and white photography would not have done them justice. They were a greenish hazel with golden specks that glittered in her irises. With all she had going for her, she need not have been jealous of my youth. In scenes we played together, when the camera was favouring me, she managed to mess my hair so that it would hide most of my face. Ms Carol knew the shot would be unusable and the camera would have to turn around on her and that would be the take, which would appear in the film. The director did not dare to interfere.

The original filming had taken place on the island of Capri and foundered there on its sea swept craggy rocks. The producer was Ronald Rietti. Klaus Kinski, who I'd worked with before on *Traitor's Gate* was again playing a 'baddy'. He arrived one morning on the set with his wife and a gorgeous little four year old girl, his daughter, Nastassja. Her doll-like little mouth was made up with bright red lipstick, her tiny nails painted scarlet and I don't know how it was possible considering her size, but she wore stiletto heeled sandals with her painted toenails peeping through. On occasion, a cigarette was placed between her fingers but she only pretended to smoke it. Nastassja was destined for stardom.

Mr Rietti was generous. We stayed in an expensive hotel made mostly of marble. It couldn't last. After only two weeks, money ran out and we made an ignominious exit off the island. All the other participants flew back to their respective homes but I was told not to return to Munich as Rietti was sure he would get further funding and the filming would continue. I rang Steffie from Rome and she didn't seem bothered. I'd been paid for the previous two weeks.

'He's picking up the tab, so you have nothing to worry about. Enjoy yourself. Rome is a beautiful city,' she said.

I was put up in a more humble hotel somewhere in Rome's northern outskirts. Rietti lodged there as well but we hardly ever saw each other as he was cruising offices and film studios with a begging bowl and I was taking Steffie's advice, enjoying the city's '*dolce vita*' and dancing in nightclubs until four in the morning. I'd return to a darkened hotel, with a sleepy porter unlocking the front entrance, and go to my room from where, at about two in the afternoon, I'd ring room service for my breakfast, after which I'd brave the brilliant sunshine and take myself for a walk – returning in time to have a bath, put my face on, dress in something appealing, and be fetched for another night out on the town. What a life. I knew it would have to end. On one of my sorties, I was stopped by the manager when leaving and asked who was going to pay the bill.

'Mr Rietti, of course,' I answered. 'He's the producer. I'm under contract to him, so he's responsible for the payment of my room. Why, is there a problem?' I asked.

'We have not received payment since your arrival.'

Gulp. I was fortunate to have had a cousin of my mother's whom I called 'uncle' living in Rome. He too was in the profession as an actor and spread his wide wings in protection over me. He was known to our family as 'Popo' but as Count Esterhazy to all others. By chance, after the talk with the manager we were to meet for dinner. Popo brought two German friends to the restaurant. During the meal I told him of my fears. He looked at his friends and a certain collusion took place between them.

One of them said, 'Tonight?' and looked at me.

'What tonight?' I asked.

'We're leaving tonight to drive back to Frankfurt. But we can stop in Munich on the way. Can you make it? We'll be going after we've eaten and drunk a few strong coffees.'

Popo nodded towards me as if to say, 'You'd better'.

I kissed him goodbye, thanked him and got in a car with two virtual strangers who drove me to my hotel.

'Where's your room?' I was asked. By chance, it was on the ground floor. I pointed to the window.

'Enter as if all is as usual. Go to your room. Pack your cases and drop them from the window. Climb out yourself and with luck, we'll be off.'

Best directions I ever had and I followed them faithfully. Each suitcase was hastily filled, hoisted out of the window and snuck to the parked car. I climbed out without much grace and jumped the short distance to the ground. In very little time we were on the *autostrada* heading north. Another ignominious exit. For years I was frightened to go back to Rome in case I was on some record for non-payment of debt and be arrested.

When I was safely back in Munich a few months later, Rietti miraculously found more finance to continue the filming. Only now, instead of glamorous Capri, our locations were to be shot in Czechoslovakia.

The cast, except for Martine, Anthony Steel and myself had also been changed. My Italian boyfriend became Jess Conrad. Klaus Kinski was replaced by another German actor, Carl Möhner who travelled with his own 'inky dink' which is a tiny spotlight attached to an existing light stand. It is shone directly into the irises during a close-up to give the allusion of extremely bright eyes. Jess and I had hours of fun standing in their piercing glare to cast a shadow or moving it just a titch to give him a glowing nose, much to the annoyance of this ultra vain actor. Years later, I would work with him again in London. We played husband and wife. He took his revenge by sticking his tongue down my throat every time we had a screen kiss. My inherited diplomatic genes did not permit me to embarrass him in front of the crew, not even on the occasion I gagged and the director had to cut. Thank God, the film didn't concentrate on an erotic marital relationship or I'd have been forced to bite off his tongue. I'd kissed on the screen before pretty convincingly without having to exchange saliva. Talking of which...

When I was nearing my 21st birthday, I met a beautiful man. He must have been because when the press wrote about him which, as a wealthy playboy they often did, he was referred to as probably the most handsome man in Bavaria. At 42, he was 22 years older than me, with prematurely white hair, blue eyes that sparkled without the help of an inky dink, a mouth that seemed constantly to smile and, when gesturing, hands which expressed an almost feminine sensitivity. He was the first man since S that I felt utterly attracted to. But it would take time. So much time, in fact, that after three months of dates to theatres and restaurants, little journeys to the countryside, and only an innocent kiss goodnight when he delivered me to my parents' door, that I received a brooch which he had ordered to be made by a jeweller of an 18 carat gold hedgehog with ruby eyes.

'You are like this little animal, very difficult to touch,' he told me. 'Put your needles down. I promise I won't hurt you.' But I was still frightened. Not of the act... of the aftermath.

We continued to see each other and in mid-winter he invited me for a weekend to a posh hotel in a Bavarian ski resort. Again I resisted telling him my parents would never allow me to accompany a man on my own.

'Come with your brother in that case. I'll invite him and anyone he'd like to bring.' Heinrich had met Paul before and liked him. When I mentioned the invitation, Paul was enthusiastic.

'Come on, Catherine, you've got to lose your virginity some time. Why not with Heinrich? He's a really cool guy.'

I'd not told anyone but Penny about my incident with S. As far as everyone was concerned, because I behaved like a virgin they thought I was one. Mommy was too busy with her own private life to enquire too deeply about the coming weekend. Once again she was in love, this time with a near neighbour who was married but his wife, ten years his senior seemed actually to encourage the relationship. They were also, importantly, in the bridge clique and spent many evenings together. Daddy didn't ask questions of her and he avoided interrogating me.

Paul owned an old Volkswagen Beetle. It was so antique that it still had orange, finger-like indicators that waved up and down either side of the car to warn other drivers of his intended manoeuvres. The rear oval window was so small, he could hardly see the vehicles behind him. The tyres were bald and we were soon to discover that the battery was virtually empty. This was our conveyance to get us to the hotel. To Paul's delighted anticipation, Olga was coming with us for the ride. Snow on the roads that weekend caused the VW to waltz on its slippery surface. We were incredibly fortunate that very little traffic was coming in the opposite direction. As we neared our destination and the sun had set behind the mountains, Paul was obliged to use his headlights. We moved on and it was soon noticeable that the beams of his lights were getting dimmer and dimmer until we had to crawl as we couldn't see anything at all and had to drive by the light of the moon shining on the snowy surface of the road. Arriving at the resort, we stopped at a petrol station/garage. There not being mobiles in those days, we had to find a public phone. The Beetle was not going to be able to cope with the hill it had to climb to reach the hotel. The garage owner very kindly gave me the number and I telephoned Heinrich to say we were stuck lower down and could he come to fetch us.

'*Aber natürlich, Liebling. Ich komme sofort.*'

His top of the range Mercedes glided into the garage forecourt. Our luggage was transferred to the boot. Paul left the Beetle in the trusted hands of the garage owner who would do his best to recharge the battery.

With delicate discretion, two rooms had been reserved for us. One with twin beds, another with a single. Olga and I nabbed the twin, leaving the single for Paul. That was a disappointment for him. He'd hoped for something larger that, perhaps, he and Olga would be sharing. But the night was young. We retired upstairs to bathe and change into something more suitable for the evening and joined Heinrich in an elegant dining room to have a sumptuous meal of *foie gras*, lobster and venison fillet with chanterelle mushrooms, all washed down with the best of French wines. After dinner, we retired to a nightclub in the basement. There was a grand piano on one side of the dance floor. The disc jockey, having made a pause, left a pianist to entertain the guests. His playing didn't stop people from dancing. On the contrary, the smooching music he coaxed from the keys saw many couples swaying in a close embrace.

Paul and Olga were already dancing. I was still at our candlelit table with Heinrich when he called over a waiter and asked for a piece of paper. The waiter returned and I saw Heinrich write something and then fold the paper with a 50 Mark note enclosed within. The waiter was sent to the pianist who acknowledged the contents with a broad smile and a nod to Heinrich. Within seconds, he was playing and singing Frank Sinatra's 'Strangers in the night'.

'I like to think, this is our song,' Heinrich said, lifting me to my feet and leading me to the dance floor. He was right as far as intimacy was concerned. We were still strangers.

Sometime after midnight the four of us piled into the lift to go to our rooms. Paul headed for his single, Olga and I for the twin. It was then that Heinrich took my hand saying, '*Nein, meine liebe. Du kommst mit mir*,' and led me gently to his room which was on the other side of the corridor.

Paul turned around, winked at me and said, 'Have a good night, little sister.' Olga gave me a knowing smile. I wondered if they also were to have an eventful night.

There is little so attractive for me than to see a man caring for his children. I hadn't realized that Heinrich had custody of his two young sons for the weekend. They had been put to bed the previous night before we met up for dinner and he had not mentioned them. I was still in bed in the morning when the boys knocked on Heinrich's door. He was already up and answered. Two boisterous urchins came tumbling into the room. They stopped dead when they noticed a presence in the bed. Heinrich introduced us. I was 'Katrinchen', a very good friend. They politely shook my outstretched hand, gave a little bow and then continued their rushing around. Sadly, I no longer remember their names. Heinrich offered me his silk *peignoir* which I wrapped around myself and while the boys looked the other way, I moved to the bathroom to dress. Breakfast was ordered and soon the four of us sat around a table in his suite munching boiled eggs, ham, cheese, bread, buns, jam and honey with juice, coffee and, for the little ones, rich hot chocolate. It was a memorable breakfast with animated conversation. The boys were not in the least bashful. I wondered if the lads were used to seeing their father in the mornings with a 'very good friend'. After our meal, he zipped them into their ski-wear and Olga and I joined them on the *piste.*

Poor Paul had spent a lonely night, a lonely breakfast and now, a lonely wait until we returned from the slopes. He and Olga as a couple were not to be.

We left the hotel after lunch. Heinrich drove us down the hill to the garage. He insisted that I ride back with him and his sons until just around the corner of our house, where I would transfer into Paul's car. The Beetle's battery had been recharged. He was assured it would get him back to Munich but Heinrich preferred that Paul drive behind him. In case there was a problem, at least, he could drive us home.

All went to plan. But Heinrich and I did not become an item. I was grateful for his tenderness, yet doubted that our relationship would ever deepen. His eyes wandered too much in search for other conquests. I accepted the experience as remedial therapy carried out by an expert therapist.

Czechoslovakia must have been a popular destination for filmmakers. I found myself there again but this time on a different project and staying in a Prague hotel a short walk from Wenceslas Square where, in 1968, the Russian tanks put down the Czech uprising and the Prague spring turned to deep winter.

We were filming a musical version of the German folklore character, Till Eulenspiegel, for German ZDF Television. I played his girlfriend and proved two things: I was capable of moving gracefully enough to music and my singing ability can turn the complexion of sound engineers green... not with envy but with nausea. I had to sing to a playback. Tape recordings of the songs were given to me in order to practice doing them in synch to the person performing them on the tapes. When rehearsing on my own, I thought I did them rather well. I learned to take breaths when the singer took hers, to copy the words so that my lips would move exactly as hers, to sing loudly or gently when it was required. Voicing the music in the scenes was necessary to look authentic. Just moving one's lips was not enough. During the takes, I gave it my all in the hope that, perhaps, I needn't be dubbed after all. I would be asked to record the songs myself. The expressions on faces of the soundman and his assistant who was following me holding the boom shattered all of my aspirations. My parents were right. I was the only member of the family who couldn't hold a tune.

During the three months of filming, I met and befriended many of the natives. Some were in the business, others were not. But all told me to be careful of who I spoke to and what I said. My make-up woman, with whom I'd worked on *Hell is Empty*, admitted to me secretly that a meeting had taken place at Barandov studios before my arrival. Everyone from the Czech crew had been warned about me. They were to watch me and report any anti-government conversations. My father was an employee of the CIA's notorious propaganda outlet, Radio Free Europe. My mail was likely to be opened. I hinted at this in a postcard I'd written to Derek. He replied with a letter. On the top of the page in bold writing was, 'Greetings to all of our readers!'

I was invited to the flat of a South American diplomat. He was engaged to a Czech woman and both were waiting for the government's approval for them to be allowed to marry. It was very soon after I entered that he gestured with his index finger to a chandelier on the ceiling and with his other index finger to his lips. It was clear. We were being listened to.

The best instance, though, in case one had doubts about hidden snooping devices happened at the hotel. Our rooms were bugged because most of the occupants were foreigners and the state wanted to know what we were up to. An intercom system connected the restaurant to the reception desk and to the telephone operators. We would often hear the name of guests being called to the phone or the head waiter to receive reservations.

One morning while breakfasting some unintentional sounds emitted from the system: heavy breathing, a woman moaning, a man grunting, even heavier breathing, more moaning, more grunting, certain erotic vocabulary groaned by the man in German to the ever faster rhythm of a creaking spring mattress. The head waiter went pale and ran out of the restaurant just as the exuberant cries of orgasm being enjoyed by the couple ended our morning's entertainment. Someone employed to listen had messed up, to say it politely. I was alone at my table and the only woman in the room. Some of the men seemed, literally, to blush and I could feel the thought they exuded, 'There but for the grace of God...'

The hotel welcomed 'tussex' girls. These were prostitutes who sold their expertise for 'tussex' stamps. There were shops in Prague that one needed to exchange, at a ridiculously low rate, hard currency to buy the stamps with which one purchased the goods on sale: beautifully coloured and blown Bohemian glassware, Russian vodka and caviar, Georgian sparkling wine, imported goods and fashions, etc. The women were encouraged to begin relationships with foreign businessmen. In their own little way, they worked for the state. I can only imagine that a few men at that breakfast had had experience of these women and hoped their encounters had not been registered on a tape which could be used in the future as blackmail.

I was sad to leave Prague, even then, one of the most beautiful cities in the world. I'm proud to have crossed the Charles Bridge which spans over the river Moldau and to have marvelled at the exquisitely carved stone statues of saints guarding either side of my path from where I climbed to the imposing castle gleaming brightly in the sun and later, reflecting the ochre glow of the sunset on its walls.

I fell in love with Prague's Art Nouveau architecture, even though, many of these buildings were in dire need of attention. I fell in love with the paintings of the artist, Mucha, who the Czechs claim as the originator of the Art Nouveau style. I also fell a little in love with a sweet man who reminded me, in looks, of my father when he was young. It was difficult to go but I knew my future was not to be in this place. I still remember the little of the language I was taught: *Děkuji* (thank you) *Hezký den* (have a nice day) *Dobrý večer* (good evening) *Dobrou noc* (good night) *Miluji tě* (I love you).

To my surprise, I returned the following year to Czechoslovakia to film more scenes for the inadequately shot *Hell is Empty*. Our location this time was a castle up on a hill overlooking a bend in the Moldau. By an incredible coincidence, I was acquainted with the son of its former owners. The Communist state had requisitioned the property and all of its belongings. It had been one of the estates of a very noble Austrian family belonging to the remnants of the Austro-Hungarian Hapsburg dynasty. I had met the son on a visit to Vienna with my mother. He came to visit me at my parent's in Munich. She salivated at the thought I might become a Duchess. It was not to be. With Peter's illness, I was paranoid that the gene pool of the aristocracy was dangerously deficient. Unlike my mother, I was not impressed. But he was a nice young man with impeccable manners and I genuinely liked him.

We were only allowed access to certain rooms in the castle. All else was forbidden. On my own one day, with nobody about, I risked an exploration and discovered some stone steps which spiralled up inside a tower. At the top was an ancient, heavy, wooden door. I tried the latch and to my surprise, the door opened into a round room with stone walls. It contained children's toys, dolls, little wooden guns, teddy bears, all manner of stuffed animals. It was a cornucopia of children's Christmas and birthday presents sadly neglected.

There was a guardian of the castle who lived somewhere on the premises. I was introduced to him. He spoke fluent German and we struck up a conversation. I admitted knowing the son of the previous occupants and asked if it would not be possible to take some small token back to him, nothing of value but something he might remember. I was thinking of a teddy bear.

'I will see what I can do. It is not allowed but I will try,' he said and added conspiratorially, 'Please be discreet.'

'Of course,' I whispered in response.

But I couldn't stay that quiet. When I was sure we weren't being listened to, I told some of my fellow actors what I had been up to. They thought my intentions were noble.

We continued filming for another few days. I didn't see the caretaker again during this time and thought, perhaps, taking something from the castle was too risky for him. It was disappointing but didn't really matter. My friend in Vienna had no idea that I was in one of his ancestral houses. He had no expectations.

On the last day of the shoot we finished mid-afternoon. I was leaving the castle with some of the cast to go to our car. The driver was politely opening the back door for me when I heard my name voiced and turned around. It was the guardian, holding a rectangular package covered with brown paper.

'You forgot this, Frau Schell,' he called out.

I went to him and he handed me what seemed a heavy parcel. Thanking him, I took it to the car and placed it on my lap where it lay burning my thighs all the way back to the hotel. The desire to rip off the paper and see what lay underneath was overwhelming. My colleagues knew better than to ask me any questions. One never knew how much English our drivers could understand and the last thing I wanted was for the caretaker to get into trouble.

Back in my hotel room, I carefully unwrapped the parcel. Revealed, to my delight, was a leather bound album with the family crest embossed on its cover. The castle had been a part of a glorious hunting estate. All of the black and white photographs glued within had been taken of successful shoots with the trophies of wild boar and deer surrounded by the hunters, their rifles still slung around their shoulders. Names of well-known people were written in ink underneath the pictures with the dates of the hunt. I believed this would be a treasure for my friend.

The Czech border guards at the airport had a nasty habit of opening passenger's suitcases as well as asking to look in their wallets when they were leaving the country. They weren't that interested in contraband entering. It was more what was leaving that mattered. Czech money, the Krona, was not allowed to be exported. It had to be reconverted to hard currency and once again at a falsely low exchange rate. Who would want to leave with Kronas? They were worth less than the tissues we blew our noses in. We were warned as well to keep our bills from the 'tussex' shops in case we were accused of smuggling out precious artefacts or antiques. I stood nervously in the queue and prayed my luggage would not be examined and had already decided that if it were the case, I would admit to having stolen the album. As it was, my bags were ignored and I arrived in Munich with the treasure. Weeks later another friend from Vienna came on a visit. He was part of that aristocratic clique and I told him about the parcel, saying it was a surprise gift for our mutual friend only exaggerating a wee bit of the dangers I had undergone smuggling it out of the country. He would be more likely to see our friend before me and could he, please, deliver it? He was delighted to do so.

I was never thanked nor did I ever hear from the recipient again, even though I was assured it was in his possession... and here I thought he had impeccable manners.

CHAPTER IX

The term 'senile dementia', or Alzheimer's, had not yet crept into our family's customary vocabulary, even though it was known that my paternal grandfather's life ended with him wandering lost on his estate and forgetting his name. It was seldom spoken of. Such debility of one's mental faculties could never happen to someone of high intellect, vast experience and wit. We were so ignorant.

Daddy had retired and we moved from the spacious house to a flat on the tenth floor of a newly built apartment block. RFE were kind enough to offer him part time employment which would help, of course, financially but we were no longer lodged at their expense. There were savings of $10,000 which, when translated into Deutschmarks at that time, and with his pension, meant they were reasonably comfortable. As I was living with them, my mother asked for a contribution which, for the sake of my conscience, I readily agreed to.

The new flat was still in Bogenhausen, our old stomping ground. We began to notice that Daddy's driving was becoming erratic. If I could, I took him to work and picked him up. But sometimes, he had to do the journeys on his own. Mysterious dents and scrapes appeared on the car's bodywork which had nothing to do with my driving. When asked, he had no memory of the incidents. I put it down to other cars causing damage to his when it was parked. I never saw insurance claims, but then, work was taking me away for weeks at a time. On my return home, subtle changes would be noticeable, those odd moments when he would repeat himself. Always helpful, he'd lay the table but on occasion the knives and forks would be meticulously placed at their opposite positions. Bread was tidied away into the oven and the butter dish on the grill above. These were small things that we laughed about.

The temporary work Daddy went to the office for was just that, temporary. He began to notice he was no longer as competent. His concentration and memory were suffering. He gave in his notice and said goodbye to his colleagues and Radio Free Europe, which had treated him as a family member, and spent more time at home – even trying to write his memoirs, but the lack of concentration was an impediment. We always had an uncomplicated and talkative relationship. I loved asking him about his past and listening to his stories of the First World War which he was fortunate to have only had a brief encounter with. At 17, he enlisted and, because of his family, was immediately made a lieutenant. It was glamorous to join a cavalry regiment and so he left Nadgyda with two warhorses. He admitted to me that he was never a keen rider. It was part of his education as a nobleman but horses frightened him. One of the pair was docile and kind. The other, un-rideable for his meagre equestrian abilities. But in the end, he never had to charge into whizzing bullets and artillery fire. It was soon discovered that he suffered with his lungs. The regimental doctor diagnosed tuberculosis and he was decommissioned, spending the rest of the war in a sanatorium high in the Carpathian mountains.

The tuberculosis was cured but not long after, he began to go blind in one eye. Although, not noticeable to anyone else, the blindness developed to the point that he could only distinguish between light and shadow. As a diplomat, he travelled extensively and in all the major cities, London, Paris, Rome, even Washington he visited eye specialists. His lack of sight was a mystery to all. At the age of 39, he finally returned to Budapest. It was dangerously near to the outbreak of World War Two. He visited a Hungarian specialist. After an examination, the doctor asked if he'd ever had tuberculosis. Daddy replied, yes, when he was 18.

'That's it,' the doctor said. 'Tuberculosis always leaves a scar, usually on your lungs but it could be anywhere. In your case it's the eye which was affected.'

When he told me this story he was quite proud that the answer for his blindness was finally explained to him by a fellow Hungarian.

Daddy spoke with happy nostalgia about his American experience. He loved blondes and if they had dark eyes, he loved them even more. There were a few of those among the New England socialites. He was too discreet to tell me if any of his female acquaintances became sexual partners but admitted to being very popular. I could imagine why. He was extremely presentable and the title 'Baron' would not have been a hindrance for him being accepted as husband material for the daughters of the most elite families.

Invitations rained onto his desk. One of these was to a party given by two sisters who had become great friends of his. It was to be a weekend 'do' in their parents' family mansion, not too far from Washington. The guests were allocated rooms and his was next door to Noël Coward's. It had a connecting door.

The sisters decided, as a joke, they would introduce Daddy to the rest of the guests as a woman. For the fun of it, he agreed to their subterfuge. They took terrible care to find just the right wig. Being of slight build, there was little difficulty in fitting him in the perfect dress and with small feet, the shoes were no problem at all. On the night, while secluded in one of the sister's rooms they applied make-up, plucked his eyebrows, varnished his nails, rouged his cheeks and gave him a scarlet cupid's bow mouth. When the transformation was completed, he descended the grand staircase for his introduction like a well-turned-out transvestite. All eyes turned to him. Some men looked interested. The girls had done an excellent job. He looked quite beautiful, but Noël Coward had suspicions. During the party, Daddy was unmasked to everyone's amusement. It was at that point that Noël showed interest, offering his solicitous attention. Daddy's Champagne glass was never to be seen empty. The dear boy was absolutely forbidden to go upstairs and redress in more masculine attire.

The festivities ended in the early hours of the morning and the guests who were staying the night retired to their rooms. He was just about to turn out his bedside lamp when the connecting door swung open and Noël Coward, completely naked, danced like a ballerina into the room with his two arms making an arch above his head. He moved with short little steps on the tips of his toes and then took a flying leap onto the bed.

Now, this is when being a diplomat makes all the difference. My father was able, in the nicest possible way, to explain that he was not of the same proclivity but had complete understanding and had absolutely no prejudice towards those people who had those tendencies. Some of the greatest authors, poets and artists were homosexuals. What about Michelangelo? Rumours abounded. Daddy's wig had been thrown onto a chair near the bed. Noël reached out for it and placed it over his private parts. He stayed resting there on top of the covers while my father, underneath, kept them up to his chin. And thus they talked until dawn.

At the end of this story, his eyes seemed to gaze back into the memory and he burst out laughing. 'Can you imagine? Noël lay there with a blonde curly wig covering his penis and we managed to converse as if that was absolutely normal.'

I don't know if they saw each other again but they did correspond. According to my father, Noël was a great letter writer.

'Do you still have the letters?' I asked, in excited anticipation.

'I did for many years,' he answered. 'But moving from one country to another, from one address to another, they were somehow misplaced. Anyway, once I went back to Hungary we stopped writing each other.'

What a loss! I often wonder if the wig incident was ever mentioned in a letter, written in his uniquely clipped voice.

Sometime in 1938, news came that Daddy's father was dying. He surrendered his post at the Embassy and returned to Hungary. The rumblings of war had already begun. Hitler had remilitarized the Rhineland with flagrant disregard to the terms in the Treaty of Versailles. France and England were powerless to demand his army's retreat. American friends had advised my father to stay, warning him that Hungary would be swallowed up or be forced to side with the Axis powers. He was not naïve and realized his diplomatic career had come to an end. Representing an ally to a fascist country would have been out of the question.

It was my mother who told me how they met. She was in a popular restaurant when he walked in with three gorgeous women. They were treated like royalty and the head waiter showed them to the best table. It was his birthday and the lady friends were taking him out for a treat. Mommy was intrigued and asked who he was.

'That's Kepi Schell,' she was told. 'You mean you've never met him?'

She hadn't but she was determined to. Mommy would not have known him before his absences as a diplomat. There was a 16 year age difference between them which would have made her far too young to have moved in the same circles. She asked all around her about him and received some tantalizing accounts as to his person. He was rich, single, charming and very well liked. He spoke other languages, was intelligent and could also be extremely naughty. Having made tremendous gambling debts, he had to sell his hunting estate, Kelemes, to pay for them. Hmmm, she thought, very interesting.

By chance or strategy, they were both invited for a hunting weekend at a country house. He had an accident while shooting, escaping from a furious wild boar. In Hungary, these creatures were allowed to grow to monstrous proportions. Because of the challenge, it was the only game that he enjoyed hunting. The injury was not serious enough for him to be taken to hospital but a doctor was called and prescribed bed rest. It was actually only a bad sprain. Mommy decided to take it on herself to nurse him. She did an excellent job. They became a couple and would eventually marry. How ironic, that their life together began by her nursing him and would end in the same way.

Dementia can take a long time on its journey to the terminus. The strain would have been unbearable. I was happy that, at least, she could spend some time with her lover. The family doctor helped by managing to engineer some time for him to enter a clinic. The insurance paid and it gave her a period of remission. I had flown the nest and offered once to invite him to me when I was between jobs. With my first husband, I was living in Twickenham, just outside of London. When I picked him up at the airport, I had to laugh. Mommy had placed a very obvious note written on stiff paper in the breast pocket of his suit. It reminded me of Paddington bear. The note read, 'My name is Paul Schell. I am visiting my daughter, Catherine, whose address and telephone number is...' This was just in case he'd get lost which was happening more and more in Munich.

Daddy was still very agile and liked to walk. One morning he took himself off to explore our surroundings. I didn't have the time to accompany him. He knew we were near the Thames and wanted a glimpse of it. With trepidation, I allowed him to go out but not before placing my mother's note in his pocket, just in case. Time passed and I began to worry. I needn't have. Just before noon, he reappeared, unperturbed and as dapper as ever.

'I was terrified you'd got lost,' I said, putting my arms around him.

'No,' he answered as if I was a fool. 'You have that tall pine tree at the end of your garden.' It was true. The tree towered above all of the nearby buildings and was protected by the council. The axe marks at its bottom were still visible when someone, years ago, had tried to chop it down and been stopped.

'I used it as a landmark, always keeping it in my sight. When I saw the top of the tree, I knew exactly where your house was.' He had always had an excellent sense of orientation, something I fortunately inherited and it was still with him, as some other instincts which surfaced from his depths.

We held a dinner party for him, inviting some friends. The actor, Ian McShane came with his wife of that time, Ruth. Now, she was a very beautiful woman, with the face of Elizabeth Taylor and the body of an even more generously endowed Marilyn Monroe. I placed Daddy next to her. He was his charming self, showing interest and asking her questions. The same ones, time after time, after time.

Ruth and I both had horses. This was the topic he would always come back to. 'So, you have a horse?' he'd ask.

'Daddy, you've already asked that,' I'd say, embarrassed for Ruth. But she showed a gentle patience. I wondered why, though, every now and again she would burst into sudden giggles. She told me later that he'd place his hand on her Rubenesque thigh which she would discreetly remove before it wandered further up. This was the early Seventies and the mini-skirt had not yet been entirely banished. I apologised on his behalf but she wasn't the least bit bothered. On the contrary, she was quite flattered.

'I've never been touched up by a baron,' she admitted.

I loved that time he spent with me in Twickenham. We continued our talks. I drove him around London. He recognized most of it.

Somewhere in Mayfair, he said, 'I think that's the street where my tailor was.' And in Soho, he pointed to a shop front where his shoes had been hand made for him. The place no longer did shoes. It sold girlie magazines.

He was disappointed with what he saw as the dissipation of Britain's famous gentlemanly demeanour, its manners and dress. The men were all hippies. Their hair was long, unkempt and looked dirty. They wore clothes like vagabonds, no suits, no ties and unpolished shoes. Always having been a leg-man, though, I noticed he didn't disapprove of the high heeled boots and the unladylike inches of thigh that women revealed while walking down Knightsbridge.

I put him back on the plane, writing the essential information on the reverse side of the original note and placing it in his breast pocket. Holding back my tears, lest I upset him, we said our goodbyes. When he arrived back in Munich, he discovered they were $10,000 poorer.

I don't remember who introduced us to Kevin O'Conners. He was a charming American who spoke fluent German and played a good hand at bridge. Mommy befriended him. He was welcomed into her wealthy, aristocratic entourage. I met him on a few occasions and found him pleasant company but had no idea how he earned his money. And then we found out. At some point Kevin sold Daddy the idea of investing into Bernie Cornfeld's IOS (Investors Overseas Services) scheme. He was one of thousands of salesmen selling these funds all over Europe. The most lucrative market was US ex-pats living in Germany. They were the small investors who made up, what Cornfeld described as, 'people's capitalism'. The scheme imploded and Daddy lost his life's savings. He became a statistic in the IOS disaster. O'Conners vanished, disappearing off their radar. Not that he could have done anything anyway.

No longer earning a salary, Daddy was the recipient of only his pension and the dollar was sliding down against the Deutschmark. Whatever I could send was a help and thank God for their friends. The tenth floor flat became too expensive and they had to move to a cheaper one. One of the saddest memories I have of him was when, on a visit, I drove my mother and our dog – a Hungarian Puli who answered to several names: 'Lumumba' from my mother, '*Kormos*' ('sooty' in Hungarian) from my father, '*Krampus*' (the nasty Christmas spirit) from me, and simply 'Puli' when Paul was home – to an adoptive family in the countryside, who promised us they would love and care for him. The breed may be recognized as the dogs with dark Rastafarian locks which, when fully grown, sweep the ground they walk over and, when mature, you can't tell their front from the rear. I saw Daddy on the balcony high above us, watching as we were getting into the car. A big white handkerchief was held in his hand as he wiped the copious tears from his eyes. He loved that dog and as long as they walked together Daddy never got lost. The apartment they were moving to did not allow any pets.

His condition progressed in stages. On a visit, Paul witnessed a terrible scene. Daddy was physically attacking our mother. Paul had to intervene. When he told me the story later, he said I'd never believe how strong he was. At only 5 foot 7, Daddy was considerably smaller than him, not to mention 40 years older and yet Paul had to use all of his strength to overcome him, by finally pushing him on to the floor.

'He was so quick, punching me like a trained bantam boxer. I could hardly escape his fists,' he related.

Our father was gripped in the violent stage of Alzheimer's. Mommy behaved like a saint, but there were times that she couldn't control her reactions. Arriving back to the flat for a visit, I noticed the glass door to the bathroom was shattered. She explained the damage was caused by Daddy kicking in the panel and that she was holding scissors in her hand at the time and stabbed him with them in the belly. He bled profusely. An ambulance had to be called. She was terrified that she would be accused of a crime and gave the excuse that he had cut himself on a shard of broken glass. Her testimony was accepted and no further questions were asked. Daddy was sewn up and sent home the following day. He had no memory of the incident at all. Mommy had to deal with these sort of happenings every day. She was afraid to leave him alone. By this time, to make up for the insufficient months for her to be able to claim her own personal pension from the American social security system, Radio Free Europe hired her in a librarian capacity. She went to work every day. When coming home, she could walk in to the flat to be enveloped by a bluish haze. He had turned on the stove to boil water to make tea and forgotten to light the gas. He had forgotten to make the tea as well. She received phone calls from strangers telling her they had found him lost and wandering kilometres away from home. Thank God for the notes she stuffed in all of his breast pockets. As she didn't drive and if she couldn't reach anyone to go to pick him up, these kindly people would bring him home themselves.

Poor Mommy. I can't say poor Daddy. He was oblivious and when the violent stage passed he seemed downright happy. His health was fine and he still walked up our steep hill to go to the little shop where he'd buy his miniature bottles of alcohol which he would throw, when empty, into the bush just below our balcony. This was to hide them from Mommy but she found them, anyway, hundreds of them. They made a colourful, sparkling glass pile.

Very soon after his 80th birthday, it became obvious that he could no longer stay at home. His condition had deteriorated. A place had to be found for him in a home. It was fortunate that not far out of Munich we found an establishment, run by nuns. Daddy was installed in a room with some familiar furniture, photographs and his favourite pictures on the walls. He didn't know where he was or why he was there. He'd begun to recognize my mother as just a woman who came to talk to him. I was completely forgotten. It hurt terribly.

The last time I saw him alive, I'd flown in from London. A Hungarian woman friend who was a doctor drove my mother and me to visit him. His once sparkling eyes had dulled completely. He shuffled along slowly, his feet tucked into slippers. Gone were the polished shoes, the dapper man. He didn't know me. Several times Mommy told him, 'But it's Katica, it's your Cumpika!' (His pet name for me.) 'It's your daughter!'

He looked at me as if I were a stranger and searched his memory. 'I don't have a daughter,' he said.

My God, that hurt. But he looked at our doctor friend, Lucia. For a few seconds his face lit up. She was a blonde with dark eyes. His interest, though, was fleeting.

We hugged and kissed him as we left. I turned around for another glance and saw him with an enigmatic little smile on his lips, his brow slightly furrowed and eyes staring into a void. He had no idea who we were and why he had spent time in our company. But I think he had enjoyed it.

How cruel the spirit which in his
body sheltered, to fly
Before the flesh was willing
and intent to die.

My father as a cavalry officer (1916).

My grandmother with Chibby on her lap and Uncle Jozsef (2 years old) behind her (1912).

Nagyida.

My mother's family chateau on the bank of the Danube.

My mother as a young woman on Rebel, a thoroughbred she won in a bet.

My parents' engagement photograph (1939).

Chibby before her incarceration as punishment for our escape.

Mami and Paul.

Water baby, splashing in the Danube (1946).

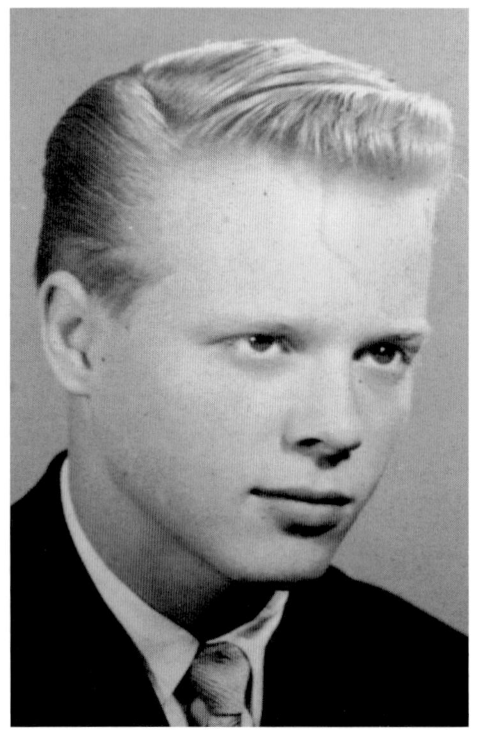

Peter

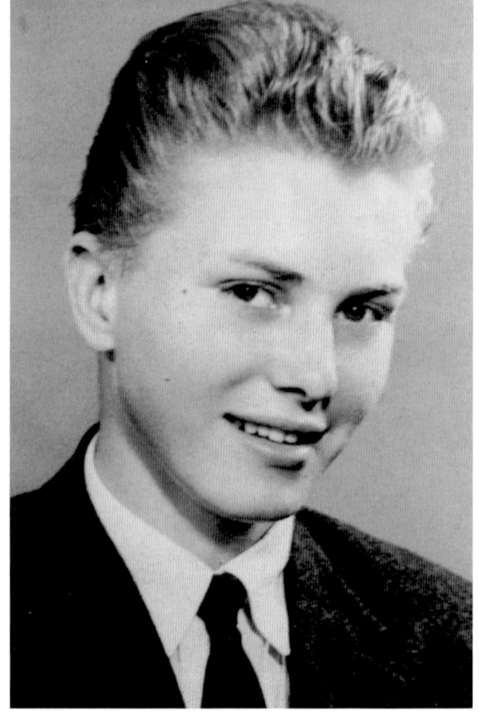

Paul

Me at 2 years old.

I am wearing the pearl necklace given me by Jolie Gabor (1954).

Our first Christmas at Uncle Peter's in New York.

1953 with my parents in New York.

RADIO FREE EUROPE
OPERATIONS MAP
P
USSR
CS
H
R
B

My father at work in Munich.

My second horse Rocky.

My first horse Paprika.

Daddy on an outing from the care home with my mother just a short time before his death.

In front of the registry office as Mr and Mrs Hays, with Michael Becker and Linda Marlowe (witnesses) and my mother not looking well pleased.

My mother (left of centre) being greeted upon her return to Zebegen.

High school play *The Importance Of Being Earnest*.

From my first "glamour" photo session with a Hungarian photographer.

Promotional material for *Lana: Queen of the Amazons*.

With Bill Marlowe in *Amsterdam Affair* (1968).

In Hammer's Wild Western in space, *Moon Zero Two* (1969).

As Nancy in the James Bond film *On Her Majesty's Secret Service* (1969).

I was taking amphetamines to stop me eating because I thought I was fat.

Lady Sinclair to Roger Moore's Lord in *The Persuaders!* (1971).

Shooting a scene with Gene Barry for *The Adventurer* (1973).

1970's still.

Press call for *Napolean And Love*, with (L-R) Susan Wooldridge, Ian Holm, Nicola Pagett and Billie Whitelaw (1974).

Laughter and fun times with Peter Sellers (1975).

A selection of images of Maya from *Space: 1999* (1976).

Mommy and me in front of the English speaking theatre in Vienna (1978).

A promotional photo from the Eighties.

As Mrs Mortenson in the ITV comedy *Mog* (1985).

CHAPTER X

The last film Steffie negotiated on my behalf was released as *Amsterdam Affair*. Its working title was 'Love in Amsterdam' and as such, it was portentous.

A newly discovered actor, William Marlowe, starred in the film. He had appeared in Stanley Baker's production of *The Great Train Robbery* and, relying on the boast, 'Stanley Baker, star maker,' Marlowe hoped to follow in Michael Caine's footsteps. Michael had been Baker's discovery for the film, *Zulu* which launched his career into galactic stardom.

Marlowe was completely out of my familiarity zone. His origins were from an East End working class family. He had an older brother, Ted, with whom he'd lost contact. Their father had been a stevedore in London's eastern docklands who eventually drank himself to death. Marlowe left home at the age of 17 to join the fleet air-arm and served on the original air plane carrier, *Ark Royal*. It was while he was on board that ship that he was notified of his mother's death by suicide. No longer having sons to protect her against a violent husband, she ended her life by placing her head into the gas oven. It had been the turmoil which permeated the family home that caused Marlow's departure.

As a child he'd been quite beautiful with enormous eyes and a full lipped wide mouth, a little like Mick Jagger. Unfortunately, in adolescence he was afflicted with acne and was one of the first boys to be treated with extreme antibiotics, which had little effect. But the salty sea air on the ships helped somewhat.

I could feel that he was damaged and wanted to heal his wounds. Still only 23, he was 14 years older than me. I fell madly in love and naively thought I had the strength to massage away all of his complexes to lighten his load. But they had become a part of him and, I would discover, he was very much his father's son.

There was post-synchronizing to be done for the film in a London studio. I packed a large suitcase, told Mommy I'd try to find work in England, and gave her my ex-stand-in Fiona's telephone number. Although officially adult, I didn't dare risk my mother's wrath by telling her I was going to live out of wedlock with a man, especially one who had absolutely no aristocratic credentials.

It was December 30th, 1967 when the plane touched down at

Heathrow airport. Marlowe was there to meet me and took me to a flat in Baker Street. It was the address he shared with his wife, Linda. Also an actress, she was away working and we were to stay there until he could make other arrangements. They had started divorce proceedings but it was not yet absolute. In England at that time, serious reasons had to be proven before a divorce could be pronounced. Adultery was a popular excuse. Their proceedings were so amicable that Linda chose to be her own correspondent. She hired a private detective to follow Marlowe and his mistress, dressing in a dark wig to play that part. The masquerade went as far as the inevitable midnight knock on the door that Marlowe answered opening it wide enough so that the detective could catch the sight of a semi-nude woman in the bedroom displayed on the marital bed. The signed report of the incident was handed into the court by the weeping wife and the divorce was favourably considered. As there was no argument about alimony, she not asking for it, and their young son, Ben happily living with his maternal grandparents, there was no conflict at all. It was agreed that the custody of their toy Yorkshire terrier Cassius would be shared. Eventually, on occasion, I'd be the mistress of a canine who could sit in the palm of my hand and if I wasn't careful, shit in it too. He was pathologically un-housebroken.

By two o'clock, I was in unbearable pain. My lower abdomen was in agony and I was glowing with fever. Marlowe telephoned the family doctor whose first reaction was to ask if I'd recently had an abortion. Once he was convinced it was not the case he agreed to open his surgery and examine me. It only took a few minutes. I was sent with a note to be admitted as an emergency patient in the gynaecological service of St George's Hospital. Without any proof of identification, I was given a bed in a ward with seven women occupying the other beds. I begged for medication against the pain but was told, until I had been examined by the specialist in the morning, the night nurse on duty could prescribe nothing. Not to wake my fellow patients, I chewed on the pillow until I was finally seen. The diagnosis was an acute ovarian infection with a suspected fallopian pregnancy. I knew the latter could not be the case as I had been celibate since the ending of the film a good six weeks ago. A nurse arrived holding a syringe filled with antibiotics destined more for a horse than a human. My buttocks were pierced three times a day, each cheek taking consecutive turns. All went well until one nurse managed to stick the needle into my sciatic nerve. I am convinced it was not an accident. Even I would later learn where not to puncture, having been briefly shown. I had a friend who was diabetic and could have been called in an emergency to administer an insulin injection. The pain of that misjudged jab stayed with me for months. Nevertheless, I was cured. The fever disappeared as did the pains. Now, I only had to worry how I was going to pay for this hospitalization. I was discharged by the specialist, said goodbye to the good ward nurses and to the poor woman I had got to know during her nightly promenades up and down the centre aisle of our dormitory. She had undergone a hysterectomy and was suffering painfully from wind. Not wanting to disturb us, she wandered through the ward in her white nightie, like a midnight ghost, in search for a convenient niche to discreetly fart.

I found the ward sister in her glass cubicle and asked where I had to go to pay, thinking all the while, how was I going to pay. Marlowe was coming to fetch me. Perhaps, I'd have to borrow the money from him and hoped he had enough in his account to cover eight days of treatment.

'But, dearie,' said the sister. 'This is the National Health. You don't have to pay.'

I couldn't believe it. By this time Marlowe had found me speaking with her.

'Didn't you know? This is our system,' he said. I don't know why the subject never came up between us. He was working and found little time to visit. Perhaps I was frightened to ask.

I was bewildered and felt very guilty. When the machinations of the system were explained to me, I realized others had paid for my treatment out of their taxes. This country had to rank as one of the most generous in the world. I thought of Peter and wondered how beautiful it would have been if Germany had had similar health care. He may have been able to stay near to his family. Obviously, I became a staunch supporter of the National Health in my would-be adopted country.

The post-synching sessions were completed and, as Linda was returning, I flew back to Munich, leaving Marlowe to find somewhere for us to live on my return. He found a furnished basement flat on south Eaton Square which was the lower ground floor of a terraced property belonging to a production manager in our business. I was impressed. Basement or not, the address was in the most exclusive part of London but it only had wooden floor boards to separate us from the living room above. I only mention this because they, upstairs, would have overheard some desperately loud rows. Living with Marlowe was much more difficult than loving him.

I don't remember going through any bureaucracy when I worked on *Traitor's Gate*. It was done without my participation. I was an import and the production office did all the necessaries. Now, however, in order to work as an actress, I needed to have a permit and to belong to the actor's union, Equity, and the union could not accept me as a member without the work permit. I was also obliged to leave the country every three months to have my passport re-stamped. After all, until things were settled, I was on a tourist visa. It meant my travelling regularly back to Munich which pleased my parents. It made the severance easier to bear for them.

The solution for my continued future in Britain was marriage. Once the decree absolute was issued, Marlowe was free to re-marry. I had to introduce him to my parents.

So that everything remained proper, I stayed with them and Marlowe was reserved a room in a local *gasthause*. Daddy came to pick us up at the airport. I thought it safer to take the keys off him and drove us back to our address, stopping briefly at Marlowe's lodgings to get him settled in with the promise I'd be back soon to fetch him.

My mother had a peculiar, almost perverse sense of mischief. When I was four years old, and an apparition of a white-shrouded form making ghost-like noises (whooo... whoooo... whoooo!) came gliding into my bedroom... Well! It was not surprising that, between her phantoms and the nuns' devils, I suffered well into adulthood from a terror of the dark. She loved frightening people.

What she did to introduce herself to Marlowe was not as classic as the time she crouched, hiding under the kitchen table when it was covered by a blanket and a sheet which hung to the floor and waited patiently for our maid, Ursula, to begin the ironing. Just when the maid felt relaxed enough, thinking she was alone, gliding the iron back and forth, beginning to whistle a little tune, Mommy grabbed her ankles from behind the hanging sheet. The woman, already suffering from heart problems left us that afternoon. Needless to say, Mommy had to finish the ironing.

My maternal grandmother had a pug dog which she adored. Sadly, the animal died. Mommy at the age of 14 had what she thought was a brilliant idea and she, even though the youngest of her sisters, convinced them to take part in her scheme. At that time in Hungary, due to the numerous hunting estates, stuffing animals was a normal practice. The three sisters had no problem taking the corpse of their mother's darling pet to their local taxidermist. He was asked to skin the animal, leaving the head intact so that the finished object would have a flat fur body, four splayed limbs and look like a miniature version of a hearth rug. When finished the girls collected it and returned to the chateau. Their mother also had a Siamese cat, a very affectionate animal which liked being picked up and cuddled. It was not too difficult, once the girls held the cat and made soothing noises, to place the rug around it and sew it together at the tummy thus giving the cat an overcoat with a bonnet of a pug's head. Once dressed in this freakish outfit, the cat panicked. It leapt off the table where the operation had taken place and went screaming into the salon where their mother was quietly doing some embroidery. The cat yowled all the way up the curtain. Their mamma, seeing her dead dog, head dangling backwards, hanging from the pleats at the top of a curtain, passed out in mid stitch.

I am ashamed to say, I helped her in one of her japes. Thörie, the Icelandic maid after Ursula, had a boyfriend who was an American marine. He often left his uniform in her closet. Mommy had the bright notion of stuffing the uniform with scrunched up newspapers to fill it out as a body would. She then stuffed a pillow case and tucked it into the neck of his jacket to make it look like a head and pinned it all together. His cap was placed on top of the effigy and it was hung by a rope around its neck to the ceiling light. Thörie was out with girlfriends that night but due back around eleven. Daddy was sent to bed. All lights were extinguished. With the skill of a film lighting director, she opened Thörie's curtains allowing the glow from a street lamp outside to illuminate the silhouette of the hanging form. It looked like a suicide. We waited on the top of the stairs for the result of her psychotic endeavour to frighten. Finally we heard keys being placed into the front door lock. The door opened. Her room was immediately to the left of the entrance. There was no need to put on a light. One step and the bedroom door opened. Well, Alfred Hitchcock should have recorded her scream. Thörie didn't stay with us very long either.

No, compared to her usual antics, what she had prepared for Marlowe was tame. I brought him into the living room. Mommy was not to be seen. Daddy, graciously, offered him a drink. Marlowe was a vodka and tonic drinker. We had a well-stocked bar. I went to get ice and lemon. His drink was poured. I was drinking white wine and Mommy still hadn't appeared. I just presumed she was applying lipstick and perfume for her grand entrance. Nobody noticed the bulge in the corner of the drawn curtains. It was early days with Daddy's dementia. He and Marlowe conversed politely. Suddenly, there was an explosive movement and Mommy shot out from behind the curtain shouting something silly like, 'Boo!' Marlowe might have appreciated it had he had the hiccups but, unfortunately, the glass he was drinking from was up against his mouth at that moment and shattered, cutting the inside of his lip. The bleeding took a long time to stop. I expected him to be furious but he laughed, spitting out a bit of blood. My mother rushed to the medicine cabinet, brought some gauze, cut it into a wedge and stuck it between his lip and his teeth. She apologized profusely. He mumbled, 'No, no, it's quite all right.' My father pretended nothing out of the ordinary had happened and helped himself to another Bacardi cocktail while I wondered how I could be the daughter of this psychopath.

Oddly enough, she liked Marlowe. Mommy was not a snob. Of course, she'd have preferred that I marry into the aristocracy, but if that was not going to be the case, then at least, someone she could influence. Marlowe had a strange respect for her. If I ever complained about her treatment towards me when growing up, he'd rationalize on her behalf. If I complained to her of his treatment of me, she'd do the same. The two people who held supremacy over my decisions became allies. This was not a good beginning for an adult relationship. I was going from one subjugation to another.

One would have thought my assimilation into the English community would have been easy. I'd had a wonderful experience on the filming of *Traitor's Gate* but now, I was coming to live. At least, though, I didn't have to learn a different language or so I thought. My pronunciation of English was ridiculed. The word, 'bath', I was told, sounded like the noise a sheep makes but with a 'th' attached. 'Vase' had such a long 'a', it harboured a 'y'. Even though Marlowe's origins sprang within the sound of the Bow bells, he managed to overcome his Cockney accent to speak with the BBC-approved pronunciation. There were people I met who smirked at my accent. When I was brave enough, I answered them with, 'When you speak, you sound as if you have a potato in your mouth which is too hot to swallow.' Usually, that shut them up.

Do I dare admit that I found the renowned British humour difficult to appreciate? It took some time but I still find it hard to laugh at other people's misfortune. The famous 'send-up' made me wince. I was told I didn't have a sense of humour. So, how did I get the crow's feet around my eyes? Certainly not from sunshine. I didn't think it amusing to make fun of or embarrass people who were overweight, bald, had long noses or short ones, were on crutches or in wheelchairs or were, like me, foreigners. I learned, eventually, to think laterally on this subject and came to terms with it. As long as the victim was imaginary, I loved it. British wit is the *crème de la crème* and universally admired. Who couldn't laugh at John Cleese in *Monty Python*'s sketch of the Ministry of Funny Walks? Or Dudley Moore, hopping up and down on his one and only leg, when being interviewed by Peter Cook to play the part of Tarzan? The interview was going badly when:

Dudley: 'What have you got against my leg?'

Peter: 'I have nothing against your leg but, then, neither have you. Traditionally, Tarzan is played by a biped.'

I'm afraid, though, watching huge inflated breasts, the size of blimps bouncing along the countryside in the *The Benny Hill Show* was not funny. Well, I'm a woman. But the French enjoyed him. 'Ooh, ve love ze British 'umour. Benny 'ill. Bravo!'

Obviously Tommy Cooper, Eric and Ernie, and the two Ronnies did not overcome the language barrier, and Benny Hill didn't have to.

It was 1968. Anti-American sentiment prevailed. The violent riots near to the US Embassy in Grosvenor square against the war in Vietnam shocked me. I had no idea that the country which adopted my family was so virulently hated. No wonder, my accent was mocked. If I ever spoke about my American education, I was told that was an oxymoron. The Americans were still being blamed for their prejudice against their Black population, although, those discriminatory laws had been repealed, beginning with Kennedy and conclusively by Johnson. I pointed out, when I lived in Manhattan, there were many Black policemen. I had yet to see a single Black bobby on a London street. African Americans participated to the point of becoming heroes in sport: baseball, basketball, football. Where were the black players on their soccer teams? Rugby teams? As far as I was aware there wasn't a Black player on a British cricket team. America had popular Black mainstream performers earning megabucks in music and the cinema. Where were those in the

British cultural scene? Out of loyalty, I was forced to defend my American friends. Ironically, almost half a lifetime later, I would champion my British friends when living amongst some Anglophobic people. They would question my vigorous defence by telling me, I wasn't even English. Why did I bother when I was Hungarian?

'Yes,' I'd reply, 'but I know them better than you.'

On June 14th, William Marlowe and I married at Kensington Town Hall. I wore a Bavarian *dirndl* as my wedding outfit. We retired afterwards, with just a few friends, to David Weston and his German wife's flat to drink a toast to our future. Not yet 24, I was young enough so that the previous night's insomnia, drinking, crying and soul searching did not show on my face. I was beginning to fear Marlowe's explosive temper and spent much of the night hiding in the bathroom. When all was quiet, I ventured into the living room, helped myself to whatever booze was available and while he was sleeping, examined my situation. Was I really strong enough to cope with his irrational, and sometimes, threatening behaviour? The fact that I loved him was not in question, but could I live with him? He could be incredibly sweet, kind and tender. We shared our own private jokes and laughed together. We gossiped. I valued his advice, his insight, experience and sensitivity. Sometimes he was like a best girlfriend. I could tell him everything. Unfortunately, though, when he was in his aggressive state, he could turn my confidences against me. Alarm bells were ringing in my head. The dawn's insipid light was beginning to creep through the basement window. I had to choose between two duties: towards myself or him. Then his head popped out of the bedroom. He looked round the corner and saw me on the sofa, my legs curled up beneath me with a wretched expression on my face.

'Hey, silly thing,' he said and sat down beside me. 'I know we're not supposed to be together the night before we marry but I could have slept on the sofa and given you the bed.' He had completely forgotten the unpleasantness of the previous night. Being his tender self, he put his arm around me and led me to the bedroom.

'There, I've even warmed the bed for you. Now, try to sleep. I'll see you in the morning.' He kissed my forehead, closed the door and left me alone. I chose my duty to him and a future, again as an alien, in this country which could be, in actor's parlance, 'difficult to play' but which I would come to love with a passion.

Funny, I don't remember a single photograph of that wedding day.

CHAPTER XI

'I hear you've lost weight, Catherine!' The casting director called out from his office as I was being shown a chair in the lobby to await my interview for the James Bond film, *On Her Majesty's Secret Service.* He made it sound as if I'd been considered overweight. Oh yes, I had lost quite a few pounds, partly due to the change of diet. I was having to become accustomed to different flavours. The mixture of steak and kidneys disgusted me. I loved each on its own but, somehow, together I didn't find the tastes complimentary. At least as a pie, I could nibble on the pastry but when served up inside a savoury suet pudding and having learned that suet was the fat that surrounded the kidneys, the whole concoction became even more unappetizing. The experience of eating fried fish in soggy batter and oily, fat chips tucked into an unhygienic, folded newspaper could only be described as a culture shock. The British loaf, mostly soft and white tasted of cotton wool and was only good for toasting. The pink sausages which looked like fleshy fingers had no taste at all. I had come from a country where, when walking into a bakery, one was accosted by the most delicious odours and had the choice of at least 15 different kinds of bread. It was not difficult for me to eat less. I dreamt of *bratwurst* with sweet mustard, German *semmel* dumplings and *sauerkraut.* Each to his own.

What helped as well were the capsules of Durafett, a popular amphetamine, or speed, which curbed one's appetite. Linda had found a tame doctor who over prescribed, leaving her with the amount she required and sharing the rest with us. Marlowe took the capsules for the high. He was already thin enough. Linda and I were encouraged to embrace an anorexic complex. We always saw ourselves as overweight. There is a photograph of me on a beach in a bikini. You can count every rib, my hips look as if they'd be painful to touch and my collar bone stands proud from the breast plate. I thought I was fat. Today, I'd want to send that young woman in the picture to a psychiatrist.

But I got the part! Inasmuch as I didn't know which of the Blofeld girls I would be playing but I was told, along with Angela Scoular, it would be a speaking role. We were the only two of the girls who'd had considerable acting experience.

Our unit hotel was in the town of Mürren, a ski resort in Switzerland

and virtually in the shadow of the infamous peak, the Eiger. Some of its windows looked onto the north side, an almost concave wall of ice and sheer rock which, like a siren, had tempted determined climbers to scale its face. The tragedies of some of these assaults are well documented. In one's imagination, their spirits are mingled in the mists and fogs which hover around the foot of that stony edifice.

During the filming we never came across Diana Rigg. I'd briefly met her on the island of Ibiza where Marlowe and I holidayed for a couple of weeks in the spring. We frequented a certain bar called Sandy's where one could meet tax exiles from our profession. I hasten to add, she was not one of those. Her partner of that time had a house on the island. She very kindly invited us out to dinner in a local restaurant. I can't remember what the argument that ensued during our meal was about but Marlowe became very heated and, as it progressed, she suddenly retorted with something like, 'You're just using semantics!' I was so impressed. I'd never heard that word before, and had no idea what it meant, but being shot out of her mouth like a bullet, it sounded the *coup de grâce* to end the argument. Marlowe fumed silently, insisted on paying the bill and growled all the way back to our little hotel. He didn't appreciate that a woman had got the better of him. The moment we came back to England and I had a dictionary in my hands, I looked up the word, 'semantics'. Ever since its use has reminded me of her.

Contrary to what gossip columnists feed upon, we women, Blofeld's guinea pigs, all got along famously. No hissing. No spitting. No scratching each other's eyes out. Some of us formed slightly tighter circles but they were never exclusive. I found myself drawn towards Angela Scoular, Joanna Lumley and Anouska Hempel. Our rooms were near to one another's and some even had connecting doors which were, more times than not left open. This did not exclude post-Bond relationships. Jenny Hanley lived literally around the corner from me back in London. We saw each other frequently. She was a great cook and gave me some useful tips that I still use today. Sylvana, our Jamaican beauty, also lived nearby. We struck up a friendship which still lasts today.

Whether or not we had scenes to film, we tended to be sent up in a cable car to the revolving restaurant, renamed Piz Gloria, on the summit of the Schilthorn, at an altitude of ten thousand feet. The production took advantage of their captive photogenic cast. We were used as camera fodder. The amount of times we were shot by journalists or the film's stills photographer would have left reels and reels of Kodak film coiled like barbed wire across a battle field. As it was, the pictures ended up gracing pages of the international press as publicity. You know how I hated to be photographed but it was part of the job and I was trying to be professional. There was a girl, though, an American called Danny who does not appear (or I haven't seen her) in any of the publicity shots. She decided early on to not to participate in the feeding frenzy of the press. I thought she was very brave and I liked her for it. So did Telly Savalas but for different reasons.

One night, Anouska wanted to introduce us to an unaccustomed pastime, something new, something never experienced by our little group. We were invited to her room, which had a window facing the northern glacier of the Eiger, to partake in a seance.

'A seance? You mean we'll speak to the dead?' We were frightened but intrigued.

After supper, Anouska, Joanna, Angela, Sylvana and I retired in hushed reverence to her room. We did not want to alienate the ghosts. We moved a table into the middle, then each rushed to collect a chair from our room. These were placed around the square table.

'Normally it should be round,' Anouska whispered, 'but this will have to do.'

Each letter of the alphabet was penned on the hotel's letter-headed writing paper. She must have come equipped for this occasion because she cut them out with a pair of scissors. The same was done for the numbers from one to ten. The squares of paper were laid out in two rows near the edges of the wooden surface and a wine glass was placed upside down in the middle of the table.

As the intermediary, Anouska began. She said a sort of prayer telling evil spirits to leave us and that only the good ones were welcomed. We nodded and mumbled in our acquiescence. We reached out our hands and placed an index finger on the foot of the wine glass.

'Is there anybody there?' she called out. No reply.

'Come to us, ye friendly spirits,' she continued. Nothing. We waited. Again she coaxed the ghosts from the other world to join us. I was just about to have the giggles when the glass began to move, hesitantly at first and then, seemingly with purpose. It glided over the table to singular letters as if spelling out words. To begin with they were nonsensical. Nevertheless, the glass evolved a life of its own, moving swiftly around in zigzags or circles. We all looked at each other, denying that we were directing it. I'm no longer certain but I think it was Joanna who was the first to interpret a message. Then the glass continued swirling on its path. It stopped at 'K' and went to 'A' and then it zoomed to 'T'. When it rushed to the 'I', I took my finger away. It continued to the 'C' and to the 'A'. It had spelled my name in Hungarian, 'Katica'. No-one around that table could have known. I whispered to them that the message must be for me and gingerly placed my finger back on the glass. Without any pressure at all from me, it spelled out, 'DON'T LET PAUL DO WHAT I DID.' The glass came to a stop. The girls looked at me. I'd begun to cry and explained about Peter who had very recently passed away.

The next time I was in Munich, I mentioned this experience to my mother. It did not amaze her in the least. Mommy was no stranger to the occult. Back in Hungary, she had gone to witches looking for potions. Her pregnancy with me had been an unwelcome surprise. She admitted to having taken a magic concoction to bring on a miscarriage. It didn't work. Neither did the leaping from a wardrobe onto the back of a chair in the hope the shock on her tummy would have an effect. I was, obviously, destined to survive. She also confessed her fears while giving birth to me that I would be born damaged. Ultrasound was far in the future. Her relief and joy at having had a perfectly healthy baby was boundless.

At the age of 17, she visited a gypsy fortune teller. The turbaned woman told her that she could see a date in her crystal ball. January 31st would be incredibly important. It would change her life completely. It was told in a more optimistic manner than, 'Beware the Ides of March'. Her marriage to my father was celebrated some years later on January 28th. She remembered the prediction and thought the gypsy had come very near. But our escape from Hungary which was a more important life changing event took place on the January 31st, 1949.

Holding seances in her friends' houses was also nothing new. She was used to tables jumping lopsided from the floor and then landing with a thump. That was what she called the knocking effect. It was during one of these sessions that her sister, supposedly, told her from the other side that she had taken her own life by jumping in front of the train and asked to be forgiven. This was, by no means, proof of suicide. It only helped invent what became rumours and myth. As a Catholic, my aunt was buried with full religious ceremony in hallowed ground. Had there been a question, the church would not have given her that honour. But my mother always had doubts which she passed on to me.

Marlowe and I had an agreement that whenever possible, we would not be separated for more than two weeks. Not working at the time he was able to make his way out to Mürren. I rented a little flat in a chalet. The idea came from Anouschka whose husband had joined her with their two little children. The possibility of cooking in my own little kitchen appealed to me. I decided to have a cosy dinner party and invited some of the girls to join us. The goulash went down well. It was just around the time of the dessert that Joanna said something like, 'This filming lark is a doddle. I think I'm going to take up acting if it's this easy.'

Well, those words ignited an ensuing explosion of temper from Marlowe. He leapt up from his chair, shouting expletives at Jo. 'You think it's easy? How dare you insult our profession with your ignorance! We've all suffered to be where we are! It takes more than what you've got to be a real actress!' We sat in shocked silence as he shouted like a lunatic. I was afraid he'd wake up all of Mürren's sleepy inhabitants. Any moment now, I thought, we'd have a knock on the door from the municipal police.

That incident always came back to me when in the future I'd watch Joanna's marvellous performance in the hugely successful television series, *Absolutely Fabulous*. Whether she suffered or not for her career, she won, hands down.

As far as Mr Lazenby was concerned, I have little to say. He was a good looking hulk and behaved as such, maybe more hulk than humble but he'd been discovered from a commercial carrying a huge chocolate bar across his shoulder. Serious film etiquette and behaviour would have been new to him. I do admit, though, he was perfectly pleasant when we had our scenes together and did not put his tongue down my throat during our screen kiss. As the first James Bond to follow Sean Connery's, he lacked the lustre to escape the great man's shadow. Roger Moore, however, was inspired casting. He was completely different to Connery but with his characterization of gentlemanly charm and humour, he made his depiction a success. Nevertheless, *OHMSS* became extremely popular amongst Bond fans. I've heard people say it was their favourite because of the story and the portrayal of James Bond as a man capable of falling in love and showing sensitivity and emotion and not always the callous quick-witted lover one had become accustomed to seeing. George Lazenby has to be given some credit for that.

I was out of work for a considerable time after the Bond movie and we couldn't afford it. Marlowe's agent was not finding him work either. We'd moved to a flat in Kensington where the rent was reasonable but the rates exorbitant. We both had to work or one of us had to earn enough money for the other to remain unemployed for a while. I realized that I was a minnow in the huge lake of ICM's superior fish and was being ignored in their promoting decisions. I had to find another agent. A very nice man from our actor's directory *Spotlight* advised me to make an appointment with an agent who was known to bring on careers. She had a small stable of talent which was exactly what I required. Her name was Jean Drysdale.

The day I walked into her office, a no frills basement property, she was on the phone. I stood near her desk. She looked up at me and said into the receiver, 'I think I have exactly the actress you're looking for. She has just come in,' and put her hand over the phone to ask me, 'Would you be free to be interviewed for a commercial tomorrow at three?'

'Yes,' I said, hardly believing my luck. We had not even yet agreed that she would represent me. This was some omen.

'Her name is Katherina von Schell and she'll be with you tomorrow. I'll give her your address, even though I don't know if I'm her agent yet but never mind. Bye-bye.' She hung up and gave me a brilliant smile.

I went to the interview and got the job. It was the first of many commercials I would do. And Jean became my agent.

Normally, at the particular point of my career in England, most thespians would shy away from doing TV ads unless they were really desperate. Faces in commercials were not always taken seriously as actors. Of course, when huge sums were offered to famous stars, they were forgiven for accepting to become associated to a particular product, *ergo* the amusing Cinzano ads with Joan Collins and Leonard Rossiter. I didn't care. With little money coming in, I was one of the desperate and did as many as I could. Ironically, it was from some of these that, eventually, I was interviewed for TV dramas or series. The next time I would be seen, though, on an English screen in a proper acting role my billed name would have changed.

Jean had a 'sleeping partner'. It was he who owned the house in which she was allowed the use of the basement for office space. He gave her advice but was never visible during the everyday running of the agency. They had a close relationship but I don't know if he was literally a partner with whom she slept. I was invited for a meeting with the two of them in his living room upstairs. After all of the usual polite small talk, he began seriously with, 'There's a problem with your name.'

'My name? What do you mean?' I asked, astonished.

'It's too German,' he said.

I was reminded of the conversation in Berlin with Herr Wecker when I was asked to drop the name Teleki because of the negative connotations it held for some Germans.

'But it's my name, even though I'm actually Hungarian.'

'You should anglicise it,' he continued.

'How? I'm not English. Every time I open my mouth it becomes evident,' I argued.

'Katherina, I don't know if you're aware but most of our business is in the hands of Jews. They don't like *German*. It gives them bad memories.'

I looked into a face with the epitome of Semitic features and understood. 'I suppose I could lose the K for a C and drop the A at the end for an E making it Catherine,' I suggested.

'Yes, and the *von*. That's terribly German.'

'Okay,' I agreed.

'And take the C out of Schell. Leave it as Shell.'

'No. I'm not doing that.'

'It still sounds too German,' he insisted.

'Maximillian and Maria haven't done too badly in a business that, as you've implied, is dominated by Jews,' I answered. 'I'll take that risk.'

And so, we settled on Catherine Schell. What a world we live in! The name I'd chosen to act under in Germany disturbed some people who were in a position to offer me work. Now here, in England, the same scenario caused by another name presented itself... or so I was led to believe.

CHAPTER XII

As Catherine Schell, I began to work quite a lot. The change of name was irrelevant. Jean had made many friends who were casting directors as well as contacts in production offices. They got in touch when certain roles were to be cast. I remember endless interviews, sometimes *en masse* surrounded by other prospective hopefuls or singularly at an appointed time where I had no idea who my competition was. The roles I ended up being offered placed me into the niche of foreign women, sometimes playing German, middle European, northern European and often, aristocratic. The exact nationality of who I would be playing was not always specified. The accent I put on was always the same. Foreign.

Very early on, the BBC engaged me in an episode of *Paul Temple* and then in another episode of *The Troubleshooters*. Transmissions for drama programmes were no longer 'live' but tape was extremely expensive. The director had to avoid cutting during scenes which meant that the cast learned their lines as if it were a live play. We moved from set to set in the studio with cameras following or awaiting our appearance in a new location. They were exciting times and the process was intricately timed and choreographed. The director really had to have done his planning. He had to make maps. Up to six swiftly gliding cameras moving from one position in the studio to another through the intricate set designs were not allowed to bump into each other. Every camera had an umbilical cable attached to the electricity supply. If badly worked out, the cables could intertwine leading to disaster. Pressures were on the actors, as well. They could not afford to fluff a line and bring the entire proceedings to an embarrassing halt. I was glad to have experienced these times. They taught me a lot.

The lighting, though, was anything but glamorous. All of the sets in the studio were lit from a grilled gallery above. The lamps shone down onto the floor and gave the same atmosphere as you would find in a supermarket. It was not complimentary. However, when a close up was required, the cameras had a single large head-light called a 'basher'. The man driving his camera would be radioed by the director and receive the order in his ear to switch it on and thus, our faces were bathed in a kinder glow. Wrinkles, eyebags and other facial indiscretions were eliminated. I was young enough to still not be afflicted but was grateful for the basher when it erased the dark rings under my eyes from lack of sleep.

It was during this time that I had my first acquaintance with the world of science fiction. I was still hardly known in Britain, still a new face, but was invited to an interview to meet the director, Roy Ward Baker, and producer, Michael Carreras, for a film called *Moon Zero Two*. They had both seen 'Love in Amsterdam', renamed *Amsterdam Affair* for the circuits, and appreciated my performance. It was to be a Hammer film but not of their usual horror category and, I was told, the production budget would, for the first time, reach £1,000,000. I would later understand why. The elaborate sets that were built in the Elstree studios were magnificent. A million pounds sounds insignificant today but for Hammer films in those days it was a considerable amount. I seem to remember I was offered the part there and then and given a script. The storyline read like a futuristic Wild West saga, only without horses – and it took place on the moon.

I was to co-star opposite James Olson, tall, thin and athletic. In the mornings, weather permitting, he would ask his driver to stop a few miles from the studios, get out and then jog the rest of the way. As his name portrays, he was of Swedish descent and every inch of his appearance testified to that ancestry.

We got along very well. He was professional and kind to me. I was still remarkably naïve as far as film technique was concerned, and poor Warren Mitchell who played a 'baddy' would suffer from my inexperience. There was a scene where I had to defend myself against him. I had just returned from outside on the moon and was still in my spacesuit holding my helmet. Following the script, I was to hit him on the arm with it. I took these directions seriously and literally, and whacked him with the helmet as hard as I could. He screamed in pain. The director shouted 'Cut!' and poor Warren, rubbing his elbow said, 'You're not supposed to do it for real!' How was I supposed to know? I'd been taught to act everything for real. I knew very little of artifice. We couldn't have had a stuntman on the set because it was Warren who explained how I should thrust the helmet and how he would avoid getting injured. Live and learn. And have an understanding teacher.

Many years later, in the late Eighties, I was given as a gift, by a waspish gay friend of mine, a book of the 500 (I may be wrong about the number) worst films of all time. Sprawled on the back cover is a picture of me from *Moon Zero Two* in a space outfit, my face just identifiable behind the visor of the offending helmet with an expression of horror as I have just discovered the skeleton of my long lost brother in a recess of a moon mine. A cartoon balloon hovers above the helmet. It says, 'I knew what I had to do to get on this movie but what do I have to do to get off it?'

Marlowe appreciated the money entering into our account. We'd made what, I thought, was a practical solution on dividing our earnings. Eighty percent was credited to our joint account from which all household bills, food shopping, rent, income tax, car expenses etc. were paid. In other words, everything which was necessary for our lives together. Twenty percent went into our private accounts to be spent, as we pleased, for our individual needs. It didn't matter that I was earning more than Marlowe, not to me anyway. But it was the age old macho problem for him. He felt half a man because he was earning half of my income. There was also the matter of rivalry. I couldn't understand how we could compete against each other. He couldn't play the parts I was going up for and I certainly couldn't play his. It disturbed him that my career as an unknown upstart from the continent was proceeding so quickly and easily. Our rows became more violent. I was literally being pushed around. The hands around my throat were not always gentle and caressing. He suffered terribly from jealousy. If I spoke to someone at a party or function, I'd be interrogated afterwards about my conversation, even if it was with another woman. Out of self-preservation, I stopped speaking to people on these occasions, to the point that, at one party when opening my mouth to say something innocuous, somebody shouted out, 'Listen everyone! Garbo speaks!'

And yet, there were always those sweet moments which gave me hope that, eventually, he would come to understand I had every intention of remaining faithful, that I admired him and loved him. But his ego was like a burning furnace. It required stoking up with fuel so that the engine of his self-esteem could continue to chug happily along.

But we had happy times! Thanks to him, I saw hidden parts of England, Scotland, Wales. We'd bought a Mini Cooper. Sometimes, late at night a sudden decision would be made to leave before sunrise on an exploration. A suitcase was quickly packed. An AA guidebook to acquaint us with where we'd end up was our only prop. The fact that we'd have swallowed an amphetamine capsule with our coffee before dawn helped with that adrenaline buzz which exaggerated the feeling of adventure.

On these impromptu expeditions we made a few serendipitous discoveries. Driving at night in heavy rain across the Northumberland moors, I spotted a hotel sign. We decided immediately to try it. Anything was better than the weather we were travelling through. Following the arrow, we drove up a lane and arrived at an old building. I remember it as white. It must have been a coach house. The front door had a lantern which lit the few steps we had to climb in order to enter. Once inside, we were bathed in cosy lighting and on the far wall, logs were crisply crackling in a grate with a stone mantelpiece surrounding the fireplace. It was like a dream. A couple came to greet us. We asked if they had a room.

'Of course,' we were told.

'And can we have supper?'

'Of course, with pleasure,' the lady said.

We were taken by her up some creaky stairs to our bedroom. There was a four-poster bed up against a wall. Through a connecting door was a bathroom. It had an old fashioned tub, one of those with heavy brass taps and lion's legs with splayed paws holding it up. We really had found paradise. Drinks were served in the lounge below next to the heat of the fire. An archway led to a small dining room. It, too, had a fireplace in which coal was warmly glowing in the grate. The meal was delicious and we drank very good French wine. There were no other guests. The woman who showed us to our room served us. She was friendly but very discreet. In that romantic atmosphere, she allowed Marlowe and I to look lovingly into each other's eyes without disturbing us.

In the morning, we were presented with a bill which was surprisingly reasonable. We said our farewells, got into the Mini and drove away without glancing back. It was obvious that we'd be disappointed with all the other stops we'd make in the future. Nowhere could compare with the Northumberland Moor's idyll.

Some while later, we tried to recapture that moment. From the directions we assumed we'd taken, there was no corresponding mention of a hotel in the AA guidebook. When we thought about it, we never even noticed its name on the advertising sign. The word 'hotel' was all my eyes had been drawn to. We didn't get an official bill, as such, in the morning. It was just a piece of paper, handwritten with room, drinks, meal and then tallied for the price.

We criss-crossed the moors, sometimes stopping at little pubs and asking if anyone knew of such an hotel. No-one had ever heard of it. The night of our discovery, we'd been driving through pouring rain. The wipers on the windscreen splashed water against the sides. Visibility by the headlights through the smeared drops on the glass was not ideal. It was difficult to recognize the lane we'd taken and yet... I thought something looked familiar. There was no sign but a tall tree I seem to have found incongruous in its setting at the time. We turned off the road and followed the lane to come to a halt in front of a building. The façade was a neglected white, windows were boarded up and paint on the front door was peeling. The glass in the lantern above it had been smashed. Nothing was visible to have made you think it had once been a hotel. There was no 'for sale' sign. The property was just abandoned. Could we have been the last guests? It was only three or four years ago that we spent the night within its welcoming walls. How quickly things can come to ruin, a little like our relationship, only the paint was not yet peeling and we were still patching up the cracks.

The successful purchase of the house in Twickenham happened after many disappointments. It was the early Seventies when 'gazumping' was rife. We'd been looking at properties and offering the asking price which was accepted. A few days later, though, the owners would ring saying things like, 'We'd love to sell the house to you. You're the perfect couple for this place but we've had another offer higher than yours.' They'd tell us the amount and then ask, 'Can you match it?' On one occasion we did, even though, we knew we'd have difficulty raising the money. The next day, they phoned again with the same request. A madness had infected the property market. It spread like a virus. Suddenly everyone wanted their own house. At the very beginning of this craze, I tried to influence Marlowe that it was better to pay a mortgage than rent. At least afterwards the property belonged to you. It took months to convince him and by that time prices were edging steeply upwards. His choices were north of the Thames. For a good working class lad, address was very important to him. Beautiful affordable places were going in Barnes but that was south of the river and according to him, only 'losers' lived there. Today those properties are valued in the millions. I couldn't care less which side of the river we were on. Not being a Londoner, I had no prejudices. In the end we were rushing out in the morning to buy the papers with 'For Sale' ads. I'd be on the phone as early as possible. Finally we managed to make an appointment for the house in Twickenham which was very south of the river and considerably far from the centre of London. It was owned by a couple who were teachers. The three-bedroomed building was late Victorian and the last in a terrace which meant the garden was just a little larger than the others and had a wooden structure at its side used as a garage. It lay in a back street called Haggard Road. Not a very glamorous name for one's address.

The house needed extensive renovations but we offered the asking price. There was a bohemian atmosphere to the place which I found comforting. In the tiny bathroom on the first floor there was graffiti scrawled above the tub. It read, 'Save water. Bathe with a friend.' I liked that. Believe it or not, in late 1971 there was still a wooden hut, the 'thunderbox', at the bottom of the garden. We were told it was no longer in use.

The couple promised us we would not be gazumped. I wrote out a cheque from my personal account for the sum of £1,050 immediately which corresponded to ten percent of the asking price.

They were true to their word. After favourable decisions from our bank for a mortgage, it belonged to us and we sent in a builder to commence with the structural renovations. The flat in Kensington had been given up, so for the mean time, Ian and Ruth McShane were putting us up in their spacious house in Roehampton which was not far from Twickenham. For a while, it seemed Marlowe and I were at peace with one another.

It was at this time that I was offered the television series, *The Adventurer*, starring Gene Barry. Luck was really with us, as now, we had a mortgage to pay and it was extremely important that we earned.

Stuart Damon and I were playing his assistants, a bit like his 'Man Friday' people. The first lot of filming the exteriors took place in the south of France. We had not yet met Mr Barry. The evening before our first day's shoot, the production organized an introduction between us in the hotel bar. Stuart and I arrived on time but the star had not yet made an appearance. We took a seat in an armchair awaiting his arrival. He made his entrance. Out of politeness, Stu and I stood up. I watched Mr Barry's eyes following Stuart's height as he unfolded himself from the seat and heard him say, 'God! I thought you would never stop.' Stuart measured at more than 6 foot 4 inches. Mr Barry's publicity stated he was over 6 foot tall. In reality he was perhaps 5 foot 10, if not even less. The disparity in their height made him look like a midget when they were photographed together. It must have bothered him. Stuart did two episodes. In the third, he was to appear in disguise as a *gendarme.* Call sheets were printed out and delivered to our hotel rooms telling us what time we should present ourselves for make-up and wardrobe as well as noting the scenes we were to appear in the following day. Stu arrived for make-up and then proceeded to the wardrobe room. An actor, freshly flown in from London, was putting on a uniform of the *gendarmerie.*

'Hey,' Stuart said. 'You're playing a *gendarme* as well?'

'Yes,' said the actor.

Stuart searched for his uniform. There was only one of them and the other actor was wearing it. The situation was incredibly embarrassing for the dressers. They were aware of the re-casting and presumed Stuart would have been told. That was how he discovered he'd been replaced in the show. He was put on a plane back to England that afternoon. I was working, and when I arrived back at the hotel he was already gone. I never even had the chance to say goodbye.

My time to be written out of the series would come as well. High-heeled boots were still in fashion but, at 5 foot 7, I was given strict orders to wear flat shoes in any scenes I appeared in with Mr Barry. If it had been possible trenches would have been dug for me to walk in as happened to Sophia Loren when playing opposite little Alan Ladd in the film, *Boy On A Dolphin.*

I don't remember how many episodes I had done before the producers approached me with the news that I was being written out on Gene Barry's orders. They would honour my contract and so, I would continue to be paid but I was not allowed to accept other projects.

It was not the first time that my height worked against me. 5 foot 7 is not gigantic for a woman. I was in good company. Ms Sophia Loren was slightly taller and Faye Dunaway matched me. The latter had just made *The Thomas Crown Affair* with Steve McQueen. I met the producer for McQueen's next film, *Le Mans* about the epic 24-hour car race on that track. He was looking for an actress to play the leading lady. We'd already met in Munich at Steffie's and he'd remembered me. I walked into the office flaunting a mid-thigh mini-skirt and, to show off my legs, the highest-heeled knee-length boots I could lay my hands on.

He ignored my legs and looked up at me from behind his desk saying, 'Katherina, I don't remember you being so tall!'

'It must be the heels,' I said, coyly.

'How high are they?'

'Four, five inches.'

'How tall are you in bare feet?'

I unzipped my boots and stood before him in stocking feet. '5 foot 7,' I said.

'Oh no,' he said looking disappointed.

'Is there something wrong?'

'Steve McQueen will not work with actresses over 5 foot 5'. There were a lot of problems with Dunaway because she was tall. 'I don't dare risk it.' So, I was not considered for the part.

Being paid and not having to work suited me very well. We'd moved into the house. It gave me time to help Marlowe decorate. Every now and again, Jean would sneak in a commercial. They would only be one day's work, so I felt safe doing them. With these earnings, we'd managed to pay for the renovations and the mortgage was under control. It was then that I made a dream come true. I am genetically programmed to adore horses. It must be from my mother's genes. She was a consummate horse woman as were her Tartar antecedents. At an early age, sitting on the back of these animals gave me such pleasure, I felt at one with them. Unfortunately, we could never afford a pony of my own and my equine addiction had to be satisfied with the horses in summer camps, lessons in riding schools or riding out on hacks which I was now frequently doing, having discovered some stables in Roehampton High Street that the McShanes and I haunted. We rode out together in Richmond Park and Wimbledon Common. They had already bought their horses and encouraged me to do the same.

I believed I was competent enough to have my own animal and I was earning correctly. The livery at the stables cost £7 a week. I thought I could afford that. Ian, Ruth, Marlowe and I went off in search for a horse. Ruth had found the address of a mare for sale via her vet. He came with us to look her over. I was bursting with excitement. She was a pretty little bay thoroughbred who did everything possible to buck me off. The McShanes and Marlowe stayed behind in the owner's house watching me from a picture window while the vet, the owner and I walked her to a far field for the trial. I was hardly in the stirrups when she glued her ears back to her neck, stuck her head between her front legs, bowed her back and lifted her rear end in jagged movements to the sky. By some miracle I didn't come off. I stuck on like a cowboy in a rodeo. Eventually, exhausted and with heaving sides, the mare came to a halt.

I leapt out of the saddle on to the ground and asked, 'Is this her usual behaviour?'

'No, no,' I was assured. 'I can't understand why she's reacting like that.'

Oh, yeah? I thought. We lead her back into the stable and when I joined the others they were very proud of me.

'So, you tried her over jumps?' Ruth asked. 'Good for you!'

'No,' I answered. 'You've just witnessed a bucking bronco.'

Ruth, who had a tendency to act as 'Mother Earth' said strictly in her Manchester accent, 'You're not buying her then.' And that was that. We said our goodbyes. I learned later from the vet that the woman was terrified of the mare and it was for that reason she was for sale. He, then, spoke of another horse newly arrived from Ireland, a four year old chestnut gelding being sold at a reasonable price from the Red Lion Farm in Essex. He knew those people and trusted them. I made an appointment to try him. Marlowe came with me. He was impressed. At the end of an hour, I took possession of a handsome animal, 16 hands 2 inches in height and because of his fiery red coat, I called him Paprika.

It was a dream come true made possible by my own efforts. Marlowe showed his considerate side, walking beside me for the first few times I was on Paprika's back. He had become more secure within our relationship. We owned a house together. We decorated it together. I was allowed to express my preferences in taste. We planted crocuses in the garden under an apple tree. I wanted splashes of colour, pools of blue, purple and mauve with a little pink and white at the edges. They were to make a carpet of colours in the spring. When, finally, Cassius the Yorkshire terrier had peed his last pee, he was buried and we planted numerous bulbs of daffodils on his grave.

I was surprised to receive a call from Jean telling me that the producers of *The Adventurer* wanted me back in the series. Gene Barry was going to have a month's holiday so the scriptwriters were told to 'write the girl back in.'

They sent me the scripts. I was very happy but I noticed they'd written a scene in which Mr Barry and I interacted. I wondered how they'd get away with that. Never mind. It was not my problem. In his absence, I went back to the studio and filmed whatever scenes I had to. Then came the day of working together. Our paths crossed in a corridor. I was coming from make-up and he was going there.

'What the hell are you doing here?' he asked, really rather unpleasantly.

'I'm working,' I said and gave him a huge smile. He scowled in return and muttered something inaudible.

Later, on the set, I was the required height. My feet were dressed in woollen socks to protect them from the cold studio floor. It must have really upset him to be working opposite me again because he kept fluffing his lines and blaming me for not giving him the correct cue.

Every now and again I did not allow myself to be bullied. After all, my Tartar/Mongol genes sometimes came to the fore. In a way, far more polite than Attila the Hun, I asked the continuity girl out loud if I had been speaking my lines correctly. She nodded.

'I'm afraid I've been word perfect,' I said in as natural a voice as possible to him. 'It's actually you who's wasting everyone's time here, Mr Barry.' I had nothing to lose. I'd already been fired once on full pay. They couldn't fire me again.

We managed to print the scene despite the steam hissing out of his ears. When finished, he walked off cursing under his breath. As the heavy studio door slammed shut, the crew applauded. I was given hugs, congratulations and offered drinks later in the bar. I'd work on different projects with much of the crew again. It was like working with your family.

CHAPTER XIII

Does one black eye make a battered wife? I don't remember why we argued, just that I was woken up in the middle of the night by Marlowe, delirious with anger. He dragged me into the living room where he continued to shout. I remember accusations but he had no-one to be jealous about. Perhaps, I was becoming more self-assured and less dependent on him. I was growing up, finding a voice and, in a way, this was a threat. I must have said something while he was ranting which struck a violent response. In a flash, I felt his fist hit my face and was knocked backward to the floor. He came rushing towards me. I defended myself by lifting a leg in the air and kicked out, slamming my heel into his thigh. I had wanted to aim for another part of his anatomy but missed. Never having had self-defence lessons, I did the best I could. It was good enough to wrong-foot him, giving me the opportunity to escape. I ran into the bedroom, dressed as quickly as I could, grabbed a coat and ran out into the night. This happened while we were still living in Kensington. At that time, the McShanes also lived in the area, a few blocks away. Arriving at their house, I rang the doorbell. Ruth later told me when they heard the buzzer, Ian turned over in their bed and said, 'It must be Catherine'. They were aware of my volatile relationship.

I was welcomed and looked after by Ruth. The next morning their doctor visited to examine my eye which was now swollen and crimson. He told me it had not been damaged but I would have a 'shiner' for a considerable time. Later that morning, Marlowe arrived, contrite and full of regrets. The McShanes stood between us lest he become violent again. Through loud sobbing and tears, he begged my forgiveness. It was a sight that could melt a titanium heart. We left together, me with a slit of an eye that looked as if it was oozing blood and surrounded by swollen, liver coloured flesh and he, arm around my shoulder, limping.

Back in the flat, he took a Polaroid of my face. After it developed, he handed the picture to me saying, 'Keep it. You can show it to your lawyer if you ever want a divorce'. I did keep it, just in case.

This was the first time that traces of violence were visible. On other occasions I managed to escape before it went that far. Once, after a party, he became so dangerously abusive that I risked jumping out of the Mini as he slowed down for a red light, and hid in an alleyway. This happened on Kensington High Street. I then walked to a friend's house near to Shepherd's Bush. Linda, who was still living in the flat in Baker Street also offered me refuge a few times. The walk from Palace Gardens Terrace to her would take two hours. I'd arrive as the dawn's light was just creeping onto the horizon. Most of these moments happened at night. Sometimes I'd run out so quickly, not even grabbing a handbag on the way. Without money I couldn't hail a cab. London streets in the early hours of the morning became very familiar to me.

It was a time when battered wives didn't make the news. Violence within marriage was a private affair. Being a victim was embarrassing. I rarely spoke of these incidents but when I showed up at a friend's house, it was obvious why I'd come. These were mainly people I'd met through him. All of my previous acquaintances were forbidden to me but the ones I came to know were kind and discreet.

I suppose I could say that I experienced, in a much smaller way, the battered wife syndrome and sympathize with women who suffered far greater abuse than me. The question that's always asked is why? Why don't you flee?

My answer at the time would have been, 'Because he's not like that really. He's loving and kind. It's only these moments of paranoia he suffers from. I can help him. I'm strong. I love him.'

I'm sure thousands of women would have given the same reply. They would have had even greater reasons for not leaving: children, lack of money, nowhere to go. Today, thank God, there are refuges that protect those unfortunate women.

For the moment, Twickenham was good for us. After my father's visit, we invited both my parents for Christmas. The little room where Daddy had slept was too small for a couple so we put them up at the Richmond Gate Hotel, opposite the park. Mommy was impressed with the house, the antique furniture we'd chosen and the decor. The festive holiday passed *en famille* and amongst friends without a single voice raised in anger. We took them to Heathrow with promises that the next time they come, we'd have renovated the loft and they'd be able to stay with us. Two happy people boarded the plane and a happy couple drove back to the house. To say that we never argued would be a lie but the temperature of our disputes seemed a little less heated.

It was during this time that I seemed to go from one job to another. I was asked to appear in the series, *The Persuaders* in which I played

Lady Sinclair to Roger Moore's Lord. It was before he played James Bond and I must say, it would have been difficult to find a more charming leading man to play opposite. He was a delight. Tony Curtis co-starred in the series as Daniel Wilde. I was aware of his background. He was the issue of Hungarian immigrants but born in the Bronx. We didn't have any scenes to play together but he came on the set, one day when I was working with Roger. We were introduced. I said a few words in Magyar which surprised him and then I mentioned my mother and the Peterle bar in Vienna. He remembered both well and complimented me for being her daughter.

'You'll go far,' he said. 'All Hungarians do.'

Tony was an unhappy man having just separated from his most recent wife, Christine Kaufmann, and was not enjoying working in England. He did not exactly drown his sorrows, he inhaled them away. The fog of marijuana smoke emitting from his caravan on the lot could make one quite high just walking past. I'd like to have invited him for dinner to make him feel more welcome but was afraid it could provoke another violent display from Marlowe.

I saw Tony again about 15 years later in New York. The hotel where I stayed was hosting an exhibition of his art work. He had his arm around a very young woman (18?) who I don't think was his niece nor his daughter. A few nights previously, I had seen him on TV being picked out from the audience in a stand-up comic show. That beautiful head of full black wavy hair had severely thinned but he was still charmingly presentable. So, at the reception after the exhibition, I was shocked to see him wearing a white curly wig. Up close and in natural lighting his face was deformed by what seemed to have been ancient cosmetic surgery. He looked like a Barbie doll who had been through a boxing match. There were indentations in his face where they shouldn't have been. But he was a talented painter. God rest his soul.

In early '73, I was offered an episode in a series called *The Rivals of Sherlock Holmes*. It starred a young John Thaw as a detective in the Victorian era. As I have always detested watching myself on the screen, big or small, I have very little memory of the script itself but I know I was dressed in costumes and hairstyles of the period. I'm also sure I played an aristocratic woman. The series was produced for Thames Television by Reginald Collin and Jonathan Alwyn directed the episode. At the time, I wasn't aware that I was being sized up for a future role. A few months later, Jean called to tell me I'd been offered the part of the Polish Countess, Marie Walewska in a new Thames Television venture called *Napoleon and Love,* directed and produced by the duo I had recently worked for. I was flabbergasted! The last actress to play that part was no other than Greta Garbo. I was terrified to accept that role and yet proud to have even been considered.

Napoleon was to be acted by Ian Holm, and Josephine by Billie Whitelaw. To be amongst this cast of highly respected actors would be a daunting experience. I read everything I could lay my hands on about Marie. I learned that she was sacrificed by her much older husband and the Polish government to placate Napoleon. He had been formally introduced to her at a ball given in his honour when marching through Poland on his way to attack Russia. Napoleon wanted her, needed to have her and she was convinced by her husband and the government counsellors to give in to him in order that Poland would remain free of Russian aggressions. He was made to promise that Poland would remain under French protection. She was shown to his bedroom against her will but whatever happened that night she was madly in love with him the following morning. Their relationship which lasted for years went down into history as one of the most enduring love stories ever. It was the first time that reading a part on the page, I knew I would have to become it. I would be Marie.

Ian, Billie and I were flown with the producer to Rome for the costume fittings. Thames TV were given a good deal with Italian costumiers for the making of our elaborate outfits. I remember it as an expensive junket. The producer liked living well. We stayed at four star hotels, eating lunch and dinner in restaurants every day during that week. Whatever waist measurements we had to begin with would have expanded at the end of our stay. But it was a very happy experience. Although, in awe of these two pillars of theatrical society, I came to feel at ease with them. We soon laughed and gossiped together as if we'd known each other all our lives.

My contract was going to last for three months. Inasmuch as Jean never insisted on a high fee, I was happy enough with what I was earning. So happy, in fact, that I thought I could stop taking the pill in the hope to become pregnant. I was 29 and in those days it was considered high time to become a mother. Marlowe was thrilled. I began taking my temperature having heard that within a woman's cycle her temperature rises a little when she is ovulating. As it happened, my temperature varied slightly almost every day so we made sure to be together during the middle of my cycle when fertility was most likely.

Just because we were trying for a baby did not mean that Marlowe completely stopped having his explosive moments. But things were better. He, too, was working.

I answered a phone call from Ruth who invited us for a dinner party to celebrate Ian's birthday. A few of their well-known friends would also be there.

'Don't you dare have a fight in front of them,' she pleaded with me. 'We'll be mortified!'

I assured her we'd be on our best behaviour. Things were happier at home now. I wanted a bath that evening before dressing to go out. We had a problem with mixing the water. In order to have the ideal temperature to soak in, the hot water would have to flow first and then the cold water would be added. The temperature for the hot water was set extremely high. As it flowed from the tap into the bath clouds of steam rose into the air. Marlowe entered the bathroom to have a shave. An argument over a forgotten subject ensued. I was pushed backwards, falling into the scalding bath, my body making a figure of the letter U. My head and arms were raised into the air as were my legs. My lower back, buttocks and upper thighs were burning in the hot water. It must have been adrenalin that allowed me to escape from this pain. My legs folded across the rim of the tub and my arms, still in the air, pulled me into a standing position on the bath mat. It was an impossible feat realized in a blink of an eye. Under different circumstances, it could have been hilarious. Marlowe was shocked into silence.

I went to the bedroom to dress and pocketed the keys to the Mini. We now had two cars. I drove to the McShanes. When Ruth opened the door, seeing me alone, her first words were, 'Oh, no. You've had a fight.'

'It's all right,' I said. 'We've come separately. Marlowe's working. He has an early call in the morning, so he may leave before me.'

She gave me a suspicious look but when Marlowe arrived, he was all smiles and she relaxed. As the etiquette in England is to separate couples around a dinner table, we managed to avoid eye contact and spoke pleasantly to our neighbours. No-one became aware of what had preceded the party.

Marlowe did leave early. I stayed behind and when the others had said their farewells, I told Ruth and Ian what had happened. My back was still stinging but I was sure there was no lasting damage. They were the first to know that I was intending to leave him.

'I think it's for the best,' Ruth said. 'To tell you the truth, if someone were to say that he'd killed you, I wouldn't be surprised. But you'll understand, we can't look after you here. It would separate us from Marlowe and we don't want to take sides. He is, after all, also a close friend.' I completely agreed, knowing that he and Ian were best mates.

It was almost dawn by the time I got home. Marlowe was fast asleep. I sat in the living room thinking, but I knew I wanted to be gone by the time he woke up. I was not ready for another confrontation. The major thought which went around in my head was, I could have been pregnant. I had not yet had my period. All the wishing for a baby to stabilize our relationship was in vain. He would never change.

The black sky was becoming purple when I got back into the Mini and drove the 25 miles to see my horse. Paprika had become too dangerous. Because of work, I had to stop riding. There are clauses in a contract which forbid dangerous activities and riding is one of them. No-one at the livery stable was keen on exercising him. When a contract was finished, I'd get on his back. He was still a young horse and he loved to buck. It was a miracle I never came off. I eventually exchanged him for another horse, Rock Hill II, who was older and wiser. Rocky, as I called him, was having a holiday in the country while I was working. He was amongst his kind munching the green grass. It was dawn when I called out his name having arrived at the field. He came trotting towards me. Before leaving the house, I grabbed some carrots and a few sugar cubes which I shared out with his friends. Once the treats had disappeared, the others left us and I was able to pat his white neck stained with a large chestnut patch. I murmured, telling him what had happened the night before and asked him if it was time to end my marriage. Rocky gave a low snicker and nodded. He could have shaken his head but he nodded. I know it's weird to say that my decision to leave Marlowe was influenced by a horse, but so be it. I returned to Twickenham. Marlowe had gone off to work. I packed some bags and left a note, telling him not to try to get in touch. I'd let him know in time where I was and wished him luck.

That afternoon the Mini was parked in front of the building Thames TV was renting as our rehearsal space. My call was for after lunch. When the others arrived having eaten, they found me already in the rehearsal room. It was Ian who had spotted the suitcases on the back seat of the car. Obviously, questions followed. I had to admit to my circumstances, but said everything was okay. I'd find a little hotel or bed and breakfast. Richard Johnson's girlfriend at that time, Pascale, was in our cast. She sweetly offered to ask him if I could stay in the spare room of their Mayfair mews cottage. And then, a flat became vacant in the same large Victorian house where Ian rented his *pied-à-terre* for when he was working in London. The house was owned by the well-known and respected director, Mark Miller. He had bought the property in Clapham, near to the common, as an investment. In exchange for a ridiculously low rent, the occupants had to promise to move out if and when the house was sold. He couldn't afford sitting tenants. I moved into the flat, repainted its walls and bought suitable furniture. Everything I owned with Marlowe was left behind. I was starting from scratch. At the end of each month, Ian and I would meet with Mark to hand over our £10 a week rent. After the cash had changed hands, we were invited for a drink and then, later to dinner. His tastes were sophisticated. We always ended up going to expensive restaurants and he always paid the bill. There was not much profit left for him as our landlord.

Ian Holm and I were working together and living in close proximity. He was Napoleon and I was Marie. It was almost inevitable that our relationship as colleagues would undergo an eventual metamorphosis to become a romantic one. During the time that I was at my most vulnerable, Ian, also 14 years my senior, gave me an emotional security. Having introduced me to the songs of Simon and Garfunkel, I thought of him as my 'Bridge over Troubled Waters'. He took me across from the turmoil of a dark and muddy bank towards a greener one. We were both aware our relationship could not last. Ian had a partner with whom he shared two children. She was a bright and lovely young woman who I genuinely liked. In another time, we could have become best friends. Our betrayal of her weighed heavily on both our consciences. In the last episode of the series there is a scene where Marie visits Napoleon after his capture and exile to the Island of St Helena. She begs him to be allowed to stay on the island, prepared to give up her life in Europe to be with him to the end of his days. He refuses and sends her back to Poland. The tears I cried on the studio floor while recording the scene were genuine. I could not stop them. Ian was my Napoleon and I was his Marie and this was our farewell.

Sometime in the spring of 1974, I was called for an interview with

Blake Edwards who was directing and producing the next *Pink Panther* movie. We met in an office in a terraced Georgian house in a classy London borough he was renting with his wife, Julie Andrews. I'd been a huge fan of the other *Pink Panther* movies, the original and *Shot in the Dark* starring Peter Sellers as inspector Clouseau. The women who appeared in these were all beautiful and sophisticated. I tried to dress for the part.

Blake Edwards is a very funny man. After just a few minutes, I lost all pretensions of being an elegant woman and laughed hilariously at his off the wall remarks. When we shook hands and said goodbye I was convinced that that was that. You've lost the part, I thought, but you spent a very amusing 20 minutes. I heard nothing more.

Then, Jean rang to tell me I had an appointment to meet with Ridley Scott for an upcoming project. The script was in the post. Ridley and his brother, Tony were, till then, directors of Britain's most gloriously photographed commercials. Having worked in that world, perhaps that was how I'd come to their attention.

A beautiful script was sent to me from an original story by the 19th century, poetic, English/American novelist, Henry James. It was exquisitely written and the part I was to play was of a woman in an abusive marriage. She is the mother of a young child and is forced to leave her husband. Rather than allow her son to remain and be raised by this powerful, sadistic man, she kills the boy. It's a tragic tale but I sympathized with the woman and thought I could do her justice.

It was going to be a wonderful acting part. With Ridley directing, the cinematography would be sublime. I had been offered the role. The appointment to meet Ridley was made at his offices in the West End of London. I couldn't believe my luck.

CHAPTER XIV

Actors often describe their working lives as feast or famine. Months may go by without a job and then, two if not even more, will come at once... a bit like waiting at a bus stop.

It was not so much an interview at the Scott's office as a discussion of the script. I told them how hauntingly atmospheric I thought the story was and how I was thrilled to be a part of the project. Everyone was smiling. Prospective dates were discussed. The filming should begin in a few weeks' time.

In an outer office a telephone rang. A secretary picked up the receiver. Now, it is a well-known fact that every time a phone rings, no matter where and in what circumstances, an actor believes the call is from his or her agent asking urgently to speak to their client, usually with good news. So, it should not have come as a surprise when the secretary intruded upon our conversation to say, 'Catherine, your agent is on the line. It's important that she speaks to you.'

With some embarrassment, I excused myself from the company.

'Don't sign anything!' Jean said as I took the phone. 'Blake Edwards wants to meet you again. Can you make it by three today? Same address as last time. I think he's going to offer you the part.'

I looked at my watch. It was two thirty. The embarrassment when taking the call was nothing compared to how I felt when telling the Scotts why I had to break off the meeting. I admitted to having met Blake for the new *Pink Panther* movie and that he wanted to see me again. If it was going to be an offer and my agent seemed to think so, I had to accept. It was a career decision. What it must have sounded to them that I was saying between the lines was: There was a multi-million dollar movie I was being asked to star in opposite Peter Sellers and that was going to do much more for my future than being in a low budget film, however wonderful the script was, directed by someone who had only done commercials until now. I'm sure that's how my words were interpreted. Shortly afterwards both brothers would have a well deserved success in the industry. Neither ever offered me another role. I can't blame them. I'm also fairly sure that the project never came to fruition. From curiosity, I looked out for the film. It didn't seem to appear in the cinemas or on the TV screen.

Back in the garden square where Blake was still living, I was welcomed, not in the office, but asked to make myself comfortable on a plush sofa in the reception room. There was a list of actresses left casually on the coffee table in front of me. I can't imagine that someone like Blake would have done that unintentionally. As I waited for his appearance, I couldn't help but scan the names. They were well known to me. Each and every one from both sides of the Atlantic already had a glittering career to support her. What was he trying to tell me with that?

Blake entered, tall, slim, handsome in an intellectual way and a gentleman to the tips of his highly polished shoes. As he had been sitting behind his desk the first time we met I hadn't particularly noticed these qualities.

'I'm so glad you could make it,' he began. 'Would you like some wine?'

'Yes, with pleasure,' I said thinking it would relax me because I was extremely nervous. He left the room and returned with a bottle of very good white wine, placed it with a glass in front of me and began to pour.

'Go on, try it. I think you'll like it.'

Just as I put the glass to my lips and without any preambles, he asked, 'Would you like to do the film?'

I almost bit into the glass. I was being offered this wonderful movie and he asks would I like it?

'Of course!' I answered, trying not to jump up from the sofa to kiss him.

'Well the part is yours, if you're not too expensive.' He gave me a sideways glance.

'I don't think my agent will give you any problems on that account.' I took a big gulp of the wine.

He refilled the glass and looked at me conspiratorially saying in a whisper, 'Don't tell anyone I told you but we've budgeted two thousand a week for the part. So, ask for that.'

I swallowed hard. It was more than I could dream of.

'I think that would do very nicely,' I answered still controlling myself not to leap up and kiss him.

'Do you know why I chose you?'

'No, to be honest,' I answered.

'Because you laugh! You're not afraid to laugh. I want your character to break up whenever she wants to. There's even extra time scheduled for laughing. I like that. Okay?' He left the room and returned with a large, thick brown envelope in his hand. 'Here's the script. Take it away and read it over the weekend. Let me know what you think.'

There are not many moments in a normal life that a rush of endorphins invades your being and makes you sing with joy. I drove the little Cooper across Battersea bridge to Clapham with open windows shouting to the world outside, 'I'm going to do the next *Pink Panther* film!' My happiness knew no bounds.

That weekend I spent with a friend, Susan Wooldridge, at her mother's house in the country. They were aware of the brown envelope and what it contained. On the Saturday afternoon, mother and daughter left me alone in their living room to read the script. I cried with laughter. Pages swam in front of my eyes, unreadable through my tears. Having been a fan, I could hear Clouseau's distinctive accent as he was speaking. It was painfully funny. When Susan and her mother found me, I was rolling on the floor still laughing.

The script was written by Blake. It was a work of comic genius. Every moment was described in a visual sense. In my imagination, I could see the end result on the screen and anticipated that it would be one of the funniest films ever.

I rang Jean on my return and told her I was over the moon with the script and my part. Of course, I would accept and told her what fee she should negotiate on my behalf.

'Are you sure?' she asked. Jean never felt comfortable asking for large sums. She'd rather actors worked for less but worked. It was a lot for me but I'm sure the ladies I saw on the list would have cost at least three times that amount and they didn't need the money.

'Go for it,' I told her. 'I'm sure you'll get it.' I didn't mention from whose mouth the figure had spouted.

That afternoon, she rang me back having spoken to Budge Drury, the casting director who was also charged with fee negotiations.

'You're being offered a thousand a week,' she said. 'No more than that.'

'Demand two,' I insisted. 'That's what I've been told to ask for and that comes from...' I had to admit to her, 'Blake himself.'

Shortly after, I picked up the phone again.

'You silly woman,' Jean said from down the line. 'He meant dollars, not pounds!' It could have been true. Those were the days when one pound was worth two dollars.

There was nothing I could reply to that and so £1000 a week it was and I was still grateful for the £885 I would receive after Jean's ten percent and the National Insurance stamp were deducted.

Another meeting was convened between Blake and myself. His first words to me were, 'What happened? Did I give you too much wine? I told you how much you could ask for.'

'My agent said that after she had spoken to Mr Drury, you had meant dollars and not pounds.'

He shook his head and in between tut-tuts, he said, 'That Budge.' It was too late to do anything about it, so he added magnanimously, 'Well, you can keep your costumes and we'll spend a bit of money on those.' And the costume department did. After the shoot, I hung these expensive designer outfits in my closet. Most of them stayed there until I took them to a charity shop. They were fine to dress the character Claudine, but somehow, as the person, Catherine Schell, I was not comfortable in such flamboyant wear.

To celebrate my good fortune in landing the film, I invited some friends to my favourite night club/discotheque called Tramps. It was in Jermyn Street. One had to descend a long staircase to arrive in a huge, plush, decorated basement where the establishment was situated. So, saying, 'I like going down to Tramps on a Saturday night,' could raise a few eyebrows.

This night, we spotted a lonely figure sitting at a table not far from ours. My friends became very excited and whispered in my ear, 'That's Peter Sellers. Go and introduce yourself.'

The Champagne had given me courage. I walked over to him and said, 'Hello, Mr Sellers. I think we're going to be working together.'

'Catherine!' he shouted out. 'What a pleasure. Blake told me. It's lovely to meet you.'

I invited him to join us but he had already made a date and was waiting for the people to arrive. Another bottle of Champagne was placed in the ice-bucket. We were told it was courtesy of Mr Sellers.

We were not to meet again until the filming in Gstaad, up in the Swiss Alps. Carol Cleveland, also a member of Jean's stable and known for her appearances in the *Monty Python* series was part of the cast. She and I were very friendly and determined to take advantage of whatever entertainment, out of our working hours, this ski resort had to offer.

Peter was sitting on a stool at the hotel's dimly lit bar. Carol and I along with other members of the cast gathered there before our evening's adventure. We were going to a highly praised restaurant a few kilometres outside of Gstaad.

'How are we going to get there?' I asked. 'We're going to need two taxis.'

'No we won't,' she said emphatically. 'You're going to ask the production office for transport.'

Peter was listening to us but not participating.

'I can't do that!' I answered.

Carol looked at Peter who was smiling.

'Yes you can. You're a star. Now, act like one. Ring the office and make demands.' She ordered me. I saw Peter nodding his head.

There was a phone for interior calls on the bar. Carol lifted the receiver, spoke to an operator and asked for the production office. She handed me the phone. It was answered by the production manager. I took a deep breath. All eyes were on me.

'This is Catherine Schell speaking,' I began in a neutral tone.

'Hello, Catherine!' he answered. 'Have you got a problem?'

'Umm... I'm going to a restaurant with some of the cast. It's outside of Gstaad.' I added hurriedly, 'Not too far, mind you, but is there any chance of transport being laid on for us?'

I waited for the obvious answer which would say, 'Can't you call a taxi?' But it was not that which I heard as a reply.

'Sure. How many are you? And for what time?'

I told him.

'There will be two cars waiting for you outside the entrance. Have a nice evening.'

It was that easy to make a demand. No wonder stars can become unbearably spoiled.

Now that all was arranged, we talked Peter into joining us. He had hesitated at first saying things like, 'I don't want to spoil your evening.' Peter Sellers, spoil our evening? Who are you kidding? In fact, I think he was afraid he would end up standing for the bill. The accepted etiquette amongst actors for such gatherings was everyone paid for themselves. He, being the wealthiest, may have had qualms.

We were all in great form. I remember laughing a lot but what impressed me most was Peter's appreciation of other people's humour. He genuinely found the conversations funny. I sat next to him and listened as he quietly repeated some of the punchlines of the jokes to himself. He was storing them up for future use which was a compliment to those who had said them.

The bill arrived and was split evenly. Peter had had an amusing evening. Thereafter, he was never again shy to join us on our outings.

We were leaving Gstaad for Nice. The day before catching our transport – Blake, in his private helicopter, Peter, in his chauffeur driven Rolls and I, in a bus with the rest of the crew, Peter asked me which hotel I was booked into during my stay in Nice. I told him. He was horrified.

'You can't stay there! That's the unit hotel!' he said, indignant on my behalf. It didn't matter to me. I was quite happy being near the crew, most of whom I'd made friends with.

'I'll arrange something more suitable for you.' He walked away.

My timidity at making demands had obviously affected him. Within half an hour he came back to say proudly that I would be in a five star hotel, the same as his on Cap Ferrat. I thanked him profusely but hoped there was no ulterior motive to his action.

When I arrived at the exclusive, luxurious hotel I was relieved to be introduced to his girlfriend at that time. She was a lovely young Scandinavian woman called Titi. He kept her very much to himself and, I think, on a short leash. I hardly ever saw them at the hotel and when by chance I did, Peter only waved at me. He didn't invite me to join them. I was eating my dinners alone. The unit hotel in Nice was too far away. I regretted not being around their friendly, boisterous company.

One day, though, when I wasn't required on the set, I sat sunbathing at the pool with Titi. She was sweet to talk to and we conversed happily together. Just before Peter was due back from work, she excused herself and said in an embarrassed tone, 'I have to go back to our suite. Please don't tell Peter we've been talking together. He doesn't like it if I make friends with someone... even another woman.' I was reminded of Mr Marlowe. It surprised me. I thought Peter was more stable.

It wasn't until the first day that we were to work together that I met Christopher Plummer. Blake told me at one of our pre-production meetings that Lord Lytton, the phantom thief was originally supposed to be played by Douglas Fairbanks Jr. but when he had decided to cast me as Lady Lytton, he felt the disparity in our ages was too pronounced. Mr Plummer and I would look better suited to each other.

Christopher was every woman's idea of a handsome man. His reputation as an excellent actor was well established. He was always polite, if a little distant but it was up to him to decide what company he kept. Off duty, he seemed to have a reasonable head of hair. What no-one understood was: why did he insist on wearing a wig for the part? Did Blake suggest that he saw Lord Lytton in a bouffant hair style? And why did he wear it going home to his rented villa one evening while driving his rented Rolls Royce cabriolet? The hair department were frantic with worry. If the piece had been blown off while driving along the coastal road and been squashed in the traffic or ended up in the Mediterranean, there was no double for it. Filming scenes with him would have to be postponed until a new wig could be manufactured and flown in from London, but he arrived the following morning with the piece in good condition. No harm done but a sleepless night for the hairdresser.

There was an affectionate scene we had to do together which ended with a kiss and a few words. Running my fingers through his hair was out of the question. I was helping him pack in the bedroom. He was anxious to fly off and investigate who had posed as the 'Phantom' to steal the pink panther diamond. The scene was shot during the day. We filmed in a villa and the bedroom had two windows. In order that the interior was not obscured by the brilliant sunlight outside, the lighting director had to compensate. The large filming lamp called the 'brute' can light thousands of watts in strength. It also gives off the corresponding heat. There were two of these monsters in the room so that we could be photographed in what appeared to be natural light. We were working in sweating temperature. Christopher's make-up was a darkish tan in colour. Mine was a more natural tint. We did the preliminary dialogue and then went into a 'clinch'. Two faces glowing with perspiration were going to leave smudges around each other's mouths. When parting from the kiss, I had dark stains and Christopher, lighter ones. Make-up girls arrived and with their sponges did their corrections. We did another take. Exactly the same happened. We persisted to a third take. At the end, Blake said, 'Cut and print!' But the kiss and the following dialogue was eventually cut from the film.

Blake had told me that he scheduled extra time for laughing. I would come to experience the necessity for that. We had moved to another villa to film the scene when Clouseau arrives disguised as the 'chief trouble shooter' of the Nice telephone company. After destroying the doorbell which Clouseau is incapable of using, the door is opened by David Lodge as the Lytton's butler. He is holding the bell with a spaghetti of wires wrapped around it and hands it to David. I arrive as the lady of the house and Clouseau introduces himself in his peculiar accent as the 'chief trouble shitter' of the Nice telephone company. He then utters a name which he cannot himself pronounce. It was written as 'Fleurnoi' in the script but ended up becoming a very laboured 'Fleurdenoyed'. As an actress, I can't help but react to the truth. I am Lady Lytton. A strange 'trouble shitter' arrives at my door. Over his shoulder, I can see a ridiculous three wheeled vehicle. He has demolished our doorbell and chosen a name for his disguise which is unpronounceable. In the script, I was never fooled as to his identity but I could not control my laughter at Clouseau's idiocy.

I don't remember how many takes we'd shot before Blake suggested a break. I had laughed. Peter had laughed and David who had been stoically trying to hold in his laughter eventually also succumbed. We reconvened after a two hour pause and recommenced. Everyone was on their best behaviour. We managed to get three quarters of the way when a muffled giggle could be heard from behind the camera. This time, it was Blake who had lost it. He could hardly say cut through his laughter. We took another pause. After a good half hour we were back in position. The clapper board clapped. I don't know how high the take number was which was called out. Everything was going smoothly until almost at the very end Blake shouted, 'Cut!' We turned around, not knowing why the scene had been brought to a stop.

'Who was that?' Blake turned violently to the crew. 'Who was stifling a cough?'

A crew member looked toward him sheepishly. 'It was me, Guv. Couldn't help it. Sorry, but I had to cough.'

'Well then, cough, damn it, if you have to! This is only a movie!'

My respect and appreciation for him as a director was already considerable. Now, it was boosted a thousand fold. I remembered those lines, 'It's only a movie' when I'd work with directors of lesser talent who didn't give a damn about their actor's safety. A pity Mr Cziffra didn't have the same philosophy when he directed *Lana: Queen of the Amazons*.

CHAPTER XV

The end of 1974 and all of '75 would be an eventful time. Some of what happened determined my future career and one specific decision, the rest of my life. I was offered an episode of a television series being filmed at Pinewood studios. I'd never heard of it but I certainly recognized the stars. *Mission Impossible* had been one of my favourite programmes. When I was told I'd be working with Martin Landau and Barbara Bain I was thrilled. The series was called *Space: 1999* and the episode, 'The Guardian of Piri'. Piri was a planet which was ruled by a computer called the Guardian. My role was the servant of the Guardian and although I looked every bit human, I was not.

I remember a meeting with the designer of the series Keith Wilson, and Sylvia Anderson, famous for producing with her husband, Gerry, the successful series of *Thunderbirds* which starred puppets. I think this was the first big project they were producing with real people. The meeting took place in the design department. We were there to determine what sort of costume I would be draped in. I was asked my opinion on what parts of my anatomy I was not too proud of.

'Almost all,' I said. 'Except for my neck. That's why I was cast as one of Modigliani's models in the BBC's drama documentary of the artist. He's the one who painted all of his women with extremely long necks.'

'We're thinking of making your costume quite revealing,' Keith said.

I then launched into all the complaints I had concerning my physique:

'Somebody once told me I had American footballer's shoulders.'

'My legs are okay but I should have high heels to make them look longer.'

'The upper thighs should be covered.'

'My waist is not tiny. I'm sort of straight down to my hips.'

'The boob department is childlike. I just pretend I need a bra.'

Keith was taking notes as I spoke. He put his pen down and began to take my measurements. I noticed his hands were trembling as he slipped the tape around my waist. I didn't think it was anything to do with the impression I was making on him. Was he ill? Was the trembling the result of a hangover? He didn't seem the type who took to the bottle. There were some wonderful drawings of costumes and sets strewn on various desks. They didn't seem to be made by a hand that trembled. I would appear in a creation which contradicted all of my misgivings and I have to say, it was stunning.

The design of the set for the planet of Piri was surreal. One could have thought one had walked into Christopher Ray's lighting emporium. There was a forest of thin, twisted, metal, tree trunks carrying pale glowing orbs of different sizes at their crowns. It was either fantastical Kitsch or simply out of this world. Whichever, it was highly photogenic, a gift to the lighting cameraman.

For a while, a photograph of me in the fetching outfit was hung in one of Pinewood's corridors of fame. When the episode was finished, I said my goodbyes to cast and crew. It had been a very pleasant couple of weeks. A pity, I had not said *auf wiedersehen* or *au revoir*, as that would have been nearer to the truth.

In early '75 I found myself once again in a situation of having to choose between jobs. Jean had sent me off to an interview. I was to meet two men I'd never heard of in the lobby of a central London hotel. They were from Australia. One, I presumed was the producer. The other, Peter Weir, was the director. They explained their project to me with charming enthusiasm. I was told much of the film would be shot in Australia's outback. The temperature could become extremely hot. I would be dressed in late-19th century costumes with tight corsets and petticoats. Would I mind?

'No.' I answered. 'I was dressed like that while working in Africa on *The Search for the Nile*. I survived.'

The outback was known for dangerous creepy-crawlies. Was I frightened? I said I would rather avoid them but, I had worked in worse conditions, like the Brazilian Amazon. At the end of the meeting they handed me a script. The title read, *Picnic at Hanging Rock*. I was being offered the role of the French mistress in a girls' boarding school. The story follows a school picnic near to a strange rock formation which, according to Aboriginal legend, is haunted. During the picnic some girls and a teacher mysteriously disappear while exploring the rock.

As I mentioned before: feast or famine. I was also being offered a five-part television drama at the same time. I had met the director, Bill Hays, for the project two weeks previously. Our interview was very cosy, even though I arrived to it with one cheek blown out like a chipmunk's. I'd been undergoing some gum operations at the time and had said to Jean to postpone the meeting but he insisted it didn't matter. He knew exactly how I looked and was acquainted with my work. He also admitted to genuinely wanting to cast me before but nothing suitable had ever come up. Bill was attractive with a sense of impishness about him.

I like to draw portraits, so, when I look at a face I really study it. He had dark wavy hair but had he been blonde and wearing scarlet lipstick on his cupid's bow mouth and had plucked a little from his arched full eyebrows and been wearing mascara on his long lashes which surrounded hazel-green eyes, I could have been talking to Marilyn Monroe. He even had her beauty spot on the left cheek of his perfect oval face.

When I mentioned his name to friends they were encouraging. All actors love working with him, I was told. The job, if I accepted it was going to be challenging. The serial, called *Looking for Clancy*, was written originally as a book by Frederic Mullally. The story refers to two young left-wing journalists who begin their careers at the same time, and how one of them, Clancy, surrenders his original principals to become seduced by notoriety and the power which can follow. I was to play Clancy's wife. As the story spanned a few decades, my character had to age from 19 into her fifties. The two reporters played by Robert Powell as Clancy and Keith Drinkel as Dick Holt had far more important roles but, nevertheless, the wife was, by no means, forgotten. She did have an influence in the story.

I was once again on the horns of a dilemma. *Clancy*'s contract would last three months but it was *only* television. *Picnic* was a shorter contract but it was a film. *Clancy* was being directed by an established, popular director. Not even my agent had ever heard of the director presenting *Picnic*. *Clancy*'s scripts were straight forward. They told a story of a human predicament. *Picnic* was a tale of such mystery, not offering conclusive answers. Did the director have the sensitivity to portray this enigmatic, haunting story on the screen? I asked Jean to help me decide. To her shame and to mine, we were ignorant of Mr Weir's successful launching of *The Cars that Ate Paris* which had just arrived with many good notices on the film circuits in Europe and Australia. With the lack of information, I made the decision to remain in England and accepted *Looking for Clancy*.

Picnic at Hanging Rock became famous and Helen Morse who played the French mistress was deservedly lauded for her performance but I never regretted my decision. Some people would say it was fate. I don't believe in that. Throughout our lives we make a myriad of decisions, sometimes even unconsciously and it is those decisions that put us where we are. Because of my ignorance, I chose a more secure path. I was not to know that my role in *Clancy* would be secondary to the role I'd play in the future as mistress and wife of Bill Hays to the end of his days.

Blake Edwards re-contacted Jean. After cutting his first version of *The Return*, he decided to write more scenes for the character, Claudine. They were to be filmed in a studio just outside of London. I was already under contract for *Clancy* so the scheduling would overlap. Discussions took place between his office and Bill's. Together, they found dates when I could rush to the studio from the BBC rehearsal rooms in Acton or vice-versa. But there was a problem. I had cut my hair. Whereas, previously, it had fallen almost to my waist, it now sat in a page-boy on my shoulders. Not a wig but a hair-piece had to be conjured to match my former appearances. There was a well-known wig makers in London which catered to the film and theatrical industries. After a few visits they manufactured a hair extension which was placed on the crown of my head with my own hair combed over it. I defy anyone to notice the difference. Even the colour exactly matched mine.

My extra scenes were all to do with Clouseau. I was allowed, once again, the luxury of unrestrained laughter when he approaches me in a night club with only half a moustache. The other scene was in the living room of Claudine's hotel suite where she manages to slip a drug into his drink which renders him catatonic.

During the filming I was made aware again of Peter's generosity as an actor. I'm sure I'm not the only one who experienced this. On many occasions, he would turn to Blake suggesting that the camera should be pointing on Claudine at a specific point in a scene. Not every star would be so considerate.

While still on location in the south of France I was interviewed on film by Barry Norman, the renowned critique and film buff who had his own weekly television programme. I'd spoken highly of my experience working both with Blake and Peter. I was unaware that it was aired as pre-publicity for the forthcoming release of the movie but Peter had seen it. I received a phone call from him. As I'd never given him my number, he must have asked the post production office.

'Hello, Catherine!' he began. I had no doubt who was on the other end of the line and was surprised to hear his distinctive voice. 'I've just seen the interview with Barry Norman. You were so kind to say what you did about me. I didn't deserve it. I should have paid more attention to you.'

'It's fine. I meant every word and, anyway, you were very busy.' I replied politely but I did think of the times at the hotel on Cap Ferrat when I'd have liked to join him and Titi for a drink or even a meal, with the understanding, of course, that I would 'go Dutch'.

'Catherine,' he continued. 'I'm invited to a dinner party tonight with people I hardly know but it's important that I go. I need a laughing partner to get through the evening. Would you like to come?'

I was free and happy to accompany him. By that time, I'd moved to a house in Fulham which had been renovated into two separate apartments. Linda, my 'wife-in-law' moved into the upper one and I had the ground floor flat. We were in an unpretentious little street called Gowan Avenue which was off the Munster Road. It would become infamous in the future, well after Linda and I had moved away. Jill Dando, the television presenter, was murdered on her doorstep a few houses down from our old address. The two story bay windowed Victorian houses formed a terrace on both sides of the road. They had tiny front gardens with a bigger one in the back. As Peter's chauffeur driven Rolls glided to my front door, it caused quite a few white laced curtains to quiver. The nosy faces behind them were not yet accustomed to such automobiles parking in their midst.

We had an entertaining evening. I was the audience Peter needed for his jokes and his presence at the dinner table was much appreciated. He dropped me back home with a peck on the cheek and a promise to meet again soon. Thus began a platonic relationship between us which gave me an insight into his very complicated character. It was not unusual that my phone would ring in the early hours of the morning.

'Catherine, I need someone to talk to.' His voice could sound despondent.

'It's three in the morning,' I'd say. 'I was asleep.'

'Please, I'm a bit desperate.'

'Sure, Peter, I'll be right there.' And I'd get out of bed, dress and drive to his flat which was in a modern complex somewhere in Westminster, sit down opposite him and listen to a litany of regrets.

'I should never have left my first wife. She was the one who really supported me.'

I didn't think he meant financially but rather his fragile self-confidence.

He mentioned Sophia Loren. It had been rumoured that they'd had a fling when filming *The Millionairess* together.

'She really loved me,' he said. 'Imagine, that beautiful woman was in love with me.' He had a forlorn expression on his face. 'But she went back to Carlo Ponti. You know who he is?'

'Yes. Her husband. The Italian producer who discovered her when she was very young. He's a lot older than her.'

'It broke my heart,' he added sadly.

He then went into a tirade of abuse against Titi. She was only interested in his fame and money. He'd bought her expensive jewellery and she never returned it when she left him which proved his point that all she had been was a 'gold digger'. The person he described did not at all fit the impression she'd made on me.

I don't remember him ever mentioning Britt Ekland in these sombre moods but I was made aware that they shared a daughter and was once asked to accompany him to help the child with her packing. I have no idea why he would have thought I was a specialist. Brit had to suddenly fly back to Sweden, leaving the girl with a nanny in a house she had been renting. He, as a dutiful father, thought it best to give her a visit. She would be flying back on her own later in the day to join her mother. I was introduced to a beautiful young girl, perhaps eight or nine in age, who commanded me to follow her to her bedroom. We walked up some stairs. An empty suitcase lay open on her bed. She then pointed to a chest of drawers and a wardrobe. I was ordered to remove clothing from them and told how to fold the articles as I placed them into the case. She hadn't needed anyone to help but I played the game, finding it amusing to study this young person demonstrate an enormous amount of self-confidence and the beginnings, perhaps, to a budding complex as a control freak. Peter, eventually joined us and chuckled at her bossiness.

I was not only called to be a comforting presence in his blue moods. On one occasion, before we were to meet Roman Polanski for dinner, I arrived at his flat. He'd decided, because he was on a 'high' to ring Spike Milligan in Australia. Halfway through the conversation, he handed me the phone to say 'hello'. I can now boast, I spoke to Spike or, rather, he spoke to me. I was too tongue tied to say much. He was charming. Peter must have mentioned me before because he encouraged me to remain a good friend.

On our way to meet Polanski at the restaurant, I told Peter of my one and only encounter with the famous Polish-born director. It was during one of my early excursions to London before I finally settled there. I was, perhaps, 21. My old stand-in Fiona, from *Traitor's Gate,* loaned me her flat for the week. Dennis from ICM was representing me while I was in England. I received a phone call from him saying Roman Polanski and his Polish producer, Gene Gutowski were in town casting for their next venture. They'd like to invite me to dine with them that evening to speak about the project. He gave me the address of a Chinese restaurant on Kensington High Street.

They were already at the table when I arrived. Sitting with them, next to Gene was a young woman about my age. She was breathtakingly beautiful. Her face was faultless, full mouth, beautiful eyes, perfect nose and dark hair which hung loosely in waves to her shoulders. If we were up for the same part, I haven't got a chance, I thought. I was asked to sit next to Roman, opposite the girl. We ladies were somewhat ignored during the meal. The two men spoke in Polish throughout. I tried to start a conversation with the beauty, asking her questions. She replied in monosyllables. After a while, it became evident, she did not want to speak. At the end of the meal, the men turned to us and apologized in very heavy Polish accents.

'We haven't spoken to you at all. Very sorry. Shall we go back to the hotel? We can talk about the film there.'

Always the naïve, I said, 'Sure.' Beauty said nothing. She nodded with a resigned expression. That should have warned me.

They were staying at the Dorchester. We took the lift to a certain floor and walked down a corridor to Mr Gutowski's suite. On entering, Gene offered us a drink from a well-supplied bar. He and the beauty sat on a sofa. Roman and I hovered about. I waited for the subject to be broached about the film. The two on the sofa began to kiss. Their tongues were behaving vigorously, as if cleansing each other's throats. I looked on, mesmerized, not even noticing that Roman had disappeared but began to feel just a little bit embarrassed when Gene's mouth came unglued from hers and said, 'Catherine, what are you still doing here? Roman wants to interview you. Go to his room. It's just opposite my door.'

Still the hopeful innocent, I discreetly left and knocked on Polanski's door. It opened slowly. There was a view of a large bed but I couldn't see him. I took a few steps forward. Suddenly, the door slammed shut behind me. Roman had been hiding there and he was stark naked. To escape him, I ran into the middle of the room. He leapt on to the bed. I made my way back towards the door. He jumped off the bed to bar my path. I ran back to the other side of the bed. He leapt back on to it. I couldn't help but laugh. There was something so ridiculous about a little man who looked like a pixie jumping around, on and off the bed, completely nude with his willy bobbing up and down. He must have seen the comedy in the situation because he laughed as well while chasing me about. I never really felt threatened. He was a lot smaller than me. Eventually, I did get to the door, opened it and ran down the corridor to the lift.

I didn't get the part. And the beauty did. Never having spoken about the film, I didn't even know its title but years later, by chance, I saw a low budget, black and white movie on the telly. It was directed by him and low and behold, there she was in a minor role. It must have been the film they had been planning and later still I saw her unforgettable face playing a major role opposite a Hollywood superstar in a multi-million dollar movie. Good for her.

'I don't think Roman will try anything like that tonight,' Peter said after listening to the tale.

He was already installed when we arrived. Peter introduced us and he stood up politely to shake my hand. There was not even an inkling of recognition in his eyes. I could not have made much of an impression those ten years ago.

Over the dinner, though, I noticed his English had improved. He and Peter made jokes throughout the meal. It was difficult to swallow the food for the amount that I laughed. When we'd finished eating, we were offered a liqueur on the house. It arrived in small shot glasses. Peter swallowed his immediately. While Roman and I were still sipping ours, he stood up. Our table was in the centre of the room in full view of the other diners. All eyes were attracted to him. Everyone knew who he was. He began a speech in a squeaking elderly voice welcoming Roman, myself and all others there to the annual ophthalmologic convention. Amused expressions all around. He ad-libbed cleverly in his old man's voice about the need for these events in order to exchange ideas to ameliorate the population's eye sight and ended his oration with the usual respectful toast to the Queen.

'Ladies and Gentlemen! Please be upstanding!' he commanded Roman and me. Surprisingly, those nearest to us also stood up. Holding the shot glass in his right hand and lifting it into the air, he said loudly,

'To her gracious Majesty!' and brought the little glass directly to his right eye while throwing back his head. It's true, the glass did look like an eye bath but only someone like Peter could have used it to such comic advantage.

CHAPTER XVI

'If they've come for me, tell them that I'm not here,' Linda whispered one Sunday morning as she crept down her stairs to my flat. We were the only residents in the house, so we tended to keep our doors open. She had looked out the window from her first floor living room and seen a parked police car with two uniformed officers walking towards our front door. There were two bells: one in the name of Marlowe and the other in Schell. They buzzed Marlowe. She quickly snuck back up the stairs. Linda often had little problems with the law, usually to do with traffic offences. I opened the door for the two policemen and was not in the least affected by their presence on our threshold.

There was a mumbled question of identity. Expecting it to be Linda's, all I heard was, 'Blah, blah... Virginia Marlowe.'

'No, I'm sorry but she's not here,' I answered. Then I realized they'd said, 'Catherine Virginia Marlowe.' Linda and I had not only shared a husband (at different times, of course) but also identical middle names which were printed in our driving permits.

'My God, it's me you're looking for!' I admitted.

'Madam,' one of them said officiously. 'We have come to arrest you for contempt of court.'

'What? What do you mean?' I couldn't believe what I was hearing.

'You received a summons to appear for a hearing in court due to a drink-drive offence. You failed to show up.'

'I never received it! I promise you!'

At this point Linda came stomping down the steps in her high heeled shoes having forgotten that she shouldn't have been there.

Ever loyal, she said, 'There must be a mistake! Catherine wouldn't do something like that.'

They looked down at the warrant and read out the date when I should have been present at the proceedings. I remembered very well the incident when I was stopped and breathalysed on the King's Road. The balloon read positive and I was taken to the Chelsea Police Station for the usual blood test. I'd been to a dinner party with a great friend, Eddy Stacey, who had been a stunt man on *OHMSS*. We'd kept in touch. He was someone I completely trusted. I could cry on his shoulder and he'd put comforting arms around me, never asking for more. We were also great dancing partners. After dinner, copious amounts of port was poured into our glasses. We left saying our thanks and farewells while I felt my head was still capable. It was the time I was driving my yellow MG. The car was parked outside of the house which was near to an intersection. When getting in, I noticed a police car waiting opposite for their lights to change. Just before I'd have moved off, the front door of our host's house opened and our hostess came tumbling out, obviously in a temper and not too steady on her feet.

'What's the matter?' asked Eddy, winding down the window.

There were a series of loud curses, mostly to do with what she thought of her partner. She was leaving the bastard.

Eddy, always a gentleman, asked her where she was going. Her intention was to get a taxi at Sloane Square. As that was a little distance away, he offered her a lift. I didn't think it was a good idea. The car was a two seater. Nevertheless, she climbed in still shouting, with arms and legs waving about. It was no wonder that the scene attracted the police car's attention. They waited for my light to become green. She had folded herself onto Eddy's lap with a bit of her bum too near to the gear shift. I drove off, signalling to turn right and continued on to the King's Road. I think it was while changing gear from second to third and trying to avoid her *derrière* that I did a little zigzag in the road. It was enough to turn on the blue light and siren of the panda car which had snuck up behind me. I came to a stop. Two burly policemen climbed out of the car and placing their caps on their heads, they approached the MG, asked me to wind down my window and offered me a breathalyser to blow into. I knew it would read positive. I was told I had to go to Chelsea police station. It was understood that Eddy would be taking over the driving of the car. While we walked from one side of the car to the other to exchange seats our hostess slunk away to disappear into the night. It was her hooligan behaviour that attracted the attention of the police in the first place. No goodbye. No sorry. No thanks for the lift.

As I was being collected on a Sunday morning, I was going to spend a day and a night in jail and because it was a Sunday it was impossible to contact a magistrate to allow me bail. The police were apologetic but they said, 'We could have come yesterday, the Saturday, which would have meant two days in detention.'

They walked me to the car. Once again lace curtains were tweaked by the curious. I was grateful for my reputation not to be in handcuffs.

Linda stood helplessly at the open door of the house, wishing me well.

Just before I climbed onto the back seat, I turned to her and shouted, 'Tell Peter!' – thinking if anyone could rouse a magistrate, he could. I was taken back to Chelsea Police Station but my sensibilities were spared. They did not put me into a cell. That would come later.

There was a shocking incident which I witnessed while waiting for the black Maria to take me to Paddington police station. Some holding cells were just off the reception area where the officer's desks were situated. A corner of one of these desks was cleared for me to sit on. The atmosphere was very jovial. I was actually having a good time. But then, a man entered the station and was led to a cell which was opened by an officer. He was allowed to go in. The next thing I became aware of was the sound of fists hitting flesh and the whimpers from the recipient of these blows.

The officers present knew exactly what was happening and ignored the noises but they disturbed me to the point that I asked one of them to intervene.

'No way,' he said. 'That's the kid's father. He mugged an old lady, shoving her to the ground. If it wasn't the dad dealing out the punishment, it would be us.'

How telling, I thought. A violent father makes a violent son. And did the police really rough up some of their prisoners? They'd been ultra-polite with me. I still wanted to believe I could trust my neighbourhood Bobby.

Just before I was taken away from Chelsea, Linda arrived with three full packets of cigarettes. She was in a state of distress on my behalf and when handing them to me, she assured me that cigarettes were prison currency. I looked down at my unexpected bounty but all I could say was, 'How long do you think I'm going to be in there?'

I was the only detainee in the black Maria to be transported to the remand cell in Paddington. As I had not yet been pronounced guilty, I imagined the cell to be like a little hotel room just to spend the night in before the ordeal of the trial the following morning. I didn't really expect curtains or a telly, although that would have been nice. A police woman sat on a bench opposite me in the back of the van. She was a very pleasant escort and we joked about my situation quite a bit. When the van came to a stop at the station she turned to me and said, 'No more laughing. This is serious. Don't put anyone's back up. They may not have a sense of humour.'

I descended from the van and was handed over to a keeper who would look after me during my stay. She was a stern looking woman built like the proverbial exterior latrine. After handing over my cigarette lighter, I was marched down the stairs and along a dingy corridor with heavy metal doors on either side. We came to a halt in front of one of these. It was opened by her and I was unceremoniously pushed in.

'But... but...' I stammered. 'I have claustrophobia.' Which was not a complete lie. I'd had an attack in the New York apartment when I was young and had locked myself into a bathroom by accident. The knobs on both sides of the door had fallen off. It took a long time for Mitzi, who was already partially deaf, to hear my screams. By the time she arrived to release me, I was a sweating, trembling, hysterical child.

'You'll get over it,' said the wardress.

'How do I light my cigarettes?' I asked in a panic.

'You push that button over there,' she said, pointing to it. 'And I'll come with a match.'

'You're going to be very busy,' I said.

She shrugged, closed the door and left me alone. And, my God, did I feel alone.

The reality of the cell was much different to my expectations of a simple little hotel room. From cement floor to ceiling, the walls were covered with off-white tiles. Against a corner was a thin bench with a plastic mattress. A rough blanket was folded at its foot. Hanging from the high ceiling was a bare bulb which cast a harsh glow. The toilet was in a cubicle but there was no door. Conversations between other inmates were going on beyond. They seemed not to be strangers to each other. I listened in fascination to their exchanges which were voiced in accents from across London's poorest boroughs. If there was any woman there who had committed a crime more heinous than shoplifting or nicking drugs from a chemist, she kept very silent.

I was desperate to smoke a cigarette and pushed the button. The solid latrine came surprisingly quickly in answer.

'Yes?' she asked, unlatching the metal window.

'Can I have a light please?' I proffered my cigarette through the opening.

She lit it, closed the hatch and walked away down the corridor. There are only so many cigarettes you can chain-smoke if you're not used to it. At some point, the one I was lighting the next one from had to be extinguished which meant, after a pause, I'd have to push the button again.

The wardress arrived and the same procedure took place. I continued to listen to my fellow prisoners and heard they were in need of a smoke. Till then, I had not contributed to their conversations.

I rang the bell. The 'outhouse' answered. She opened the hatch and gave me five matches.

'You're old and ugly enough that I can trust you with these,' she said. 'You get a light by scratching them in the grouting between the tiles.' What things one learns as a guest in Her Majesty's prisons! Not only from overheard conversations but now this as well. I have never looked at grouting in the same way since.

Before she closed the hatch, I gave her a full packet of cigarettes to hand around to my fellow detainees. They were extremely grateful and so, with time, I began answering their questions. What was I in for? I told them.

'Ah, alcohol! That's a bitch.'

What did I do in the daytime? What a strange question, I thought. Did they lead double lives? I was an actress, I told them.

'Yea? What you been in?' they asked.

'Some films. Lots of telly,' I answered.

'Yea? Like what?'

I listed some of the programmes – *The Adventurer, Rivals of Sherlock Homes, Napoleon and Love* and more. They had seen everything I'd done, making comments about hairstyles, costume and even the plot. I decided they must lead double lives after all, thieving in the daytime and studying the television at night.

We were given something to eat through our hatch at about six in the evening. It was disgusting: congealed baked beans, pink, fleshy, finger-like sausages, and soggy chips swimming in oil. I couldn't eat it. Half an hour later, the heavy iron door opened with a loud warning for me to stand back. Linda, her son Ben, and Marlowe were ushered in. Knowing Linda, she would have called everyone I knew about my predicament but I was, nevertheless, surprised to see Marlowe. We had started amicable divorce proceedings which would take two years before the *decree nisi* would be issued. But I was touched that he had bothered to come. It was sweet how they worried about me. The door slammed shut behind them.

'Peter's really sorry but there's nothing he can do as far as a magistrate is concerned,' Linda said, handing over a warm brown paper bag. Inside it was half a roast chicken and chips. Very knowingly, she said, 'Food is rubbish in these places. We thought we'd get you something decent. The big woman rifled through it, though. I guess they're afraid we'd have smuggled some arms in it.' Then she added, as an afterthought, 'but her hands looked pretty clean.'

I was happy for that. The smell of the chicken was giving me an appetite.

Ben, who was only 14 at the time, dug into a jacket pocket and lifted from it a quarter-size bottle of cognac. They hadn't bothered to search him.

They were only allowed to stay for a few minutes. When I was alone, I sat on the bunk and ate some of the chicken and nibbled on a few chips. I took a swig of cognac but it wasn't my favourite drink. How was I going to get rid of the bottle? As it had been smuggled in against the law, I could hardly call the wardress to share it around with the other women. Eventually, it was hidden under the U-bend behind the toilet. I hoped I wouldn't get another visit from the police, charging me with possession of contraband during my stay in the cell.

That night, I couldn't sleep at all. The bare bulb glared down at me relentlessly and the hatch was opened several times with loud metallic clicks.

In the morning, I got to meet my neighbours. We were all transferred in a small bus to the court in Marylebone. As they considered me a celebrity, the women begged me to go to the press and reveal the inhuman conditions they were made to suffer during their arrest and when in remand. I told them I didn't think the press would be interested in anything I had to say and thought to myself, 'inhuman' was an exaggeration. Uncomfortable may have been more to the point. Little did I know that my short *sojourn* at her Majesty's pleasure would hit the front pages in London and the news travel all the way to Los Angeles. The reason for this 'scoop' was Peter Sellers' appearance in the public gallery of the courtroom. Linda was with him and would be called 'the unknown woman' in the papers.

There is always a journalist who hangs around with the hope of getting a story from the proceedings in the courts. A list is posted of the day's defendants. My name would have been on it as Catherine Marlowe which was not newsworthy. But when the reporter recognized Peter, he began to make some deductions; there must have been someone whose hearing was scheduled who had a connection with him. I was called and entered the courtroom. The reporter was there and listened. The magistrate asked why I had not appeared at my hearing. I answered, because I had never received the summons and explained that when the offence had taken place I was living at my Clapham address but that I had been in the process of looking for a flat to buy. It could be that I would have moved by the time the summons was issued. I had mentioned this to the officers and promised to leave a forwarding address, which I did. Not hearing anything from the police, I'd hoped perhaps there had been a glitch with the computer or, by miracle, my blood test had proved negative or been lost. I felt it was not up to me to contact the police. After all, they manage to find murderers. I had told them I was an actress and the name I was known by. Let sleeping dogs lie, I thought. It was only after I re-taxed the car giving my new address that they came to arrest me.

There had been enough publicity during the making of *The Return of the Pink Panther* that it didn't take a genius to conclude that Catherine Marlowe was Catherine Schell who had once been married to William Marlowe: *ergo* her name in her driving permit.

The magistrate allowed me four weeks to make a case for my defence and another date was made for the hearing, but the next day's papers were full of the story and that was only because Peter had wanted to give me moral support. In his mind he imagined getting up and making a speech on my behalf, defending my good character. How wonderfully amusing that would have been. He even admitted to having rehearsed something to that effect during the previous night.

The press behaved like vultures picking on a corpse. Everyone wanted a bit of flesh. I gave interviews on the doorstep or on the phone. Thinking of the poor women who had been my fellow detainees, I stupidly talked about the conditions of my stay: light on all night, deplorable food. I resisted saying there were no curtains on the windows but there weren't any windows, anyway. It was no surprise that I received a negative press, some articles asking if I'd expected caviar and Champagne. I had a manager in Hollywood for a brief time. As the incident was mentioned in a Hollywood paper, he telephoned me.

'You know, Catherine, all publicity is not necessarily good publicity. I'm trying to sell you as this elegant, aristocratic lady and you spend a night in jail because you were drunk driving a car!'

He didn't remain my manager for long and I never worked in LA.

I began to hear less and less from Peter and suspected that he had found a romantic involvement. During a visit from my brother Paul, I was invited to a film premiere with a gala dinner afterwards. The invitation was for two so Paul was thrilled to be my escort. It was the time I was still on the 'A' list. We saw the movie and when leaving, I heard my name called out by a familiar voice.

'Catherine!' It was Peter a little further up the star encrusted staircase. We waited for him to join us and, sweetly, he gave me a big hug. As he was not alone, introductions took place. I presented my brother and, he introduced us to a gorgeous young woman, Lynne Frederick. Peter asked if we were invited to the dinner. I said yes, and he suggested we share his car and his table. It was obvious he was very much in love. Also obvious was how adept the still teenage Lynne was in tying him round her little finger. Or even better said: if Peter were a guitar, she knew exactly how to pluck his strings to her advantage.

Peter's agent was the great Dennis Selinger who I had left years ago. Around our table, I heard her tell him that Dennis, who was sitting at a table across the aisle from us, was totally against their relationship. She was also part of ICM's stable and he promoted her as an innocent young woman.

'He hates the fact that we're seeing each other. He says you'll introduce me to drugs.' She was stirring better than a *saucier* in the kitchen of an exclusive French restaurant. I witnessed how upset he became, threatening to have words there and then with Dennis.

'Not now,' she purred. 'You'll ruin the party. Think of what the papers will say.'

Dennis had been his agent for years and was also a friend. In time, I was told, she managed to separate him from the people who could influence him. Even his wonderful chauffeur with whom I celebrated my thirtieth birthday because I'd kept it a secret from the production when filming *The Return* in the south of France was fired. He was more than a driver for Peter, he was a devoted friend.

I did work with him again in 1978 on a remake of *The Prisoner of Zenda* which was written as a comedy by the renowned duo, Ian La Frenais and Dick Clement, famous for their British sitcoms, *The Likely Lads, Auf Wiedersehen, Pet* etc. He was now married to Lynne and she played the starring female role. I replaced a well-known French actress who couldn't cope with the comedy lines in the English language. When entering my hotel room at Vienna's Hilton Hotel, a basket of fruit, some chocolates and flowers welcomed me. A note from Peter reading, 'So 'appy to be seeing you again – Guy Fleurnois' was attached.

When we met later that evening, he told me he had mentioned my name at the very beginning for the role and had been disappointed not to find me as part of the cast. I had re-joined ICM at that time after leaving Jean Drysdale and was being represented by a friend of mine within their offices. But I was out of work for almost a year, so I left and joined another agency called CCA. Within the first week, my new agents rang to tell me the good news that I'd been offered a film with Peter Sellers, *The Prisoner of Zenda* being filmed in Vienna. It was ironic that only after having left the agency which was involved with the pre-production and casting of the film that I should now get the part I'd been originally suggested for. I was thrilled for my new agents.

By this time, it was known Peter was suffering from heart problems. He had a pacemaker inserted and could only work for a few hours a day. I was invited once to join the two of them for dinner at a Viennese restaurant. I have to say, Lynne was always polite to me and the evening was full of humour.

Many of the scenes we appeared in 'together' were shot with me acting opposite Peter's stand-in. These were sometimes saved for the afternoons when Peter would have been taken back to the hotel. As much as he tried, the stand-in was not equal to Peter's comic timing and my reactions were not the same. But one scene I will always remember which we did do together. We were running around at night in a forest and had to signal our positions to each other. As it was at night he asks me if I can imitate the hoot of an owl. I tell him truthfully, no.

This question had come up with the director. There was no way I could do an owl. He asked me which bird noise I was capable of. I told him, I was pretty good at chickens. He asked me to give a sample. I did. He was impressed, and that's why Peter and I, in our 18th century costumes, wander about amongst the trees on a moonlit night clucking like chickens.

Some people told me that they were not too impressed with the rest of the film but the squawking chickens in the woods was a classic.

CHAPTER XVII

It was Sunday. I was invited to friends for lunch. Normally, I would have hung around afterwards to chat but on this occasion something niggled at me to go home. There wasn't a reason other than I felt I needed to be within my own four walls. As I left, my hostess who was also an actress, called after me, 'Your agent won't ring! No-one gets a job on a Sunday!'

She was a lousy clairvoyant. Within minutes of my arrival, the telephone rang. It was Jean.

'Catherine, I've just received a phone call from Gerry Anderson. Are you free tonight? He wants to talk to you about a part in the second series of *Space: 1999*.'

I told her I was free.

'I'll ring him right back and you afterwards.' She hung up. In my excitement, I had just the time to light a cigarette before the phone rang again.

'He'll send a car to pick you up at seven.'

The neighbours were treated again to the sight of an expensive car gliding up to the entrance of my house and a chauffeur with cap and white gloves walking to the door to ring the bell. He drove me 20 or 30 miles out of London to a restaurant in a village on the river Thames where the head waiter escorted me to a table. Gerry stood up to greet me and I was invited to sit down. The restaurant had a very formal feel to it. 'As it's quite late, I thought we could eat and talk at the same time. I hope you don't mind,' he said.

'Not at all,' I answered. A menu was placed in my hands. It was a 'lady's menu', without the prices. I regretted having had lunch earlier. The choices were exquisite. A bottle of Chablis was placed into an ice bucket on the white linen tablecloth. Gerry poured me a glass and we began our conversation. He explained how, with the arrival of Freddy Freiberger from America as co-producer and writer, the second series would contain changes. Some of the original characters had been written out and others introduced. One was a female alien with extraordinary powers. Her scientific brain could function better than any computer heretofore invented by Earthlings and, more importantly, she had the ability of metamorphosis and could change molecularly into other forms of life. Her name was Maya and she would be known as the *metamorph*, a word which was unknown in the English language but was invented for the series. Fascinating, I thought, and as far as I was aware, a first. He didn't mention Tony Anholt's participation as security officer. Perhaps, no decisions concerning his role had been made yet.

'Would you be interested in such a role?' Gerry asked.

'Of course,' I replied, thinking of the possibilities.

'What about appearance? You'd have to look considerably alien.'

'I understand,' I answered, 'as long as I'm not given pointed ears like Mr Spock in *Star Trek*.'

He smiled at that and said, 'You'll have a lot to say about your make-up. Of course, Keith Wilson will still be the designer. He'll have his ideas as well.'

'Another thing...' he hesitated for a moment. 'Barbara Bain is aware that we are thinking of casting you. She and Martin have a right of veto. You are similar in type to her... blonde, tall, classy. She would prefer the role to be played by someone totally different to her.' I could understand that. It made sense. She was thinking professionally as an actress.

We had our dinner and talked some more. He mentioned that Sylvia would not be producing the series with him. There had been a separation. Gerry was the epitome of a British man: always a gentleman and utterly discreet.

I was sent back home with the chauffeur and a request. Could I do a drawing of how I saw Maya as the alien?

I couldn't wait! That night, sleep alluded me. I was too excited, thinking of the character and how she could appear on the screen. I decided, if the building blocks of existence were there – oxygen, hydrogen, carbon, nitrogen, etc. – life on another planet would not look so different to our own. She could have a similar physique with just a few differences. Everything the human body has today is the consequence of evolution and some mutation: colour of hair, skin, eyes, height. I reckoned most of these differences were determined by natural phenomena and brought about by geography, too much sun, too little sun, extreme heat, extreme cold, light, lack of light, vegetation, diet, etc. I had an idea that her planet was much older than Earth. If races ever existed, they would have intermingled. She would have a mixture of pigmentation. Maya had to look different from Barbara but her make-up should not take too long. In the next few days, I drew a picture of a face with darker pigmentation in the form of a deep widow's peak and a triangle on both cheeks which originated from her ears. The darker colour then went down from her jaw in a V across her throat, ending in a point at the middle of her clavicle. A little dark peak made a cleft in her chin. Her short hair resembled a sheep's fleece, thick, white and curly. There was something raccoon-like to her face. But what would make her truly alien were her eyes. Instead of round irises, hers were in the form of a star. If Mr Spock had pointed ears, Maya would, literally, have stars in her eyes.

I gave the picture to Gerry. Looking at it, he asked, 'You're willing to go this far?'

I told him yes.

Discussions over the contract followed between Jean and the producers. Make-up tests were scheduled. I arrived early one morning at Pinewood studios and underwent several transformations. The ideas were mainly Keith's. I was given a rainbow coloured complexion. It was a startling look but would have been difficult to copy every day and remain in continuity. Also, it took a long time to paint on. My idea, minus star spangled eyes and curly white wig was tried. The dark pigmentation making the widow's peak, shadowed cheeks, ears and neck was applied. My own hair was drawn back into an elaborate bun. Every time the make-up was finished, I went to the sound stage to be placed in front of a camera. I was not alone. A parade of women from various ethnic origins were being screen tested. Barbara and Martin were going to look at the results in the coming days. If they were testing for Maya, I felt sorry for them. I had already been told, but for contractual accords, the part was mine.

Keith directed my make-up sessions throughout and one of his particular ideas for the alien 'look' was to have several pieces of a rubbery, flesh coloured fabric placed on my face. They were cut into geometric designs and glued to my forehead, cheekbones, temples and chin. The material had small bumps, a little like pimples. Natural make-up was then applied to my own skin and on the pimples. I couldn't believe that Keith would have dreamt up this idea for a female alien who was supposed to be attractive and was going to have a flirtatious relationship with the security officer. But I had to go along with it. As I left the make-up chair to go in front of the camera, I turned to Keith and said, 'I suppose, if you want acne to become popular, it could work.' Both Barbara and Martin were horrified when they saw the test.

In the end, the make-up would be a compromise, my shadings and

Keith's bumps for my eyebrows. His excuse for their existence was that the power and ability for my molecular transformations originated from them. I don't think this was ever made clear in any of the episodes. They were referred to by me as 'octopods' because they were very akin to the underside of octopi tentacles.

The producers were keen on the iris in the form of a star but for that I would have to wear contact lenses. In this case, they would have to be 'piggyback', as the black star had to be painted on a hard lens and that, in turn, would be placed on to a soft one which would adhere to my eye. I had many meetings with ophthalmologists. With one lens on top of another, my sight was changed. It was no longer 20/20. To compensate for this, both lenses had to be prescription. My pupil was measured minutely because the centre of the star had to remain clear, otherwise, I would only see black and be blinded. I was given the final lenses with their bottles of treated water to practice wearing them and told to strictly adhere to a schedule which was something like one hour in and three hours out. It was a nerve wracking experience having to place foreign objects into eyes which had perfect vision with the result of disturbing that vision. My eyes cried profusely in defence. But I persisted to the effect that on one occasion in a restaurant, the time came for me to insert them. I excused myself from the table, having forewarned my friends for my momentary absence. I stuck the soft and then the star-painted hard lenses in my eyes. By now, I'd become quite proficient.

When returning to the table, I kept my eyes lowered. My friends had already seen me with them in on other occasions, so it wasn't shocking for them. We continued to converse as if nothing unusual had taken place. At the end of the main course, the waitress came to clear away the plates. When passing mine to her, I looked up to say 'thank you'. She dropped the whole lot on the floor and ran screaming into the kitchen. The eyes certainly made an impression. They definitely looked alien. I knew the owner of the restaurant and explained the unfortunate incident, offering to pay for the broken crockery. She was too enthralled with my eyes to accept payment. I don't recall ever seeing the waitress again when visiting the restaurant in the future.

Gerry asked me how I was getting along with the lenses. The production had scheduled a film test with me wearing them. I told him I was ready. I couldn't admit to being one hundred percent comfortable but I was sure, with time, it would be the case. Once again, on the same sound stage, I was placed in front of a camera. Everyone was very impressed. The story of the waitress had done its rounds. The lights went on and were directed towards my face. The camera rolled silently. I was told to move my head from one side to the other and then look directly into the camera. My eyes began crying so much, it was a miracle the lenses didn't swim out.

'Cut!' The camera man stopped. 'Are you all right?' I was asked. My eyes were shut, tears streaming down my face.

'I think it's the lights,' I said. 'My eyes are very sensitive to light.' We tried again to no avail. Every time a light was shone into my face, I wept. It was a good idea but with my peculiar sensitivity, it couldn't work. I could just about take bright lights for a close-up but with foreign objects in my eyes it became too irritating. The production invested a lot of money for the lenses and I felt very guilty. On the other hand, had my eyes suffered any damage, a law suit could have followed. I'm pretty sure this is where the idea for Maya's transformations originated, to appear first as a close up in the pupils of her eyes. And no... the eyes you see on the screen for that effect are not mine. We tried but once again, I failed them, so a model was hired for that well-lit, extremely close photography.

I had not yet signed the definitive contract. Jean had established a fee. English actors worked on our union, Equity, contracts. We did not have the advantages of American agreements. There were lawyers, nevertheless, who, even in Britain, specialized in show-biz negotiations. I mentioned to Jean, as this was an important series with all manner of possibilities, that, perhaps, I should speak to a lawyer.

'No, dearie, you don't want to do that. It would put people's backs up,' was her reply. I was still innocent enough to take her advice.

My fee was ridiculously low but camouflaged by the third extra in lieu of repeats. Only if the series was networked in the US would we ever earn again from its sales or on the third showing by a British network. It was never shown on a network in America but had multiple syndications. The British actors did not receive a cent from America. It took 30 years, until a company which had something to do with Michael Jackson bought the rights, before we Brits received a payment. I was notified by an ex-agent, John French, who had a client on *Space*. He rang up to tell me that these payments were being made to his actor and that if I wanted, he'd negotiate on my behalf without the usual ten percent demand. John had looked after Bill Hays and me for a while. By the time he rang, Bill and I had moved to France and we were very grateful for the phone call.

The first contract that Jean sent on to me was returned without my signature. I knew enough arithmetic to calculate that if I was to appear in 24 episodes, each taking two weeks to film, but the time stipulated in the contract was only 42 weeks, and I was being paid weekly, it meant that some episodes were being filmed back to back. I demanded payment for 24 episodes. A new contract, more correct, was issued.

I had a problem with transport. As I had lost my license, I no longer had a car. Pinewood studios is a good 30 miles from where I was living. On what I was earning, I could not have afforded taxis. The production office did not want to give me a chauffeur driven car. That was not what I was asking for, I told them. They were given a choice: either I would ride my horse to work or they could lay on a unit car with the understanding that it was not exclusively available for me but would pick me up in the morning and take me home at night. They were horrified at the idea of me riding down the M4 motorway to get to the studios, so, it was agreed that a young driver called Steve would chauffeur me when required. He was an excellent driver, very helpful, and became a confidante. When finally my year of exclusion from the driving classes came to an end, it was Steve who found the perfect car for me to buy. After putting it through its paces and finding it 'useful', he negotiated a price for me.

'You can't go there yourself,' he said. 'They may recognize you and put up the price.'

After I finished work, he drove me to the address. I stayed in the car and gave him the cash. He handed the notes over to the sellers, received the keys and papers which he then gave to me and that night I drove home with my newly issued driving license in a Bermuda-yellow coloured Mini 125, the one with the longer bonnet. It had a black sun roof and smoked windows. I found it very racy in every sense. The best thing was, the producers remained ignorant of my purchase and Steve continued to drive me.

There was one other hiccup with the contract which was resolved after I'd already begun working. Once again, Jean had not advised me as she should have. I was going to appear in an expensive Anglo-American series with innovative and well-designed special effects. Our Eagle spaceships were crying out to be sold as models. Our lunar mobiles (my name for them) could be sold in miniature kits for children. There was going to be a business around merchandising. It was obvious but nowhere in the contract was there a sentence that I would have a stake in these sales. I imagined, correctly, Maya dolls. I can't remember exactly who it was that talked to me about it. Was it Martin Landau? He was very aware of the differences between the American and British contracts and gave advice accordingly. I had nothing to lose, so asked Jean to negotiate. She was, as usual, very hesitant. To the credit of Gerry Anderson, he complied and I was given a small percentage of his merchandising profits. I was also told I'd probably never see a penny, which until very recently remained true.

There was a moment well into the filming when I had a meeting with Gerry and Freddy Freiberger. I liked Freddy. He was a warm, friendly person, almost paternal. We had something in common, we sympathised with each other. I have no idea how this conversation was broached but both of us had ear problems as children which followed us throughout our lives. We were very prone to ear infections. I mentioned the scars I had behind both my ears which came as a result of an operation to remove the mastoid bone. I was still a baby in Budapest. My parents' connections at the American embassy procured penicillin for me to deal with the constant infections but, alas, an intervention became necessary. I'm sure that he told me that, he too, had had his mastoids removed.

At the meeting, I was told that a spin-off series on the character of Maya was being considered and was highly likely to be realised. Obviously, I was very excited.

'Now we're going to give you some advice,' Gerry said and Freddy nodded. They both looked earnestly at me.

'Yes?' I said cautiously.

Gerry continued. 'If the spin-off becomes a reality, you're really going to have to change your agent. You'll need a more powerful person, someone who can negotiate terms to your advantage. You should also see a lawyer. And this is the enemy speaking.'

Freddy nodded in agreement and then said, 'We were perfectly aware that it was you who stipulated the corrections in your contract.'

In a way, I was already having doubts about Jean's capabilities. It was a cruel place for her to be, having launched someone's career and then, not being able to deal with their success. I had grown fond of her and was going to find the severance very difficult but I was not her only client in the same predicament. There were other matters which determined my final decision.

It was a matter of repeats. In every contract one signs as an actor there is a clause that any residuals received from further sales of the programme would be paid directly to the agent who had negotiated the deal. It was up to the agent, after retaining their percentage, to forward the remaining amount to the actor concerned. I had been receiving phone calls from my parents in Munich telling me they had just been watching me on their television screen. Acquaintances from other European countries and even Americans were sending me magazine clippings from various programmes being currently shown on their TVs. I'd always wait a while before ringing Jean in the anticipation that she'd have sent me a cheque with the statement of the company and programme. When after a considerable time had passed, I'd finally pick up the phone and each time I'd be given the same excuse: she did her accounts on the Friday of every week and on that particular Friday after having received the payment, she was suffering from a flu. It was a matter of a simple oversight and she would send a cheque immediately. It was amazing how often she was struck down with a flu, severe colds or bronchitis.

As things turned out, there was never a Maya spin-off. After the completion of the series, I was invited to lunch with Jean. A friend of mine, who had been a producer and was joining ICM as an agent, persuaded me to become a client of his. Perhaps, I should have waited for the coffee to tell her of my intentions but I thought it only fair to broach the subject at the point when she could have walked out of the restaurant and not been obliged to pay. I was there on her invitation and felt very guilty. So, while the menus were still in our hands, I told her that I was leaving. She turned ashen. I'd never seen anyone change colour so quickly and, for a moment, was terrified she'd fall off her chair in a faint. But she recovered and we had our meal. The atmosphere between us was somewhat cooled. She asked me why and I told her it was mostly to do with her reluctance to stand up to producers. I said all I had to say, as diplomatically as I had been brought up to do, and never mentioned the repeats she had held on to until I rang her about them. That would have been an accusation of dishonesty and I didn't want to believe that about her.

Not very long after having left her, I received an instruction from Inland Revenue to present myself for a meeting with a named tax inspector to be questioned about my latest income declarations. This always puts the fear of God into actors. We are not very good at keeping accounts. I had become a company when beginning the filming of *Space* and had a wonderful woman, Peggy Thompson, who took charge of all my bookkeeping and a sympathetic, kind and patient accountant,

Ronald Parker, who worked with her for her clients, all of whom came from show business. Ronald accompanied me to the interview. As far as I was concerned, my declarations were honest. I had never earned cash. All payments were received via my agent and after the retention of the obligatory 10 percent were sent on to Peggy who put an amount into my private account, keeping the majority for the company which paid the mortgage, the taxes and all deductible bills, etc. Her bookkeeping was pristine. We, her clients, were not allowed to even touch the company account. She held the cheque book. We were allowed a credit card but only on our private account. The statements would be perused with a magnifying glass and if there were payments made that she could legitimately claim as 'business', our private accounts would be reimbursed.

For this reason, Ronald and I were surprised that the inspector asked me where the extra £900 had come from which had not been declared. I couldn't give him an answer but assured him, all payments came via my agent. If there was an amount missing, I couldn't have received it. I told him, as he knew there were monies undeclared, he would also know the source they had come from. All British companies had to present their accounts and payments to actors would be amongst the information. He played it cleverly, perhaps in the hope I'd confess to a forgotten cash payment for opening a supermarket or some such thing celebrities were often called on to do. I assured him it was not the case and must have convinced him because, although, he never divulged where the extra amount came from, he settled on my giving him a cheque for one third of the outstanding claim which was equal to the unpaid tax on the £900. It was either that or a re-examination for the past seven years. After the cheque was in his possession, he enquired about a particular business claim: the plane tickets for my trips to Munich. I explained, I had an agent (Steffie) who looked after my career on the continent.

'Why are there no hotel bills?' he asked.

'Because I stay with my parents in Munich,' I replied.

'So, these are not private visits?' I was asked.

'Sometimes, yes, but you won't have the tickets for those. My agent feels she can set up interviews for me knowing I can live with my parents.'

He accepted this statement of events and became extremely helpful.

'Do your parents have a car?' he asked.

'No. My father can't drive anymore,' I told him.

'So, how do you get to your interviews?'

'I catch taxis.'

'I don't see any receipts for those,' he said, looking through the folder.

'Because I didn't know I could claim,' I said and then he became even more helpful. Ronald, my accountant, sat quietly listening intently to the proceedings.

'Are taxis expensive in Munich?'

'I suppose only a little cheaper than in London.'

'How many would you take?' He was leading me and I followed his cue.

'Oh... three interviews... there and back... six cabs.'

He wrote it down. 'What about your agent? Surely you would have invited her to a restaurant.'

Usually it's the other way around but I nodded knowingly in agreement. 'Yes, of course.'

'And restaurants in Munich? Are they expensive?'

I was well primed by now. 'Yes... exactly like London.'

He wrote that down. I don't remember if my tax for that particular year, after the initial £300 cheque, was less because of my Munich expenses but he had told me I could claim for transport and restaurants in the future and I should keep my receipts.

Ronald and I went afterwards to a pub to celebrate. The goodwill we had been shown by the inspector was invaluable.

Peggy Thompson wrote an official letter to Jean mentioning the inspection and stating that monies received for me had not been declared and ordered her to search through her accounts for any repeats or residuals still owing. If further payment was not forthcoming she would set the Inland Revenue hounds upon her as well as denouncing her to Equity which would risk her losing her agent's license.

One week later, Peggy received a cheque for the amount of £2,000.

CHAPTER XVIII

I am so often asked by fans of *Space*, what it was like working on the programme. The reply is: it was one of the happiest years of my life. Perhaps, that's why it's difficult to write about it. Conflict makes for interesting stories and there was very little conflict on the show. People want to know if Barbara and I got along. I think they'd like to hear that we fought like cats and scratched each other's eyes out. I have to disappoint them. We had a very cordial working relationship. I was told she had some clauses in her contract which pertained to me. I was never to appear out of the Maya persona as myself. So, when receiving the script for 'The Beta Cloud', I was surprised to read a scene towards the end of the episode where Tony Verdeschi is recovering from an injury and lying in bed in Alpha's infirmary. To amuse himself, he is paging through some old magazines from Earth. Maya enters the ward to give him a visit and notices his interest for a particular page. There is a glamorous publicity shot of a woman who is an actress. He shows Maya the page. It is a picture of me. Maya is not impressed with whom she sees and when leaving, she transforms into Catherine Schell, making a remark about some people having poor taste and walks out in a jealous huff. I wondered how this scene was allowed to remain. It didn't for long. Another script was issued for the story and the part of the scene where I turn into myself was cut.

At the end of most episodes there is a shot of one of the cast which becomes frozen and lasts a few seconds. Obviously, Martin and Barbara had the majority of these stills which establish the end of the programme. Zienia Merton, Nick Tate, Tony Anholt all had their moment. Not a single episode ended on a mug shot of Maya. Was this also in a clause of Barbara's contract? It didn't matter, though. The only important thing was the atmosphere on the set and that was pleasant.

There are always times between scenes on a set that can last a good few moments. Instead of disappearing back into my dressing room, I would often remain in the studio under some lights and either read a book or do English cryptic crossword puzzles. I read the *Guardian* newspaper and on the back page was such a puzzle. They were invented by different setters who assumed a pseudonym, the most famous of whom was Araucaria and the most evil was Bunthorne. It takes time to understand the devious clues which make nonsense sentences with every word, a code in itself. The greatest requirement for solving them is the ability to think laterally. Achievement takes extreme concentration and Barbara noticed my nose in the paper, pen poised and brow furrowed. She, too, had discovered these enigmas and became fascinated with them. I began to help her decode the hidden messages in the clues. She would arrive in the morning, smiling proudly having filled in a few of the answers but, eventually, she became very adept. People who can't do the cryptic crossword and are envious of those who can often say, 'You don't have to be intelligent to solve them.'

I tend to reply, 'But it helps.'

It must have been while struggling with one of these puzzles and having my eyes lowered that someone quietly entered the studio and stood up against the wall out of the light, keeping his presence discreet. When thinking for the answer, I raised my eyes and saw this person lurking in the shadow, watching what was happening on the set. A strange thought entered my head. As I studied him, he seemed vaguely familiar but I was sure there was something wrong with his ears. They didn't stand out, they weren't too large and then it struck me: they weren't pointed. I recognized him then. It was Leonard Nimoy! He had come as Martin's guest. They were friends in LA and I was eventually introduced. Tall, very good looking in an un-macho way, he oozed sensitivity. I remember a charming smile. We conversed for a few moments. He was impressed with my alien make-up and then I was called for a scene. He left shortly thereafter. Much later, I noticed his billing as director on films and regretted never having worked for him. I'm sure it would have been a joy.

Martin had a wonderful sense of humour. He could make me laugh to the point that my make-up girl would sometimes have to drag me away to correct the damage inflicted by the mascara seeping down my cheeks caused by uncontrollable tears brought on by laughter.

The most memorable moment that we shared in hilarity was when the two of us happened to be watching one of the monsters Maya had turned into being disrobed of its costume. Sitting in our canvas chairs, we both looked on quietly, absorbed by the sight. Two dressers from the wardrobe department were unzipping, unbuttoning, removing Velcro from the huge furry costume to liberate the person within it. The monster was so tall that a step ladder was used to assist the dresser who had to remove the grotesque, enlarged head from the shoulders that were more than a metre wide. The entire effect was of an extra-terrestrial King Kong. The head, more gargoyle than ape, was lifted off and the costume unzipped and peeled away to reveal the person inside. Martin and I burst out laughing. Without a word said between us, we were struck with the same sense of the absurd. The enormous stunt man who had been hidden inside had an uncanny resemblance to the monster costume he'd been wearing. We didn't see the need for the elaborate disguise. The first assistant told us politely to either pull ourselves together or leave the studio. We made an exit still doubled up with laughter.

Laughing between scenes could be a pain for the make-up department but it was not as bad as corpsing within a scene. Unlike Blake Edwards, the producers of *Space* did not schedule extra time for it. Directors were under pressure to have the required amount of minutes in the can at the end of the day. Laughing fits were not appreciated. I'm afraid I was a naughty girl when filming the episode 'All that Glisters'. Ray Austin, the director, had some difficulties but not only with me. Patrick Mower, who was guest-starring as a geologist, Nick Tate, Martin and I found the storyline such a stretch of the imagination that it was hardly possible to speak the lines without giggling.

Having left Helena and Tony behind on Alpha, we landed on a bleak, stony planet for a geological survey searching for a mineral called milgonite. Communication between us and Helena remained open. Our sometimes frantic dialogue consisted of such memorable lines as, 'Maybe the rock is angry.'

Martin showed his thespian prowess by managing to state with conviction, 'That rock has energy, intelligence and purpose.'

At one point, Maya turns into the rock in order to communicate with it. When she transforms into herself again, she says, 'The rock refused to co-operate.' It took a long time to get that line out with a straight face.

Back on Alpha, Helena tells us, 'The rock has control of Tony.'

'Maybe when they panic, they behave like humans.'

She is then held hostage by the rock. We can hear her say, 'It's moving around, exploring our storage supplies... and fixed itself to the water supply.'

It turned out the rocks needed water. Well they would, wouldn't they? So, before disappearing out of the planet's orbit, we kind Alphans sprinkled rain-making granules into the dense cloud-cover hovering above it. Within a minute, a torrential downpour took place and the rocks happily soaked up the liquid and glowed in satisfaction. Well, they would, wouldn't they?

In 1976, England enjoyed an uncommon heatwave and then suffered a drought. I remember many of us ironically coming down with colds.

It was decided by the producers in England and America that I would be sent to the States on a publicity tour. I was given some time off from filming and a budget to buy a glamorous outfit for my TV appearances and to purchase a set of stylish suitcases – so I wouldn't feel disgraced when bellboys carried my luggage up to the suite reserved for me in my five star hotel. I was told I'd be flying first class.

I have mentioned my stepson, Ben, who kindly smuggled in the quarter-bottle of Cognac when I was imprisoned in my Paddington cell. We got along really well. I loved his sensitive, warm and humorous company. For a 16 year old, he was not yet showing the underside of adolescence. I suggested to the producers that instead of a first class ticket, I was prepared to fly economy if they also paid for Ben's fare. The hotel suite was no problem as there was usually a little spare bedroom. If not, he could always sleep on the sofa of the living area. We would be flying into New York, staying there for three nights and then on to Los Angeles. Ben had a school friend there and would stay with him until he needed to come back to England to start the autumn term. The friend's mother, Nina (from Nina and Frederik, a popular singing duo from the Sixties) would organize his return trip.

I don't remember the name of the hotel we stayed at in New York but it was very old-time classy. We were shown to our suite and I barely had time to unpack when the telephone rang. One of the reasons I'd wanted to bring Ben was so that he could act as my assistant and be my chaperone. I asked him to answer. He looked at me, panic stricken.

'It's all right,' I told him. 'They speak English here.'

He lifted the receiver and said a hesitant, 'Hello'.

The next thing I knew, I was holding a telephone to my ear and listening to a deep, melodic female voice with just a hint of a foreign accent asking me if I was Catherine Schell.

'Yes,' I said, intrigued.

'I am Maria Schell,' I heard her say. Oh my God! I was speaking to one of my favourite actresses.

'I think I have received flowers which were intended for you,' she said.

I had to admit I had been a little surprised that there was nothing to welcome me in the suite. That was unusual.

'There is a note attached to a Miss Schell, but from a production company that I have never heard of. I have known about you and wondered if there was not a confusion, so I telephoned the desk and asked, by chance, if there was not a Catherine Schell booked into another room. They told me yes, so I will send your bouquet down to your room.'

'Thank you, thank you!' I said in a grovelling tone.

'Would you like to come up to my room for a drink?' she asked.

I'd have climbed the Empire State Building to get there. Ben was too shy to accompany me, so I took the lift alone and knocked on her suite door.

It was 1976. Maria would have been 50. She had a beauty which radiated from the inside. Her face completely matched the balmy, gentle voice with which she spoke. She had generous, kind features. Even her startlingly blue eyes, normally a prerequisite for actors playing Nazis, exuded warmth.

We spoke about our common name. She, her brother Maximilian, the other siblings Carl and Immy, as well as her mother had become aware of my existence when *Lana: Queen of the Amazons* was being launched in the cinemas, creating press publicity. Of course, in Germany my name, Schell, had a von in front of it. I explained it was to differentiate me from them.

She asked why I hadn't taken up the offer from her mother to join the repertory company she ran in a small Zurich theatre. The mother had rung Steffie after reading about me in the papers with the offer of a six month contract. I told Maria, I was only 20 at that time and Steffie had heard of the in-house director. He was not the most pleasant of people and she was afraid I would not be able to cope. I had argued with Steffie that it would be good for my experience. I'd be doing 'rep' but she was adamant and she was right. After my nightmare on *Lana* I was still too green to stand up to a tyrannical director and would have really given up the business.

Oddly enough, their family name and ours had originated from the same part of Germany called Schwaben, only our side had been ennobled in the 18th century. In the very distant past, we would have been related. I'd spent a delightful hour and was privileged to have met her.

While in New York I was asked to have interviews with reporters at breakfast and lunch. Having been taught not to speak with my mouth full, very little food reached my stomach, as most of the questions required long answers.

I was taken to dinner by the American backers and met Truman Capote. He joined us at our table. We were in the original Joe Allen's. I listened, fascinated by his squeaky voice expounding on his book, *In Cold Blood,* which I had avidly read. I regretted not having it with me for his signature. I don't think he'd ever have remembered me. My awed silence of the great writer would not have made an impression.

Poor Ben was back in the suite during my outings but he was happy over-dosing on American television, Coca-Cola and hamburgers delivered to him by room service. We flew together to LA where he was picked up by his friend and Nina.

An appearance on the Johnny Carson show had been scheduled for me but it was not Johnny who hosted that evening. Perhaps, the cast list was not interesting enough for the great presenter to trouble himself. Never mind, I walked on the stage in a glamorous dress, bought for me by *Space*. The host for that night was charming and the audience clapped enthusiastically on my entrance. They also laughed at witticisms made by the host or sometimes by me. It all went splendidly well and I never saw the directions given to the audience on large cards reading, 'Clap! and/or Laugh!'

I left Ben in LA which had been the plan. On my way back to New York, I made a quick stop in Chicago to visit a friend of my brother Paul from the Munich days, Voya Skakic. He had become president of the third biggest PR firm in the US and had arranged an appearance on a talk show for me in the windy city. Uri Geller, an Israeli magician whose speciality was bending metal by thought alone was also a guest and I witnessed him warp a house key placed in the host's pocket. When retrieved at the end of the show, it was intriguingly bent and made useless for opening doors.

I'd kept in contact with Ben, making sure all was well and learned that he was anxious to return with me to England. His friend was no longer the same boy he had known and he felt uncomfortable staying in LA. He was afraid of being overheard and spoke in a sort of code on the phone, leaving lengthy silences which I had to fill with questions that he could answer to with 'yes' or 'no'. I spoke to Nina with the excuse that Ben had to return earlier because there was shopping to be done which we had forgotten about, for uniforms and sports gear before the beginning of the Stowe term. She made all the arrangements for Ben to meet me in New York and we flew back with Air India who upgraded us into first class. The production company had booked all of our flights with Air India whenever possible. They were probably cheaper than other better known western airlines and every time, they kindly upgraded us.

We shared the first class fuselage with a Maharishi whose adoring followers were mostly in economy class but that did not stop them from visiting and kneeling in supplication to him in the centre aisle. As far as I remember, the Maharishi only sat belted up in a seat during take-off and landing. The rest of the time, he sat cross-legged wherever his widely separated knees found place. The crew acquiesced to all of his needs and his acolytes murmured sweet sounding prayers around him. Ben and I studied this in fascination and accepted all the Champagne the beautiful stewardesses offered. As we approached Heathrow, we flew over an unrecognisable English landscape. Instead of an emerald green carpet, due to sufficient rain, we flew over a brown, lifeless straw matting. To assuage any complaints we might have made against the Maharishi's followers invading our space, we had been told that he was coming expressly to England to pray for rain. I was not tempted to join Hinduism, but the very next day the skies released a deluge and England became once more a green and pleasant land.

Back in the studio, filming had continued. I had no idea how successful my American excursion with interviews and television appearances had been but I don't think I disgraced myself. The producers had been generous and I hoped I had earned them the publicity the programme needed and deserved.

Peter Medak directed two episodes, 'Space Warp' and 'The Seance Spectre'. When I saw him for the first time on the set, there was something familiar about him. He was tall, fair haired and had blue eyes in a round face with high cheekbones. He could have been my brother. When he opened his mouth and spoke Draculese, I knew he was a fellow Magyar. But he differed to most Hungarians I had known. They were temperamental, explosive with uncontained personalities. Peter was so laid back he could have been carried around on a stretcher. I adored him and his wife, the excellent actress Carolyn Seymour. We three would become close friends.

I listened in fascination as Peter told me his story. He escaped from

Hungary as a young man during the 1956 uprising when Russian tanks were marauding over Budapest streets. I was 12 years old at that time picketing the Russian Consulate in New York with my mother and clutching a board on a pole which read 'Children Killers' in blood red paint. He described an account relating to his escape. In the carriage of the train he had boarded which would take him near to the Austrian frontier was a man holding a metal hammer attached to a long wooden handle. The Hungarian border guards were sympathetic to the masses fleeing but one could never be sure. Had they been given orders to shoot, they would have done so. The train stopped and all the escapees leapt off it and ran helter-skelter to cross a little river whose far bank lead to a hole in the barbed wire previously cut by other refugees. Peter looked back at the man. He was calmly walking forward on the track while tapping the rails with his hammer as if he was testing them. Tap... tap... tap he continued until he had crossed the border because the railway line went through to Austria without any impediment. It did go between the huts of the frontier guards but what were they going to say to a track inspector doing his job? His method was an example of *chutzpah* and simplicity.

There is another story Peter told me which has remained a vivid picture in my mind. His family were Jewish and they lived in a Jewish part of Budapest. Towards the end of the war the Nazis began seriously to round up the Jews for deportation. The apartment block the family lived in was built around an interior courtyard which was entered through an archway. The front door of all the flats opened up onto an exterior walkway which ran the length of every floor and was connected by zigzag metal stairs reaching from one level to the next.

The family had sat down to a lunch of bean soup at their kitchen table when they could hear the sound of trucks screeching to a stop in the courtyard beneath. Soldiers were shouting in German and their boots stomped along the lower walkways. Rifle butts crashed against doors and people, screaming, were dragged from their homes. The family leapt up from the table and ran out of a back door which opened on to an interior staircase to the basement and then on to the street, out of view of the soldiers. They escaped into the countryside where a friendly family looked after them. At the end of the war, Peter and his family went back to their apartment. They entered their home. Nothing had been touched. All was in place as they had left it. Even the bean soup, congealed and cracked like dry cement, remained in the plates. The slices of bread, rock hard, were scattered on the table top. Peter was a young boy at the time but has never forgotten that sight.

At the beginning of the filming, Martin and Barbara encouraged me to go to 'rushes'. At the end of every working day, yesterday's developed but unedited takes would be shown in a little theatre. Martin and Barbara religiously attended these little sessions. They were so serious about it, they even took notes. I told them I so hated to see myself on the screen that it was more prudent for me not to go. But I was told I'd learn so much. In order to prove that I, too, was professional, I relented and joined them one evening. It was torture. What was I supposed to learn? Everything I saw myself do was wrong but I couldn't make the demands of reshooting those scenes. I was learning that I had a lousy, boring voice and my delivery of lines was atrociously amateur. There was not a single angle of my face which was photogenic and I was best captured from the back of my head. Botox did not exist at that time, so I had no possibility of paralyzing the nerves that worked the facial muscles in order to calm the gymnastics my expression lines were exercising during my close-ups.

Anne-Marie Hanschke had tried to stop me from moving my face too much as I was delivering loving lines to an ashtray or a plant in her little apartment. My mother was known to slap me when I furrowed my brow. From a woman who was incapable of lifting her eyebrows, I was told I'd appreciate the slap in later years when I would have a miraculously smooth forehead. Nothing worked.

At the end of these torture sessions, I'd be asked if I had enjoyed what I had seen. I could only tell them that their performances were marvellous. Eventually, they noticed the depression I'd arrive in the following morning and it was agreed that, for me, it was best to stay away.

Martin and Barbara would both go on to win awards for their film performances. But I witnessed an Oscar winning performance of Martin's in an Italian restaurant. Bill Hays and I had become an item, albeit secretly, but everyone in the business was aware of our relationship. He was still married but spent more time in London than at his home in Kent. This was mainly due to his work as a director.

Bill was going to be in London for his birthday. I suggested that we celebrate it with Martin and Barbara at our favourite Italian restaurant, La Famiglia. I would pay. So it was that the four of us sat around a table in animated conversation and eating wonderful food. I can't remember why Martin decided to show us a transformation. He wanted to prove, without any aids like trick photography or make-up, it was possible to change from Dr Jekyll into Mr Hyde just by expression alone. It was incredible. We witnessed the pleasant, intelligent face of Dr Jekyll slowly develop into the menacing, demented monster, Mr Hyde. The entire transformation took, perhaps, five minutes. Bill and I looked on, spell-bound. Without the slightest artifice Martin managed his metamorphosis only with the manipulation of his facial muscles.

I bet he wasn't slapped as a boy for making wrinkles on his forehead.

CHAPTER XIX

I loved my little flat in Gowan Avenue but I also loved buying pictures, some from artist acquaintances or just from galleries. My taste in art is not *avant garde.* A painting from Francis Bacon would give me nightmares. I like to feel comfortable gazing at the images on my walls but have developed enough maturity to avoid the fluffy puppies or kittens with their cute little heads sticking out over a *trompe l'oeil* wickerwork basket. When I ran out of wall space to enjoy my acquisitions, it was time to move.

Linda and I had made friends with our mortgage broker. It was not easy as an actress to get a mortgage but Dennis Bernard could manage it for us. I told him I was looking for a larger flat and asked if he could arrange a loan. Not only was he optimistic but also sure he knew the very person who would buy my flat. I managed on my few days off from the series, or on other days when I finished work early, to look at properties. My flat had been bought for £10,500 and I placed it on the market at £13,500, not a bad profit for a year and a half but prices were rising. Dennis sent me the prospective buyer, a young woman of Scottish descent. She knew how to negotiate. I had to settle for £13,000 and pay half towards repairing some damp in the bathroom. But by that time I'd made an offer for an apartment that the bijou Fulham flat could have fitted into the enormous 540 square foot living room alone. I couldn't believe the price for this spacious, elegant flat conversion consisting of the lower and upper ground floors on the left side of a double-fronted Edwardian building. The living room had high walls with the original rosette in the centre of the ceiling and an elaborately carved frieze running along the top of the four walls. Light entered by three huge windows placed in an alcove or bay. Above the picture rail on the opposite wall of the windows was a row of lovely little leaded lights. The entrance hall still had its original stained glass window and its multi-coloured Art Nouveau stone tiles. I couldn't complain about my flat going for £13,000 as I was only paying £3,000 more for this three-bedroomed palace. The reason for the price being so low was that it had housed squatters who had left it in a deplorable state and an exterior wall which ran down the length of the stairs to the lower floor was black with fungus. I wasn't afraid. Every problem was surmountable. I'd made friends with a couple of blokes who had done the decorating at Gowan Avenue. They'd have a lucrative job at 1 Challoner Crescent. I was going to leave a little tree lined street with workmen's cottages on both sides of the road to a more built-up area in West Kensington, known as a rather shabby bedsit land. The outside has never been important for me. I don't live there. I live inside my walls and it's up to me to make them pleasing.

But there was one problem: I was not yet divorced from William Marlowe. We had agreed on a 'do it yourself' divorce with a two-year separation and the filling in of legal forms by ourselves. In those days, although much easier than his and Linda's had been, a reason still had to be stated. In our case I allowed him to divorce me on the grounds of desertion and never used the incriminating photograph with the black eye. He had actually visited a lawyer who told him that I could be sued for alimony, as I had been the one who had earned most of our income. To his credit, he declined the suggestion.

Marlowe was now living with another woman, more his age and certainly more his sexual fantasy. She had a much more rounded silhouette than either Linda or me and darker skin with luxurious coal black hair. It was not her name but I always referred to her as Fatima.

All actors are superstitious. We rarely talk about prospective jobs because we're terrified that, by doing so, we would be cursed and the part would not materialize. At this point, in my case, it was a matter of a signature on a piece of paper which would determine my future. I chose my priority. The flat was more important than the divorce. Thus, until Challoner Crescent became a reality, I held back with my signature on the divorce documents. They remained in a drawer out of sight.

One day, after work, my phone rang. I answered but there was no-one on the line. I hung up and the phone rang again. This time I could hear, between my hellos, someone sobbing. Then the line went dead. Just then, Linda had come home and before going up the stairs to her flat, she opened my door to greet me. I told her of the strange calls I'd been getting. At that point, the phone sounded again. It was Linda who picked it up and listened. She, too, heard the sobbing and hastily hung up. Turning to me, she said she was sure she knew who it was.

'It's Fatima! She's been desperate that you sign the divorce papers. We've got to go to her house. I think she's done something silly.' Because of their son, Linda kept in contact with Marlowe and was familiar with what was going on in that relationship.

We were in Fulham and had to make our way to Teddington. During the half hour drive, Linda explained that Fatima was not always stable. She could be prone to taking an overdose, especially if she and Marlowe had had an argument. As far as Linda knew, he had never been violent with her. She was a big girl and, if anything, it may have been the other way around. I liked the idea of the 'biter being bitten'.

It was dark when we arrived at the bottom of their pathway. Light glowed dimly through the ground floor windows. As we neared the front door, we noticed it was slightly ajar. Linda gently pushed the door open while calling out a 'Hello!' There was no reply. I'd never been to the place before. I had no reason to do so but Linda knew the house well. She had gone there several times to speak to Marlowe about Ben and even had the dubious experience of having been thrown out of it. I allowed her to lead me into the living room. My eyes were immediately drawn to a candle flickering on an improvised altar. A photograph of Fatima's husband, Roger Delgado, who had died two years previously was placed against the lower shelf of a bookcase. He had been an actor, famous for his interpretation of an arch villain in the *Doctor Who* series. A note written by her extolling his virtues and her undying love for him was laid across an altar cloth strewn with flowers from her garden. It had not been terribly long ago that this shrine had been assembled as the candle was only half way burnt down and the flowers were not yet limp.

Fatima was known to imbibe a lethal cocktail of vodka and sleeping pills. I said to Linda, who was still calling out to alert anyone there of our presence, that I'd go into the kitchen to search for an empty bottle of vodka and whatever pill jars I could find. She said she'd go up the stairs to the bedrooms.

The kitchen was just off the living room. I put on a light and glanced around for evidence of a suicide. My search was interrupted by a blood-curdling scream. It was Linda. She had omitted to switch on the overhead light and bumped into a prostrate body three quarters of the way up to the first floor. Fatima was lying unconscious across the stairs and breathing very shallowly. We slapped her face, calling out her name hoping to revive her. Linda almost found this fun, as it was Fatima who had unceremoniously shown her the door that time, but her compassionate nature won over and she went to call the ambulance being better able than I to tell them the exact address.

I'd never really taken first aid lessons but there was something I didn't like about her head being so much higher than her legs and was worried that her brain would be starved of oxygen. She lay in a coma state and I presumed her circulation would be weakened. When Linda came back, we decided to bring her down onto the landing where, at least, she could lay more horizontally until the ambulance arrived.

Linda took hold of her ankles and I, behind her head, raised her arms to lift her shoulders off the floor. Linda pulled. I lifted. Her weighty body slid down one stair but her head, which I couldn't support, went thud against the step. Linda heaved, I hoed and her head went bump again. We continued. Heave. Ho. By the time we reached the landing, Linda and I were hysterical. Her head had bumped down at least five steps. Thank God the stairs were carpeted. It lessened the risk of giving her concussion.

The front door had been left wide open for the ambulance men. Two of them walked across the threshold and saw the inert body stretched out on the landing. Linda's and my eyes were red from crying, not from sadness but uncontrollable laughter.

'I wouldn't waste any tears for her,' the stronger of the two said as he came up the stairs. 'We've dealt with her a few times. She'll pull through. She makes sure of that.' And he hoisted her like a full sack of potatoes over his left shoulder and went back down the stairs. We followed him outside as he made his way down the path to the ambulance.

I never saw her again. The last image imprinted on my mind was of her upper body hanging down from his shoulder, her limp arms stretched downwards bumping with the rhythm of his stride against a buttock and the back of her head, long thick black hair falling to her elbows, her face thudding against where his left kidney would have been.

She was unceremoniously manipulated into the back of the vehicle. Both men climbed into the front and with blue lights flashing, they drove off to the hospital.

Linda and I went back into the house. I found some paper and wrote an angry note to Marlowe telling him where he could find Fatima. Before leaving Gowan Avenue, I had grabbed the divorce papers and against my superstitious nature, I signed them and left the note and papers scattered on the makeshift altar. For safety's sake, we blew out the candle and left the house.

The West Ken flat did work out and in the not too distant future, I became a divorcee. Later, I would even work with Marlowe on an episode of *The Gentle Touch* in which he starred as the Detective Chief Inspector. I had been cast without an interview and it was half way through the rehearsals that I received sincere apologies from the producer in case my working with my ex-husband had caused any embarrassment. It hadn't, but I did notice that if Fatima ever came to visit the studio, she avoided any contact with me.

In February of 1977, I moved into the flat. The furniture from Gowan Avenue was lost in its palatial space but I had acres of walls to hang my pictures. After I had bought a large, dark oak Victorian dining table and surrounded it with suitable antique chairs, I invited Barbara and Martin for my first Sunday lunch concocted within my brand new kitchen. They were still in London doing post-production. I invited Linda and some other friends as well. The Landaus arrived along with their daughters. It was not often one met two teenagers with such exquisite manners. Barbara offered me a housewarming gift which she and Martin had found in the Portobello market. It was a little silver tray, elaborately embossed with flowers and in the middle was a smooth oval in which was engraved the handwritten word 'Beautiful'. It remains a treasured possession.

I don't recollect what I served as a starter or the dessert but I remember, very well, placing a platter of roast pork with its crispy coat of browned crackling in the middle of the table. It was only then that the thought occurred to me: What if they're Jewish? And Kosher! Oh, my God! In milliseconds, I tried to remember if I'd ever seen one of them eat a bacon or sausage sandwich but the image alluded me. I need not have worried. They tucked into the pork, mashed potatoes and gravy with seeming enjoyment.

When the filming of all the episodes was finished, the production held a farewell party on the studio floor, incorporating the latest sets. All the crew, directors, actors and their guests meandered about, glass in hand, between the furniture. I'd asked Bill to accompany me. By now, he knew Martin, Barbara, Peter Medak and some of the other directors as well as many of the guest stars who had also been invited. We, who had worked that last day had taken off our make-up. My hairpieces were attached by pins to a wig stand. Our costumes were handed to the wardrobe department and we emptied our dressing rooms which had become home from home of our personal belongings. They had sheltered us for almost a year. Tony's, Nick's and my room were off the first floor corridor. Martin and Barbara had a suite tucked in at the end of it. As I closed my door for the last time, I thought of the happy exchanges and mischievous chatter which had bounced off these walls. We had been a happy bunch devoid of selfish egos.

Downstairs, the party was in noisy animation. Bill was making his rounds, talking to whomever he recognized. He was not a shy person and that was just as well as he was blessed with an aura that attracted people to him. While he was surrounded by admirers, I took the opportunity to say my farewells to the crew. Frank Watts was our lighting camera man. We had worked together before and would again on an episode of *The Return of the Saint*. He was, seemingly, always employed with the same operator and focus puller. The episode took place in the South of France and we stayed in a hotel in Nice. I had replaced a French actress. No-one told me for what reason but I assume the severance had cost the company a lot of money because I was allotted a room in the hotel which overlooked a back courtyard where the rubbish bins were kept. This was unusual for an actress playing the guest starring role. But when I was shown the room, there was a lovely bouquet of flowers with a note to welcome me. It was not from the production company but from Frank and his camera crew. I looked around the tiny space and felt humiliated but the bright flowers in the vase cheered me. My suitcase was unpacked when there was a knock on the door. It was Mike, my hairdresser with whom I'd also worked before. He took one look around the cramped room and cursed.

'How could they have put you into this dump of a room? Have you complained? No way are you staying here!' He was adamant. 'I'm going to talk to the guys.'

Mike was there to talk to me about what hairstyle I would have. He was a genius in coaxing my unruly tresses into submission but still allowing them to look wild. By the 'guys', he meant Frank and his crew. They were still working but soon due to arrive. After a short conversation about hair, he left.

Later that evening, I received a phone call from the hotel director.

'We have made a terrible mistake, Miss Schell,' he said with a French accent. 'Of course, you will have a room overlooking the sea.' Ironically, it was the same hotel on the Promenade des Anglais that I had stayed in when filming for *The Adventurer*. I had had a beautiful room then. Perhaps it would be the same.

He assured me that a maid would come, repack my suitcase and deliver it to my new room. I went down to the bar where I met 'the guys' and hugged them all. On hearing my plight, they had stormed into the production office and demanded suitable accommodation for me. The following day, I did get some sheepish apologies from the location manager.

But that was still all to come. The night of the party on the studio set at Pinewood, I reminisced with Frank and his constant companions. His clapper boy /focus puller imported Hungarian Pulis and was thinking of breeding the large Komondor as well. We talked a lot about dogs as I knew the breeds well, especially the Puli. There was one person missing, though from Frank's entourage. He was the grip. I have searched the internet for his name but could not find it, so I will call him Barry. A grip carries the camera equipment from one scene to another and, when required, pushes the dolly (a platform on wheels) upon which the camera and operator is placed to capture a scene in a smooth continuous motion. When required, on an external shoot, he lays the tracks over which the dolly would glide.

It's a very, very long time ago and I'm not sure I have the exact mental image of Barry, but I think of him with a beard and much senior in age than the rest of the crew. He was a quiet man and other than polite greetings, I don't remember ever having a proper conversation with him but he was liked by his colleagues. I only found out his history afterwards.

When we had finished shooting one day, Steve, my driver, was not in a hurry to go home. I sometimes liked to have a drink in the Pinewood bar before returning to London. Several other projects were usually being filmed in the studio's numerous sound stages. The bar was a convivial place to meet with other actors after a hard day's work. Steve walked with me down the corridor which lead to it. The nearer we approached, the stranger the atmosphere became. Normally, there was laughter and loud conversation emitting from its interior. As we neared, a fog of eerie silence enveloped us. Steve walked through the entrance in front of me and immediately turned around.

'You don't want to go in there,' he said.

'Why?' I asked.

'There's something you won't want to see.' He put a hand on my shoulder, gently pushing me backwards.

'What?' I insisted and managed to look over his shoulder.

There was a circle of men gathered, looking down with concern at something on the floor. It was the first time I had ever experienced the bar captured in such an intense hush. Between the legs of the onlookers, I discerned a body and a vague figure in white kneeling across it. Ignoring Steve's advice, I inched forward. It was Barry on his back with legs stretched out straight. The white form I'd seen was the studio nurse giving him mouth to mouth resuscitation.

One of our crew approached me and quietly said, 'Oh, Catherine, it was terrible. One moment he was standing at the bar having a drink and then he suddenly let out a shout and collapsed. We dragged him towards the middle so there'd be more space and called the nurse and an ambulance. She came quickly but the ambulance still hasn't arrived.'

He looked as if he was going to cry and then said, 'I don't think he's going to make it... such a shame... a lovely guy and he's got a family.'

Just at that point the wide swing doors which lead to the back entrance opened and the emergency servicemen walked in. The nurse stood up and the men laid him on a stretcher. I will never forget the position of his head as they lifted him off the floor. It hung at an impossible 90 degree angle from his shoulders. I knew poor Barry had died and was so sorry for his wife who would shortly receive a devastating phone call which would irretrievably alter her life.

The following morning was a working day. Cast and crew who had heard the news were desolate. It was then that I learned about his past. Barry had been a prisoner of war in a Japanese concentration camp. He had been starved and during his incarceration had seen so many horrors that it was a miracle he had not suffered mentally from his experience. At least, it did not seem so. When liberated, he was emaciated. The lack of nutrition, vitamins and minerals that his body had required took a toll on his future health.

He had complained about a strange pain in his left arm for a few days before the incident and was advised to immediately see a doctor by his workmates. Had he said something to the production office, they'd have forced him to consult a cardiologist. It seems that his work ethic was stronger than his concern for his personal discomfort.

We lifted our glasses to Barry and I continued on my path of farewells. It had been a wonderful year. I felt I was saying goodbye and thank you, not to colleagues, but to my friends.

CHAPTER XX

'Love is arbitrary,' Bill said to me as we held each other close. It was the preamble to another goodbye. I asked him what he meant by using the word 'arbitrary' in this sense.

'It's irrational, illogical. It either happens or it doesn't. I never planned it but I can't help my feelings for you.'

And I couldn't help mine for him. Love doesn't flow like water from a tap. It can't be turned on nor stopped by the turn of a wrist.

Once again, we were going to try a separation. Bill loved his family. He had two children, a girl and a boy. When our affair began they would have been seven and nine respectively. When we were working together on *Clancy*, upon his return to London from the family home in Kent, the cast would be regaled with his children's episodes. He would smile and his hazel-green eyes sometimes misted up when he recalled certain tales.

One of them was of his daughter. She was coming home on a Sunday from church with a very determined expression on her face. She was moving very quickly with both arms held straight down at her sides and her little hands were clasped into fists. Bill asked her what the trouble was.

'You can only do wees in the cemetery. You're not allowed to do poos!' was her hurried reply as she rushed to the toilet.

He was proud of his son who was already showing signs of artistic talent, describing him as a silent thinker, only opening his mouth when he had something important to say.

Bill talked about his wife, as well. I remember him describing a fashion show she entertained him with after a London shopping spree.

Listening to these accounts, I was convinced he was a family man and respected him for it. The business is too full of promiscuity. It was refreshing to see a good-looking and charming man who seemed devoted to his family.

That is why it was such a surprise when he made clear his feelings for me.

'Do you remember in the pub next to the Acton rehearsal rooms? We were both working on different programmes. Our eyes met across the crowded space. We gazed at one another. I fell in love with you then.'

I didn't remember. As far as I was concerned, the first time I'd laid eyes on his sweet Marilyn Monroe face was at the interview for *Looking for Clancy*. But I didn't tell him that.

No-one 'steals' someone else's partner. There has to be a fundamental lack in the relationship which will be sought and replaced from elsewhere.

We had a very bumpy ride until he finally committed to me. On no occasion did I force the pace. I was the perfect mistress, making no demands. Whatever would have happened, he'd have always remained the love of my life. Ironically, it was not he who left the marriage. His wife had found someone else and women, being more honest and courageous in such situations, let him know. It happened at a time that we hadn't seen each other for over 18 months.

I had allowed myself to be wooed by other men. Hugh, the Earl of Cawdor, a relative of the Thanes from bygone generations mentioned in Shakespeare's play *Macbeth,* invited me to his medieval castle in Nairn. He reminded me of a panther: graceful, sleek with eyes like a cat's, absorbing, studying everything around him. I was introduced to his two eldest daughters and his two sons, the youngest of which was Freddy. In a mad moment of mischief, Freddy and I climbed up to the castle's turrets and threw our homemade paper water bombs down onto the unsuspecting tourists who had paid good money for a tour of Cawdor Castle. Hugh scolded us on our return but I discerned a tell-tale chuckle in his voice. If anyone could have stolen my heart, it would have been he but I was still in love with Bill Hays.

Through a friend, I met someone who was, it seemed to me, the epitome of the British establishment. He had been to all of the correct schools, he'd been an officer in the navy and his speech was ultra upper-class, pronouncing 'off' as 'ohrf'. His name was Peter Cameron-Webb, he was 52, and had become the co-chairman of one of Lloyd's largest syndicates named, PCW, after his initials. I was introduced to a millionaire life-style, flying in an eight-seat private jet with pilot, co-pilot and a stewardess who poured Champagne and offered us smoked salmon sandwiches during the flight. I was invited on what I called his 100 foot 'marble' yacht to cruise the Mediterranean docking at Monte Carlo during the Grand Prix. We'd make our way to Cannes or other fashionable Italian ports. I spent an afternoon sailing on his swift 30 foot racing yacht. Amongst his other possessions was what looked like a red

Formula One sports car. He encouraged me to drive it but I found the gear shift too harsh to manipulate, even when I double de-clutched.

A few weeks into our relationship, I was offered a film in Ireland called *Exposure*. A great friend, the actor TP McKenna, was starring in it and upon his suggestion to the director and producer the part of the female photographer was offered to me. It was a small budget film. They wanted a 'name' who would not ask for an exorbitant fee, someone who was not a snob and who would 'muck in' as it were... no Winnebago, no grand hotel suites, just an ordinary actress without demands and pretentions. I loved TP. We were great mates and had worked together before. I first met him when doing *Napoleon and Love*. He was in *Looking for Clancy* with Bill directing. I accepted the job without hesitation.

The filming was due to begin but there was a strike which cancelled all commercial flights from Heathrow to Ireland. What to do? I spoke to Peter about my situation. The private jet was put at my disposal. Just for fun, I invited Ben and some friends to fly with me across the Irish Sea. As Ireland's telephone operators were also on strike, the production office received a telegram (this was 1978) stating the identification number of the jet and its time of arrival. The producer's knees began to tremble when he received this information.

'I thought she was a normal person!' he shouted at TP. 'You said she wouldn't behave like a star! Does she expect us to pay for the jet?'

'I don't understand it,' TP replied. 'She's never behaved like this before.' But they came to meet the plane at the airport. TP later told me how beautiful the little silver jet looked in the sky. They saw it appear like a shining dot and then, it circled the airport once and glided lower to land. It taxied to the private terminal. The door opened and out came a ladder which unfolded to the ground. I was the first to appear on the steps in the last of the afternoon sunlight. Ben and my friends followed me down but we had to say our goodbyes on the tarmac. The pilot needed to make a quick turnaround as the jet was booked for later that evening.

TP gave me a hug when we met and congratulated me on my impressive entrance. He introduced me to the director and producer who bade me to follow them to their car. One of them took my suitcase and we walked outside to the parking lot. I had just lived the sublime and now I was to experience the ridiculous. With the case tucked into the boot, TP and I climbed into the back and, thus, the four of us were juddered and rattled all the way to Dublin in an old jalopy. But the ride was fun. We laughed a lot and I knew I was going to enjoy this job.

Between the filming TP showed me the Dublin sights. Irish born and bred, he was a hero in that city and I was proud to be in his company. I said sights but it was more the pubs he frequented that I came to know and the famous Irish conviviality. I don't think we were allowed to pay for a single drink.

We had dinner one night in Dublin's most expensive hotel. The dining room was surprisingly empty. We were the only guests until a tall handsome figure in the guise of Sean Connery sauntered into the room. He passed our table giving a polite nod and installed himself at the far end, choosing to sit down at a round table with his back to the room.

TP and I spoke to each other in excited whispers. 'Did you see who that was?' 'What's he doing here?' 'Oh my God! We're breathing the same air as Sean Connery!' And so it continued until I had a bright idea.

'I'm going to send him a note,' I announced.

'You can't,' TP said, horrified.

'Yes I can,' I answered. I was now in one of my outrageous Hungarian moods. My darling Bill had disappeared. He would have reined me in. I was ripping apart at the seams. I asked the waiter for a piece of paper and wrote a note upon it. It read: 'I suppose a shag is completely out of the question.' I showed it to TP who was aghast.

'Catherine, no! You can't! Oh, my God! You mustn't,' he hissed, still maintaining his Irish brogue.

'Yes I can,' I said, folding the note and called the waiter back to our table.

'I would like you to deliver this to Mr Connery,' I ordered him. 'Do not read it, just put it in front of him.'

'Yes, madam,' the waiter said, sounding a little dubious about his task.

We watched him walk up to Sean Connery's back. He whispered something in his ear and then, as ordered, placed the note in front of him. An opened bottle of red wine stood in the middle of the table.

We watched, mesmerized for his reaction. As his back was to us, all we could see after a moment's reading was a quick pumping of his shoulders as they moved up and down signifying a laugh. Then, he stood up, grabbed the bottle of wine and with a beaming smile made his way to our table. When arriving, he looked down on us from his magnificent height and asked in his Scots accent, 'Which of the two of you am I supposed to shag?' I almost swooned.

We spent the meal together. He had recognized us as fellow thespians, not knowing who we were but realising what we were. I don't remember what film he was shooting but he seemed happy for our company. After dinner, we were invited to his suite where we had another drink. TP and I had to work the following day. As we left, Sean accompanied us to the door. I noticed a chequered cap hanging from a hook on its back. There was a mirror to the side. I placed the cap on my head and looked in the mirror.

'Looks good on you,' he said. 'It's my golfing cap.'

I took it off to put it back on the hook.

'No, no. Keep it. It suits you better than it does me.' And that is how I ended up with Sean Connery's golfing cap which I still proudly wear today.

The strike was ongoing when we finished the filming. TP had an important appointment in London.

'No problem,' I told him. 'Peter will send the jet.' It was wonderful to be able to speak like that.

We flew back to Heathrow together, TP looking out of the window, excited like a child. I'd grown blasé by then. We were hurried through passport and customs at the private terminal. On the other side, the Rolls was waiting and TP couldn't believe the luxury he'd experienced that day. We'd had smoked salmon and Champagne in the sky and more Champagne, cooling in an ice bucket continued to flow all the way down the M4 to London. There was an advertising campaign at that time to do with Shell gasoline. Its logo was, 'Go Well with Shell'. He couldn't agree more.

I enjoyed the trappings of that lifestyle. It was a new experience and I felt after my last splitting up from Bill I deserved to be spoiled but deep down I knew this was not a life for me. There was a price I had to pay which was beyond my means. Peter was kind and generous. He was handsome, distinguished and everything my mother would have wanted for me. I'd introduced him to my parents. It was at the time my father was severely in the grip of Alzheimer's. Peter had invited them for a cruise on the marble yacht, flying them in from Munich on the jet. I took a photograph of the two standing up against the plane on the tarmac of Nice's airport. My mother beamed glamorously. My father smiled with a confused expression. The stewardess held him by an elbow. He had no idea what was happening or where he was. His eyes had assumed a shallow glaze. Peter would have been my mother's saviour. He was already promising to finance the best of possible homes where Daddy would have expert care, thus liberating my mother from her overpowering responsibility. My brother Paul had just married Hildegard Knef, the famous German actress, painter, poet and writer. *The Gift Horse*, her best-selling autobiography had been published in the late Sixties. She was several years Paul's senior. *Fedora*, her latest film, directed by Billy Wilder was closing the Cannes film festival. The yacht was sailed across from Monte Carlo to the millionaire's port of Cannes and Hilde and Paul were invited for lunch. They, too, were very impressed with him. He made them feel his generosity would extend towards them if they were to fall on lean times. In our precarious profession it was a comforting assurance. A friend of mine, an out of work actress, was already benefiting from his bounty. I began to feel I was a ticket to salvation for too many people and actually felt guilty at letting them down when I couldn't go on with the relationship, couldn't continue to share a bed with someone I was not in love with and so in order not to prolong the charade, I decided to end it. Again, Bill Hays took precedence to my affections. My days as a rich bitch were over and it was just as well. In the early Eighties, a scandal hit the headlines. Peter Cameron-Webb of the PCW syndicate and his co-partner were accused of fraudulent handling of their members' investments. Rather than submit to an investigation, Peter made an ignominious exit from England. Although it was five years after our brief relationship, a mutual friend warned that I could be contacted by the press as they had heard rumours of our affair. It was a time when selling 'kiss and tell' stories, especially with incriminating photographs, could be quite lucrative. As it was, no-one phoned me and I would have denied all knowledge anyway.

In 1978, I was asked to partake in the iconic BBC series *Doctor Who*. The four part serial would be called 'City of Death'. The series had already entertained a youthful audience for years and the Doctor had assumed many embodiments. He was now in the guise of Tom Baker. I had caught some glimpses of the series in the past when visiting with friends who had children and I could boast of sitting around the same table during a dinner party where Jon Pertwee was present who struck me as the epitome of an elegant, English intellectual. That was the sum of my familiarity of the series. I'm afraid I could not describe Tom Baker using the same adjectives, certainly not elegant. He arrived in the mornings to the rehearsal rooms boisterous and dishevelled wearing a shirt in dire need of a holiday in a washing machine. I was absolutely dumbstruck to learn later there was a romance blooming between him and Lalla Ward who was pretty, discreet and squeaky clean.

Working with Julian Glover was a delight, made even more satisfying by the frequent drags from a cigarette stuck into a long, thin holder. I had given up smoking at that time and took advantage of the nicotine fix my interpretation of the role permitted. I think it was my idea that the Countess would always be seen through a veil of smoke and, sweetly, Michael Hayes, the director, complied.

I missed out on the location shoot in Paris as all of my scenes were interiors and recorded in the BBC studios and I have to admit: like most of the work I've appeared in, I didn't watch it. Some time in the very early Eighties, I met John Nathan Turner drinking in the BBC bar. I had worked with him on *Looking for Clancy* with Bill Hays directing. He had been Bill's assistant on that and other shows. He was known to us as 'Nat Tune' the name Bill had given him. Now that he had become the producer of *Doctor Who* he did not wish to be reminded of his beginnings and did not appreciate being called by his nickname. We spoke briefly and it was then that I learned that the fourth and final episode of the 'City of Death' had achieved the highest television audience ever in *Doctor Who*'s history. He did not mean it as a compliment. On the contrary, he seemed to imply its popularity was despite my contribution as he added, 'I would never have cast you in the programme.' And thus dissolved all my hopes of ever appearing in another episode again.

Later that year, I was invited to do a play at the English-speaking theatre in Vienna. The play was *Wait Until Dark*, made notorious by the film in which Audrey Hepburn played the blind woman, Susy, in the principal role. It was that part which was offered to me. I accepted the challenge. Cyril Frankel directed and the Irish actor, Niall Buggy, played Roat, the sadistic character which Alan Arkin portrayed in the film. We rehearsed the play in a church hall just off Parsons Green in Fulham.

Cyril suggested for me to visit a centre for the blind, situated north of Notting Hill. Niall, with whom I clicked immediately, became a close friend and he accompanied me. The centre had been warned of our arrival and we were introduced to several sightless people, those having suffered from birth, others during their lives and some struck only recently.

As the play does not describe how Susy became blind, I surmised by reading the interchanges between her husband and herself at the beginning of the play that she would not have been born blind.

I was amazed at how differently each category reacted and behaved. We were invited to sit with a group in the canteen to have lunch. It became apparent that those who had had eyesight for many years coped with the food on their plates much better than those who had never seen.

No-one's face was turned to their dish. No need. I was impressed how adeptly the recently blinded cut up their lamb chop and pushed the peas onto their fork. The ones who were born blind struggled somewhat, much of their food falling back onto their plate, eventually picking up the chops with their fingers. And why not?

As diplomatically as possible, I mentioned this anomaly.

One woman answered, 'It's obvious. I still have a memory of what things look like. We can still imagine shapes and that's a great help.'

'On the other hand,' said a young man who became blind very early in his life. 'You don't have the same keen perception of touch, scent and sound.'

'Probably not,' said the woman. 'But those senses will develop.'

She then said something which came as a shock to me. 'Thank God, I'm only blind. It's much better than being deaf.' Except for Niall and I who had both faculties, there was agreement all around the table.

It was incredible listening to people comparing invalidities. For them, the loss of hearing would be too debilitating, too isolating.

'We'd be living in a fish tank, watching movement and life but not being able to really participate. We can hear recordings of plays and books. People's voices and their vocabulary paint an image that is beyond the necessity of sight. Where's the timbre in someone's voice when their doing sign language?'

In later years, I met a man who was completely deaf, almost from birth but he could read lips. It was in France. He was French and when I spoke to him, I would have pronounced words with an English accent. My lip movements were not as he expected and he sometimes didn't understand me. His sisters translated what I had said with the same sentences, still in French but with perfect lip diction. With the help of his sisters we were able to communicate.

Niall and I were even invited to one of the studio flats which was rented by the recently blinded woman. I was impressed by the practicality. I supposed, with time, one didn't need to have eyes to make use of the space. Everything had been thought of in minute detail with that lack in mind.

The whole day was a humbling experience. I wasn't sure I'd have been as brave and accepting in their situation of such a misfortune. They knew why I was there and by studying them, I determined the body language I would use to portray Susy.

Those who had never had sight or had lost it many years before had difficulty focusing. Their eyes did not move in a synchronized fashion. I had no choice, really. It would have been impossible for me to imitate those incongruous movements. I decided, definitively, that my Susy would have lost her sight one or two years ago through a trauma which affected her optic nerve. I learned to not completely focus and to keep my eyes somewhat off centre when talking to another actor in a scene.

There was another invaluable trick I discovered. When on stage the lighting shines from the front. If I teased a few strands of hair over my forehead so that they reached my eyes, too few to be visible to the audience but enough for the light to glow through the strands distorting them into what seemed like a Vaseline curtain, the illusion of blindness was consummate. I actually felt I couldn't see and, in a way, it was true. The dispersion of the light through the hairs caused a smearing effect which completely disturbed my vision.

The play received rave revues as did all the actors. Our contracts were extended twice until I finally couldn't continue. We were even offered another three months in Berlin but I had had enough. We were doing six nights and three matinees. Nine performances a week. My shins had begun bleeding from bumping into low furniture on the set. This was done on purpose. When Susy became stressed, she would forget where objects and furniture had been meticulously placed. The period the play had been cast in, it would not have been correct for me to wear trousers. I stayed in a skirt and could hear people from the audience whispering in sympathy, 'Oh look! She's really hurt herself. That's real blood trickling down her leg.'

Towards the end of the play when it is only Roat and Susy on the stage and he is behaving sadistically, the audience, sincerely believing that she was blind, shouted out for him to stop being cruel to her. At some of the performances, we thought they would climb up on the stage to protect her. Then when Susy has smashed all the lights on the set and the stage plummets into darkness which would be an advantage for her, the audience is lulled into a sense of security thinking she has overcome the killer. Suddenly, there is a horrifying moment of surprise which I will not describe here but it forced a scream from the auditorium that could blow the roof off the theatre. To Niall's and my delight it happened at every performance.

There is an 11 year old girl in the play. Her character is called Gloria. She was played by the actress, Bernadette Windsor. Bernadette was in her early twenties when we worked together. Crucial to the plot is a doll which Gloria steals out of spite. It has been brought to the apartment inadvertently by Susy's husband who is unaware that the doll contains heroin. The entire play revolves around the recuperation by the nasty Roat of the precious doll. It would have been impossible for an actual 11 year old to play the part on the stage so, a more mature actress had to be cast. Bernadette's height did not go above 4 foot 10, which classified her as a dwarf. She also had a high pitched pre-adolescent voice and a round child-like face. Other than that, she was a perfectly formed pretty little woman with wavy blonde hair and blue eyes. We shared a dressing room and I once made the mistake of calling her a midget. She argued that she was a dwarf and not a midget. I argued that dwarfs had big bodies and heads and stubby little legs and arms, just like those in Snow White, whereas, she had a perfect figure, albeit small.

'Don't tell me what I am!' She was a spunky little person. 'I know exactly!' And then she gave me the name of her particular condition of dwarfism.

After the performance Niall and I liked to celebrate. Bernadette almost always joined us. We sometimes went for a meal or, on occasion, to a disco. Niall loved dancing. Several times, I was told that my daughter did not have the right to enter the establishment and how could I be taking a young child to such a place, anyway? We made her carry her passport and upon seeing it, sincere apologies were made, usually followed by a free drink. It was the time when the hit song 'YMCA' by the Village People was popular and we danced like lunatics to it. Admittedly, some of the other revellers gave our little family unit very strange looks.

When the play closed, the theatre wanted to send us back to England by train. It was going to be a long, gruelling journey from Vienna with several changes. I went to a travel agent and found that plane tickets were actually cheaper. Flights were booked for the whole cast.

It was the first time that Bernadette would be in an airplane. She was very excited. We made a big fuss over her. When we were shown our seats, we made sure she would sit by the window.

'It may be night, but you'll see all the lights of London as we land. It's spectacular!' I assured her.

She sat next to me and as we were taxiing down the runway, I helped her attach the safety belt. The stewardess looked on attentively. The engines revved, we sped down the tarmac and were finally boosted up into the air. Bernadette looked out of her window as the Viennese lights twinkled their farewell. She was nervous but, I wouldn't say, frightened. We all praised her for being so brave.

The nice stewardess arrived with a colouring book and some crayons. She reached over me to hand them to Bernadette who took one look at the offering and shouted in her 11 year old voice, 'I don't need those! I need a gin and tonic!'

The expression on the stewardess's face was priceless.

CHAPTER XXI

I was in a walled-in garden behind an impressive Victorian terraced house in a fashionable part of Fulham which belonged to a gay couple, Anthony and Michael, who had become my close friends. Explosions of colour and scent emitting from blousy flowers added to the happy atmosphere. The interior of their house was an accolade to all that was appreciated in the world of Art Nouveau and Deco. Stone statues of these periods were placed artistically between plants and shrubs. I held a glass of Champagne in my hand. We were not many, only the dearest members in our circle. It was my 35th birthday. I was in a pretty frock with a large happy smile on my face... and then a passing pigeon shat on my head. There was a photograph taken of me, laughing hysterically with the white goo sliding down my hair.

This comparatively rare phenomenon, I was told during the gathering, was a herald of good fortune. A short time later I received a phone call. It was Bill. We had not spoken for near to 18 months. His speech was slightly slurred. He explained that his wife was in a serious relationship and that she preferred for him to leave. He packed a little bag, walked out of the house and found a bench to sit on. There, while watching the traffic pass by, he thought of his situation and wept. For the best of reasons, he had given me up and now he had nothing: no wife, no home, no family. Would I take him back?

Since the first week I'd moved into Challoner Crescent, I felt guilty with the enormous amount of space I was living in. Any of my friends who needed a room to tide them over for a while found one with me. Even Linda who had sold her flat shortly after I left Gowan Avenue and had bought a property around the corner from me in West Kensington came to stay for a few weeks until renovations in her new acquisition were completed. When Bill phoned, another girlfriend, Rozzy, was staying but that didn't stop me from telling him that if he needed a place to stay, there was the second spare room which he would be welcome to. I was willing to help him out but, I told him sternly, he had to understand that was as far as my hospitality would reach. I must have been dreaming. We were back together the following day.

Bill felt uncomfortable with Rozzy's presence but I could not tell her to leave. She had fallen on hard times. Her three children were living with her parents. There was a financial problem to do with the father of the children and until that was settled she was in a sort of limbo.

Bill became more and more moody until one morning he announced that he was leaving. He needed time to be alone and 'think' and was going to stay in a well-known serviced studio apartment block. The address where he intended to go was quite infamous. It catered mostly to bachelors who were in his circumstance or those who were waiting until they found the right woman who would supply a suitable home.

I did not allow myself to indulge in feelings of being, once again, the cast-off mistress. My Hungarian director friend Peter Medak and Caroline Seymour had moved to Los Angeles. Only one phone call later, and I was sitting on the long-haul flight from Heathrow to LA. I had no idea how long I would stay. After I left, Rozzy moved her children into the flat. Her husband was now paying enough in alimony that she could forward me £100 a week. The exchange rate was very beneficial. I could contribute for my stay at the Medak's and rent a cheap little car. I knew many of the Brits who had emigrated to LA. The car afforded me the transport I needed to have a social life. My English agents had connections with Californian ones who introduced me to casting directors and producers of important television series being made at that time. I had allowed my hair to grow naturally. It was a darkish red and tumbled in abundant waves down to my shoulders. It looked wilder than groomed, definitely not the girl next door. Everyone loved the accent but I was difficult to cast. I heard this from my agents who would have preferred me to have a more conventional look. I had suspicions when they asked if I had any personal commitments and understood, exactly, why the question was posed. It was a polite way of asking if I was free to go to bed with a prospective employer. Mr So-and-So who met you would like to invite you to dinner but if there's someone back home we'll not encourage him. I definitely had someone back home, I'd reply, omitting to say that I was not certain it was the case.

I was in LA for less than a month. During that time Bill had rung several times. The call that made me book a flight back to London was special. There was a sincerity in his voice when he said he loved me and I also believed him when he said he'd come to the conclusion that he didn't want to live without me.

I rang Rozzy. She told me not to worry, she had somewhere else to move to.

Bill met me at Heathrow and, the moment he put an arm around me, I had no more fears of future separations.

Not quite a month later, Paul phoned me to say Daddy was in a coma. He had suffered from a haemorrhage in his brain. I should fly to Munich immediately. The next morning I was on the first flight. Paul met me at the airport and gave me the news: Daddy had died in the early hours of the morning. We drove to the Catholic home where I saw his body laid out on a bed in a special room with walls completely bare but for a crucifix hanging over the bed. I cried. I wailed. I screamed. The nuns had to calm me. My mother was there as well. She had held a vigil during the night and had no tears left to cry. Paul too was overcome with grief. We had lost our father's spirit long ago; it was only just now that his body was taken away. The finality was unbearably painful. I kissed his cold forehead and a thought struck me: he did not leave me until I was safe in the arms of another man.

Mommy had decided some time ago that Daddy would be cremated. His urn would join Peter's which had been transported from America and placed in Munich's northern cemetery. Bill was determined to join me for the services. It was the first time he would meet my mother and Paul.

There was a memorial service and then an evening mass held in our local Baroque church. Bill was one hundred percent atheist, but he behaved impeccably during the mass. It was afterwards that he disgraced himself. The church was full of mourners. Daddy was popular and much loved. We couldn't invite everybody back to the flat. Only the very closest of our friends and family joined us for the wake. My cousin, Bosco, the son of Daddy's twin brother, Peter, had flown in from Paris where he worked for Reader's Digest to be with us. He and Bill hit it off immediately. They made themselves useful by taking everyone's coats on arrival, pouring drinks and doing the rounds offering the canapés which we'd made before the service. There was an equal mixture of Hungarians and Germans but all spoke English which meant Bill was not at a loss. At one point he was amongst a group of guests, which included Paul, Hildegard and Bosco. Bill wanted to know when the actual funeral was going to take place. He had attended a memorial to my father in one church and then, now, the mass in another. When was my father going to be interred?

'He's not being buried,' Paul said. 'He's going to be cremated.'

'Yes, but when? Tomorrow?' Bill asked.

'No, not for a few weeks, yet,' Bosco answered.

'Why?' asked Bill.'

'It seems there's a queue. A lot of people are being cremated nowadays and there's only one crematorium.' Bosco replied.

'A waiting list to be cremated?' Bill couldn't believe it and unable to control his dark sense of humour he said, 'but Dachau is only up the road.'

There was a moment of shocked, embarrassed silence especially from the Germans but the Hungarians understood the irony. They didn't exactly laugh but their gentle chuckling under their breath lightened what could have become a very nasty incident. For the rest of the evening, Bill was strictly chaperoned by either Paul, Bosco or myself in order that he didn't make another *faux pas*.

Mommy was not in earshot when Bill made his comment. We told her about it afterwards. There was no gentle chuckling on her part. She laughed hysterically. One could have thought with her appreciation of his wicked sense of humour, they'd have got along but, alas, it was not entirely to be the case. There was an unspoken truce between them where I was concerned. In my presence they behaved honourably towards each other but it grated on them both and I could feel the tension in the air. Nevertheless I was allowed, even magnanimously encouraged, to invite her to our flat and Bill behaved impeccably as did Dragon Lady – Bill's preferred name for her. When we were going to be married, it was Bill who chose the date. 'Let's have the wedding around Christmastime. That way, Dragon Lady will visit only once.'

We married on December 22nd, 1982. A friend of Paul and Hilde, Rudi Münster, an important personage in the luxury hotel world offered us a limousine to take us to Fulham town hall where the ceremony was going to take place and a suite at the Dorchester hotel for the nuptial night. Anthony, Michael and Linda were to be our best man and witnesses.

According to custom the bride is not accompanied by the groom on the way to the wedding. My mother sat with me in the back of the polished Austin Princess, which was decorated with white ribbons, as we made our way up the North End Road towards Fulham Broadway cruising slowly between the market stalls. It was a busy day and shoppers clapped or gave us the thumbs up as we glided past. Mommy waved out of the window a little like our dear Queen. After making our vows, during which I cried to the point of being speechless with Bill squeezing my hand until my knuckles almost broke, we exited the building and Anthony took photographs. The limo was waiting outside prepared to drive Bill and I home where a reception had been prepared. The chauffeur opened the back door for us. We had to stop my mother from climbing in to take a seat.

'No. The return journey is only for Bill and me,' I told her.

'Vat? I don't come viz you?'

'No. That's not the custom,' I pleaded.

Her disappointment was obvious. 'To hell viz custom!'

There could have been an unpleasant scene in full view of passers-by but Anthony intervened and put his hand on her shoulder leading her to his upmarket BMW which was just behind the limo. Michael, with an elegant, chivalric gesture ushered her into the back seat. She seemed placated.

It was not her only disappointment of that day. When all of the guests but one had left the reception, the limo was again waiting to take us to the Dorchester. Once again, Mommy wanted to come with us.

'But you can't!' I reasoned with her. 'It's our wedding night.'

Thank God, a Hungarian cousin of my mother who was at the reception grabbed her by the hand, stuffed her into her little car and drove away with her to a bridge party. Until a disastrous accident stole her mobility, she featured importantly at our Christmases in London and I would always manage a week in Munich when Bill was working on a foreign location.

Now that I was married to the love of my life and in my later thirties, it was high time I had his child. So far, I had not become pregnant. There was obviously something wrong. A girl friend who had been in the same situation spoke to me about a miracle professor of obstetrics under whose treatment she had been and who had, with time, successfully delivered to her a baby boy. His name was Professor Ian Craft at the Royal Free Hospital in north London. I made an appointment and was received by him in a plush office in the part of the hospital which was his domain. He asked me questions pertaining to my medical history and then, quite brazenly, he asked if I had been promiscuous. When I recovered from what I thought was impertinence, I answered, 'I don't think so... certainly not compared to most of my friends.'

'Have you had sexual relations with more than three men in your life?'

I looked across at him sitting behind his desk and almost laughed.

'Are you kidding? I'm 38 and only recently married the man I want to be with for the rest of my life. I'm afraid I was a wee bit more adventurous than only knowing three men before I settled down with him.'

'Well,' he smiled and said, 'Medically, you are considered promiscuous.'

I couldn't believe it. These 'considerations' had to have been decided by men. Nevertheless, he accepted the challenge and became my consultant. After an exploratory tiny intervention with a camera entering via my belly button which explored the interior organs essential for procreation, he announced the necessity for an operation. Some parts were not correctly positioned, others were damaged. It was physically impossible for me to become pregnant and he would put everything to right.

The operation, even to his surprise, took over three hours. When the anaesthetic wore off, he delighted in telling me the details of his corrections which I will not transmit here in consideration of the squeamish nature that some male readers may possess. Suffice it to say, I was told, 'You are now perfect. Everything is in good order.'

After eight days of recuperation in the hospital, he sent me home to Bill with these instructions: 'You probably won't feel like doing it but you must let him do it to you... as often as he wants to.'

I followed his instructions but, still, nothing happened.

I went back to see him. Now we were advised to practice abstention.

'You must not allow him near you. Keep him away for at least two weeks,' and then he added in a serious tone, 'Do you need a gun?' It was said in such a way that one could have thought it was just another service provided by the National Health. He seemed prepared to write out the prescription there and then. I saw myself walking into a pharmacy and walking out again carrying a pistol.

Professor Craft was a delightful character. There was further treatment I could undergo but it entailed the latest scientific interventions which had little to do with nature and I preferred that my child would be conceived by the biological channels that were meant for this process. That was my opinion and if it couldn't happen naturally, it was not meant to be for me. I sometimes wonder if it was not also my brother, Peter's, condition that had a subconscious effect on this decision.

The question of adoption came up but Bill was not enthusiastic. He was already the father of two children. His need was not as great as mine to give affection to a new little soul. The process of adopting a child has to be entered into passionately by both parties. If not, it can make an unendurable stress on the marriage. Many loving partnerships have foundered on that particular rock.

In my late thirties, I began to have the distinct feeling my career was slowing down. The starring parts I'd been used to turned into cameos until a project called *Mog* was proposed to me. The storyline for this comedy series was based on Peter Tinniswood's book of the same title. The scripts were written by the expert comedy duo Dick Clement and Ian La Frenais. I had not seen them since the filming of their version of *The Prisoner of Zenda*. I was invited to participate in the pilot playing the part of a Danish psychiatrist. Billy Connelly was to have the title role of a petty thief who seeks asylum from the police by hiding in an asylum for the mildly insane. He was the 'eccentric' who organized the other inmates in rebellion against the clinic's rules and especially against the psychiatrist Mrs Mortensen's dictatorial methods of therapy. The idea was brilliant and Billy Connelly as the chief instigator of mischief was inspired casting. It was a Witzend production for Central TV with Tony Charles producing. Tony was the friend who had tempted me into joining him at ICM when he had become an agent. He, too eventually left the agency to become a producer for Witzend.

We rehearsed for the pilot in London. Billy was charming and very easily amused. He was generous with his compliments and we were quite proud of ourselves when we made him laugh but there was a wee problem: with Billy's fertile comic mind, he found it difficult to stay on script. I had the feeling it was the first time he was expected to remain within the constraints of material written by someone else. He had not trained as an actor and was a newcomer to this form of discipline. His ad-libs were delightful but not conducive to the rigid structure required for saying dialogue correctly for his fellow actors to respond to while being in the right position in front of whichever designated camera that would be gliding amongst the studio sets to photograph the scene.

The pilot was shot in Central TV's Birmingham studios. The cast consisted of Billy, Tim Wylton, Alan Shearman and Burt Kwouk as the crazies, Abigail Cruttenden as my daughter, and yours truly. When finished, the pilot has to show that the project is commercially worthwhile.

It is, sometimes, shown separately as a teaser for the forthcoming series or becomes the first episode. In this case, the pilot was not even finished. We had overrun the time allotted and, as time is money, especially in this profession, the proverbial plugs were pulled. Witzend was left with an incomplete product. Nevertheless, there must have been enough to show the value of the project because Central TV agreed to go ahead with it. *Mog* went into production for 13 episodes but there was some re-casting. Billy Connelly was absent for our first read through. In his place was the actor, Enn Reitel, famous for voicing various characters in the very popular current affair puppet miming show, *Spitting Image*. Burt Kwouk was also missing. He was replaced by the Black actor, Malcolm Frederick.

I'm sure the recasting had little to do with lack of talent. Billy would go on to do wonderful work in TV and films and Burt continued to enjoy a career.

I have fond memories of those six months doing *Mog*. Once again, the cast became good friends. We were like a little club enjoying our train journeys from London to Birmingham for the recordings. Enn, at that time, was into thoroughbreds. He owned a horse and kept the animal in a racing stable near to the course at Epsom. Unbeknownst to the producer and what would have been to his horror, Enn and I went riding, he on his and I on a borrowed thoroughbred. We galloped wildly across the downs. It is something which is strictly forbidden when having signed a contract as insurances do not cover dangerous sports and flying in private airplanes. It's just as well PCW was no longer in my life.

The director of the series was a young man called Nick Phillips. As he was the youngster in our group, I had the feeling he was slightly in awe of us. I'm not sure how many comedy programmes he'd made before but he was very grateful for all the suggestions Enn and the rest of the cast liberally donated to help with the direction. *Mog* was shown on an ITV channel and attracted a sort of cult following amongst teenagers. It was never repeated and other than in the memories of those young fans it disappeared into the depths of the unsuccessful TV programme graveyard.

I have one outstanding memory, though, which has nothing to do with the actual making of *Mog*. After finishing a recording in the evening, a few of us caught the train back to London the following morning. Malcolm was with us and with the return tickets in our palms, we crossed

Birmingham station towards the platform where our train was waiting. It was the first time I witnessed 'stop and search' by the police. Malcolm had wandered off from our nucleus and was approached by two Bobbies who began asking him questions. Noticing he was absent from our group, I turned around to look for him. He was only a few yards away and the two policemen seemed to be harassing him. Malcolm's eyes were cast down to the floor and he had an expression, not so much of fear, but intimidation which was not his normal demeanour. Walking up to him, I called out his name and said something to the effect that we were waiting for him and we'd miss the train. It was said more to convince the coppers that he had a legitimate reason for being there and it worked. The two men looked at me, nodded to him and walked away. Malcolm was fuming as we hurried to the platform. I had nothing to do with his being stopped, and yet, I couldn't help but apologize.

'Don't worry about it,' he replied. 'I'm Black. I'm used to it.'

Up until then, I'd had no idea how precarious life could be, even in what I'd always considered liberal Britain, if one was a man and Black, which is, after all, just an accident of birth.

CHAPTER XXII

I don't know if an astrologist could have ever predicted the importance the year 1989 would hold for me, how the events within that year would affect me emotionally, affect my career and, eventually, instigate a monumental decision which would entirely change Bill's and my future.

In the previous year, Bill had directed the second series of *Wish me Luck* for London Weekend Television. The stories related events of the British covert involvement within the French resistance movement against the Nazis in the Second World War. It was a great success and the Producer, Michael Chaplin agreed to tackle a third series of episodes, with Bill directing, based on the daring women agents from SOE who worked undercover in dangerous circumstances in the very territories commanded by the German military. There was a good role that Bill thought was correct for me. The part was of a French speaking British agent who has been sent to France to replace the leader within an SOE nucleus. However, she is guarding a dangerous secret from her past.

These stories took place in the mountainous area above Grenoble called the Vercors. With only just a little theatrical tweaking, the episodes were based on real, tragic events. I had not yet read all of the scripts so I packed them in my suitcase to read when seeing my mother in Munich from where we would travel on a pre-arranged trip to Budapest.

Since our daring escape when I was a four year old child, this would be the first time I'd put my feet back on Hungarian soil. It was my mother's idea, even though she had vowed to herself never to return while a Communist government was still in existence. Two years previously, her sister Chibby had passed away at the age of 74. Mommy had not attended the funeral and this weighed heavily on her conscience. It was not the only reason for the visit. I was now of an age that I wanted to return to the country of my birth to discover my roots. It would be, after all, the first time I would not be an alien in a foreign land and what better way to savour this experience than with the one who gave birth to me.

Mommy arranged for us to borrow a car which, of course, I would drive. She also contacted an old friend, Istvan, who had an apartment in the centre of Budapest. He would be our host. When we arrived, he welcomed us to his flat, thrust a drink in our hands, showed us the facilities, entrusted a set of keys to us, warned us to replace any object we used to its exact spot, picked up his white walking stick and bade us farewell until later when he'd collect us to take us out for dinner. Istvan was blind and gave us a new interpretation to the word, 'hospitality'. Because the flat was quite small, he thought it best to leave it to us and move himself into a friend's flat. She, in her turn, moved herself to hospital for the duration.

Istvan accompanied us through the markets, streets and squares pointing out the well-known sights. It felt surreal to have a man with a white stick which he'd wave around to signal my attention and then point it towards whatever monument or church was of specific interest. While walking together down a particular street, he told me to look up to a sign. It read Paul Teleki *uza,* a gesture the Communists had made to honour the Minister President who had committed suicide rather than act as a puppet of the Fascist regime. Istvan always knew exactly where he was. His knowledge of every square metre of the city he inhabited impressed me. He loved Budapest. It was the reason he never sought asylum in the West, even though, he could have survived as he spoke several languages.

I learned that he was not born blind. The city was too remarkable to forget. It had burnt itself into his imagination allowing him to continue to see it through his blind eyes. It was on that form of blindness I had based my performance as Suzy in *Wait Until Dark* ten years previously.

On those occasions when Mommy and I walked down the boulevards and pavements on our own, we made our way with arms around each other's waists. She used a cane having undergone a hip replacement. When I received the call from a friend in Munich to tell me she had fallen down in the flat hurrying to answer the telephone, I burst out crying. She had broken her femur and would need an operation. It was to take place the following morning and I promised to be there afterwards.

The thought of my mother who had been the dominant female in our relationship, the one who could be a monster, a dragon but who was *y* monster, *my* dragon, and to imagine her reduced was abhorrent to me.

The friend who told her I was coming as soon as I could mentioned my tears. It was the knowledge of this spontaneous reaction which helped to soften the opinions we held of each other. It was proof for her that I genuinely loved her. That was all she seemed to need to mellow towards me and hold me in some respect which, in turn, allowed me to feel as an equal and treat her like my closest confidante rather than a domineering mother.

I drove us to what used to be the family chateau, a baroque edifice on the edge of the Danube north of Budapest in a little village called Szob. The chateau had been confiscated by the Communists and was now being used as an orphanage. Its directors had been notified of our visit and we were met by a young girl, perhaps 12 years of age whose task it was to be our guide. We were shown into an elegant reception room/ salon with a magnificent fireplace. The walls were bare, painted light blue and there were a few decrepit arm chairs and little sofas scattered about but the intricate carving of the frieze which surrounded the ceiling was enough to remind one of the room's glorious past. I asked Mommy how she felt being back here.

'Nothing,' was her reply.

'You don't see yourself and your family sitting there in front of the fire? You don't remember the furniture, the paintings, the curtains that the cat climbed up disguised as your mother's pug?'

'No.' She looked around the room and said, 'I see nothing.'

Mommy was so indifferent that tears welled up in my eyes. I was compensating for this momentous experience which required a deep emotional response. I behaved as I thought she should have felt. We were then taken into the back garden which sloped down to the river. A magnificent white stone staircase curved out of tall french windows to descend gracefully to the lawn. I took a photograph of the young girl and my mother standing together on the bottom of the steps. There but for history's capricious moments, the girl could have been me with my mother many years before.

We thanked everyone for their understanding, and left the chateau. Our next place to visit was the church, a beautiful, golden baroque structure which had been built with contributions from my grandmother's ancestors, the Lützenbachers. In the adjoining cemetery, was the elaborate, neo gothic family crypt. We went down into its gloomy interior where the coffins were enclosed into the stone walls with the names engraved on plaques of the persons resting behind them. Chibby's was the last to have been added on a stone slab. That is when my mother broke down. It had taken 40 years for her to make this pilgrimage and now she stood weeping amongst the ghosts of her family. I crept silently back up the stairs leaving her in solitude to grieve.

We later went to Zébégèn where Chibby had been lodged with the family known to my mother from her youth and visited their little peasant house. Mommy cried again when we were shown the room with its dirt floor where her sister had lived after her long incarceration until her death. Once again, only the vagaries of history determined that one sister would succeed and be comfortable while the other, through no fault of her own, suffered the consequences of a misguided political philosophy. The chateau had left her cold. I was surprised that my mother, who was normally extra sentimental would be crying more from guilt than her memories.

I then asked her to show me that part of Zébégèn where she had been called *Alma Rosza* (Apple Rose). I'd listened, enchanted, when I was a young girl to her stories of a certain Countess Karoly who was worshiped like a queen within the village. She owned much land and an entire street with painted little peasant cottages which bordered on both sides of it. Colourful flowers burst from their window sills and, inside, the wood work was painted with gay geometric designs or plants. This Hungarian passion to paint wood is something I unconsciously inherited. At any one time these little houses were occupied by the children of her aristocratic friends whom she welcomed, tutored and nourished. For most of them it was considered their summer holiday.

At the age of 16, Mommy had an argument with her parents. They had returned from a spell in a sanatorium where they had sought refuge suffering from a 'delicate state of nerves' as my mother described it. This was the direct result of the 1929 financial crisis when her father's attempt at banking had turned into a disaster and he had lost his wife's fortune.

During their absence, Mommy had taken it upon herself to sell the family carriage along with the two splendid horses who drew it in order to survive. With the proceeds, she bought a heavy working horse and a plough. Discovering at the local registry office that a largish field not far from the Chateau, actually belonged to the family, she sowed it with corn. The surrounding farmers were amazed that this young countess with the help of her maid was not afraid to, literally, soil her hands with earth. They helped her to take the harvest to the market and, so, her efforts bore fruit.

When her parents came back, instead of being proud of her initiative, they were furious. Mommy ran away and walked the kilometres from the Chateau in Szob to Zébégèn where she was welcomed in Countess

Karoly's embrace and allowed to remain once the Countess had notified her parents of the well-being of their daughter.

No-one in this little fantastical enclave was allowed to be called by their actual name and never were their titles to be mentioned. As her charges were integrated with the village children, played and were taught with them, she did not want to differentiate between their status. All the boys were given the names of trees and the girls, flowers. That is why Mommy was called 'Apple Rose'. The Countess, herself, was known as *Napraforgó* (sunflower) and she was their bountiful fairy queen.

In order to suppress those hormonal surges which were only natural in adolescence and especially with the close proximity and interaction of both sexes, the Countess imposed strenuous physical activity. The Hungarians bred small horses that looked like miniature thoroughbreds. These were put at the disposal of the children under her guardianship. They had to look after them and those who couldn't ride were taught by her. It was during this time that my mother became an excellent horsewoman.

The children were also given canoes to paddle on the Danube and would be met at a pre-set destination some kilometres later down the river where a picnic awaited them. It was never an ordinary one. These picnics were served on a linen covered trestle table with porcelain plates and silver cutlery. The Countess would have arrived with two of her servants in her Rolls Royce to set up the dining facilities. She insisted on the best of manners and propriety.

Life-long friendships were established here. Mommy befriended two sisters, the countesses Apponyi, Geraldine and Virginia. The latter became my Godmother. The former married Zog and became the Queen of Albania. Moncika, a girl from the village that my mother had played with, was the grown-up woman who would later look after Chibby in her home.

A little ceremony took place to welcome my mother back. It was organized by Moncika. All the villagers came out to greet her. She was presented with a bouquet of apple roses. Again, she did not cry but, I, when taking the photographs could hardly focus because of my tears.

Back in Budapest, I admired the graceful bridges which spanned the Danube linking ancient Buda to Pest. We crossed the river to visit the palace that dominates the hill in Buda overlooking the Danube opposite the parliament built on the banks of Pest. The elaborate structure reminded me very much of our parliament buildings in London.

We walked outside in the gardens and at one point my mother asked an elderly grounds man which was the window of the office where Paul Teleki had shot himself. 'Why do you ask that?' he said, amazed.

'Because he was my uncle and I haven't been here for many years.'

I couldn't believe my eyes when I saw this man drop onto one knee, take my mother's hand and kiss it saying he was honoured to meet a relative of the great man. It was a gesture one would not normally see today.

There is a spurious saying: if you have a Hungarian for a friend, you don't need an enemy. I don't know where it originated but I can swear to you now, it's not true. I admired the Hungarians I came across and from what I experienced, it would not be possible for them to be deceitful. They are too open, too spontaneous. They cannot hide behind a veil of sham. You may not agree with what you hear but they're not afraid to say it out loud.

Perhaps that had been the problem between my mother and me. She could not help but be herself even when she knew her behaviour may have been hurtful. I had inherited a side of my father's Schell genes which made me more reticent to speak my mind. It took a major incident, usually concerning the well-being of someone else to make me shout.

The Budapest experience brought us close together. We arrived back in Munich and shortly afterwards I kissed her goodbye to return to London. A friend picked me up to take me to the airport. Mommy stood on the balcony, waving to me, eyes red, big fat tears sliding down her cheeks. It was the last time I saw her standing on her two legs without assistance.

I'd found the time to read the scripts in Budapest and there was no doubt that I was eager to do the programme. Working with Bill was, sometimes, difficult for me. I didn't always know if I was accepted by my colleagues as an actress capable of doing the part or someone lucky enough to be the wife of the director. I needn't have worried on this occasion. Bill had a stable of actors with whom he worked frequently. On the whole they had all become friends, so I was completely at ease with my fellow cast members on this job. Bill's filming was considered more of a family get-together than work. Perhaps that is why the end result of his programmes showed an intimacy between the actors which could not have been faked. Their interplaying was real and believable.

As these stories depicted the tragic betrayal of the Vercors *Maquis* (The French Resistance) by the allies in 1944, most of the location shoot took place on its high plateaus. Grenoble, which had hosted the German military during the war, featured strongly in the stories but we had a problem. It had become too modern, its buildings richly renovated and its streets carried gleaming rail tracks upon which silent, state of the art trams smoothly glided. We had to find another French city which had not benefited from that particular facelift.

The French production/location manager chose the little city of Le Puy-en-Velay, the capital of the Haute-Loire, a department in the region of the Auvergne, famous for its range of extinct volcanoes.

In 1989 the Haute-Loire was underpopulated and its capital, not wealthy. It was exactly what the camera man needed. Tall, narrow buildings with neglected facades clung together, leaning over on both sides of cobbled streets. Old fashioned shop fronts with fading paintwork lined the narrow lanes. The production found all the views it needed to maintain the effect of a city during the Second World War. Swastika flags could hang out from windows of the *Hotel de Ville* (Town Hall) without any alterations to the square where it stood or the building itself. It was as if parts of Le Puy were in a time capsule. For our purposes, it was ideal.

We spent two weeks in that charming city, established in pre-medieval times in a volcanic crater. The narrow, needle-like peaks called chimneys which spout upwards from its basin were formed millions of years ago from cooling lava. Most wore a religious monument at their summit: a chapel, a saint or the spectacular, tall terracotta Virgin. I had heard that the architect who designed the virgin committed suicide by leaping from her crown because he had placed the Christ Child she is holding against the incorrect breast. I don't know if this is true. I'd been to many exotic cities in my life but little Le Puy was the most extraordinary.

It was not surprising that, on a day off with three others from the cast, a journey of discovery was planned. Jeremy Nicholas would be our guide, Bryan Pringle, Sid Livingston and I would follow. Jeremy had decided La Chaise-Dieu, 40 kilometres from Le Puy would be our destination. We were to visit a medieval abbey in the heart of the town which had become famous for hosting classical concerts within its hallowed walls, all due to a fellow Hungarian, a renowned pianist called Cziffra. Years before, he had visited the abbey and deplored the decrepit state of the building and, most of all, the debased, magnificent organ. The concerts were to engender the finances for the reparations required. The music festival which took place towards the end of August every year became world renowned. Stars from every continent came to sing and perform with international orchestras for little money out of respect for the well admired Cziffra.

It was en route to La Chaise-Dieu that I really fell in love with the Haute-Loire. All of us in the car marvelled at its unique scenery. We drove along the Casadéen plateau from which we could see the rounded shapes of the blue volcanoes nestling in the distance. Since Africa, I had never seen such vast horizons. The verges on either side of the road were brilliant with wild flowers and patchwork fields lapped like a sea on the shore of dark green forests of pine. I was transfixed with admiration.

On arrival, we chose to sit outside of a café opposite the Abbey's western facade before attempting to scale the steep steps leading to its Gothic entrance. By the time we found our courage, and arrived out of breath, it was too late. The door shut in our faces. It was exactly midday and, obviously in France, God goes out to lunch. We decided to do the same, to find a restaurant in the countryside nearby and return at two pm.

Outside of La Chaise-Dieu, we followed a little winding road which descended through the forests and came upon a tiny hamlet called Bonneval. Small as it was, it still boasted a church, a *mairie* (town hall) and a restaurant with a large terrace and a view of an enchanting valley.

We had a meal and after finishing were invited by the *aubergist* who had been practicing his atrocious English on us to have a game of *pétanque*. It was while waiting for my turn to play that I discovered, just below the terrace's walls, a little hovel with a handwritten note attached to one of its closed and battered shutters reading, '*à vendre*' (for sale). Two days later, when Bill had some time free, we returned to Bonneval.

The *aubergist* had been busy on our behalf. He had gathered the relatives concerned for the sale of the house who had opened the shutters and doors to give us a guided tour. The property was far larger than I had first perceived. It was built into a hillside. The structure on the southern slope was four stories high. It also consisted of two vast wagon and hay barns with their earthen floor stables beneath. Everything was in a terrible state of repair. As I walked through its interior my feet were getting colder and colder which had nothing to do with the temperature. It would take a large amount of money to renew the roof and electricity, modernize the plumbing, install a loo in a more convenient place (as the existing one was in the barn) and create a room where one could bathe or shower. All of the worm-eaten floors and ceilings had to be destroyed and renewed. The required renovations were beyond our budget. We were inheriting only the walls and the openings. Every window and door had to be replaced and yet, as we finished our tour and walked outside, Bill said, 'We'll buy it,' all because the faded name 'Valentin' was painted on the crumbling façade. His great grandfather, grandfather, uncle and brother all carried that name and he fancied the idea of being called Monsieur Valentin. We purchased the house and the rest is history.

Wish me Luck was finished sometime in September. In October, I received a devastating phone call. My mother had been knocked down by a fast moving car. She had been waiting at a traffic light. Seeing the image for pedestrians turn green, she moved into the road when a young female driver who had only recently obtained her permit jumped the light. Mommy was thrust onto the bonnet and against the windscreen. The young woman slammed on the breaks causing my mother to be thrown onto the hard tarmac suffering multiple fractures. I flew out to Munich and saw her in the hospital. She was wishing she had died. Mommy had always been convinced she would not reach the age of 75. Her parents, her sisters and brother had all succumbed before attaining that age. I used to argue with her that, at least, Chibby who had gone to 74 proved there were longevity genes in the family. If one took into consideration her cruel incarceration, the fact that she smoked sixty of the worst brand of cheap, non-filtered cigarettes made of God-knows-what junk tobacco, that she drank a bottle of fifty percent proof *schnapps* a day and managed to live over two decades on a damp mud floor had to prove she had a miracle constitution.

As it was, Mommy celebrated her 75th birthday on November 11th of that year. She was eventually able to move back into the flat and found a young woman from Czechoslovakia to live with her. Watching her move upright was painful. Our lawyer fought the guilty woman's insurance lawyers for compensation. He was not up to the task. They walked all over him and Mommy received an insulting 40,000 Deutschmarks – less than £15,000 for the suffering she would endure for the rest of her life. Complications ensued. In 1996 Paul and I managed to place her into a retirement home which was paid for by her pension and kind contributions from her wealthy German friends. One has to be able to walk into such an establishment. It is one of the stipulations. What happens thereafter does not have an effect on continued occupancy. We managed to move her with a few bits of furniture, some paintings and framed photographs of Daddy, Peter, Paul and myself. We were aware she had circulatory problems in her legs. The fact that she continued to smoke and the enforced lack of exercise didn't help. Mommy had been used to walking for a half a kilometre up a steep hill two to three times a week. It was in the little village at the top where she did her shopping and it was during the return from one of these excursions that the accident occurred. Only a few months after arriving at the home, she was made to enter hospital for an amputation. She lost her left leg from just above the knee rendering her completely bed-ridden. Thanks to her many friends in Munich she was not allowed to feel lonely. I visited as often as I could and took her out to cafés or the local *gasthaus* in a wheelchair where, if weather permitting, she could sit outside and watch the world go by. We talked, reminisced and joked. We indulged our Hungarian natures, laughing loudly and weeping unashamedly. I lost my much tamed dragon in February 1998 but I still feel her in the ether that surrounds me. Whatever one's beliefs, I like to think she has joined Daddy and Peter. Heaven, beware!

The early Nineties were, on the whole, a desert as far as work was concerned, with only an occasional oasis to keep us nourished. Bill was offered a series of TV films on the works of Edgar Allan Poe's short stories which were filmed in Zagreb. The Yugoslavian wars were not yet completely over but, other than a few of Croatia's own fighter jets scratching the skies above the capital, the city was peaceful. I flew out separately to play a part in one of the stories and on landing at Zagreb's airport, saw a stream of blue helmeted baby soldiers, the UN's peace keeping force, flowing out of a huge fat-bellied airplane and along the tarmac to the terminal buildings. They were in full combat kit but, to me, they were carrying what looked like toy rifles.

Halfway through the project, the producer was having financial problems. Bill heard that some of the actors had not been paid and stopped the shoot. We were soon on a return flight to London. With the intervention of our union, Equity, everyone eventually received their fees but some people had to borrow money to survive which included us.

A while later, Bill found himself directing episodes of the popular London soap, *East Enders*. It was, what one would call, a cushy job. He could do it effortlessly but it was a waste of his incredible talent. This was a sign of the times: there was very little classical drama being made but we were grateful for the regular income.

I was asked to attend an interview sometime in 1993 with an Italian film director/producer. The subject of the film was a loosely based remake of *Roman Holiday* which had starred a young Audrey Hepburn. The plot was a romantic comedy of a fictional European principality which was being threatened with bankruptcy. The ruler had a beautiful daughter that he hoped to marry off, regardless of her desires, for a considerable amount of money which would avoid the necessity of selling the Royal Palace to American developers as a casino complex. I would be co-starring with David Warner and Susannah York. The young princess was played by a pretty unknown blonde called Barbara Snellenburg. I mention this job because it was, truly, the last time that I was allowed to remember the taste of bygone glamour. The director, Carlo Vanzina, was a soft spoken, gentle soul. It's very rare that during the making of a film one's expenses are upgraded. The shooting took place in Austria. The British actors stayed in Vienna's Hilton Hotel... a very reasonable hotel, and yet, Carlo decided it was not good enough for us. We were moved to a charmingly elegant, intimate hotel outside of Vienna on the banks of the Danube. Our rooms were exquisitely decorated with antique furniture and *objets d'art* I admired but was afraid to touch. At the end of a day's work, David, Susan and I would have dinner in the five star restaurant. Carlo, almost always, joined us. We were not allowed to pay for anything. As this generosity was so unusual, we actors, invented a scenario: the film was being financed by laundering money for the Mafia. When the film, which I never saw, was released it had the title, *Piccolo Grande Amore*. Carlo went on to do many other films, far beyond the laundering capability of Mafia resources. He was just incredibly generous.

Back in London, I was offered theatre work but it was not enough to continue paying the mortgage on the flat and our London expenses. When Bill's contract at *East Enders* was not renewed, it was time to think of a plan. The house in Bonneval with its adjoining barns was a huge property. It could, if completely renovated, have 300 square metres of living space. We could imagine several bedrooms with bathrooms *en suite,* a large dining room and a second kitchen. There were distinct possibilities to make something like a guest house. But were we prepared to do that?

The last job that I did on British soil was a television mini-series called *The Wimbledon Poisoner*. It was during the making of this that convinced me to turn my back on the business. I'd become used to doing cameos. As a matter of fact, I quite enjoyed them. They gave me an opportunity to play roles for which I was not typecast. But to be reduced to playing no more than a glorified extra was too humiliating. The director Robert Young, who had been a close friend, was astonished that I accepted the job. The part was so inconsequential that the casting director was left in charge, rather than disturb Robert with making decisions for such unimportant roles.

'I wouldn't have dared offer you such a nothing part,' was what he said when we met on the set.

My reply was, 'I have to earn money. There was nothing else on the horizon.'

'Well, now you're with us, I'll give you lots of close-ups.'

Dream on.

I belonged to a group of couples who lived near to Wimbledon Common. We were seen rushing back and forth at night over the fields either chasing or running away from whom we presumed to be a murderer. Every now and again, we came to a stop and a camera photographed our expressions: horror, confusion, anticipation, fear... whatever.

Unfortunately, I, literally, had to hold my ground to just be part of a two-shot. The man who played my husband was larger, heavier and had very strong elbows. All of our appearances on camera were supposed to be together and he tried to push me out of them. I could have mentioned it to Robert but I felt it was my battle. The silly man should have known that with a face like his photographed with mine, I didn't have a chance. Who would your eyes have been attracted to? A middle aged fading beauty or the humanoid equivalent of a toad?

It was this experience and what was happening to Bill which convinced me we had to sell up in London and commit ourselves to another future in France. The vodka tonics and red wine were appearing earlier every day. He was consoling himself for the lack of recognition of his well established talent. There was a new generation of programme makers and too many of those were interested more in the lucrative returns from 'reality' shows. Less and less drama was being produced. We were becoming dinosaurs. He and I needed another project – produced, directed, designed, and starring the both of us.

The flat was sold and a date for the removal company established. We held a house-cooling party a week before our departure to say our farewells to our friends. Many tears were shed as people called out the toast, 'To the end of an era!' and emptied their glasses.

In order to keep the price of the move as low as possible, I decided to pack many of our belongings in the crates the company provided. Bill helped a bit, mainly with the huge collection of hard-back books which we didn't want to leave behind. I wrapped the more fragile objects and while doing that in the kitchen, folding bubble wrap over glasses and plates that I looked out of the window and cried.

I had counted the years I'd been in the profession, 31 in all and it seemed to have abandoned me. At the same time I knew that was not true. It was my fault. I was to blame. I had not heeded Géza von Radványi's advice all those years ago in Munich after my performance as Gwendolen in *The Importance of Being Earnest*. I did not forsake everything for my career. My devotion to acting did not go deep enough. It was a profession, one I was fortunate to practice to the best of my abilities but it always remained just a job, a means to an end affording me to lead my life and to love my man. It had never been an all-consuming passion and that's what the profession requires if you want to continue well into your dotage.

The removal men with their lorry arrived on January 29th. Bill and I left England on the overnight ferry from Portsmouth to Le Havre. We would arrive early afternoon on January 30th in Bonneval.

My father, at the age of 50, arranged our escape from Hungary on January 31st, 1949. He was courageous enough to envision for us a better future. I followed his example. Almost to the day and also at the age of 50, I left all I knew behind to seek a new life in another world. Bill was with me and I was not afraid.

ACKNOWLEDGEMENTS

I'd like to mention my gratitude to all the owners of the many café/bars where I spread my notebooks and dictionaries across their tables while writing this book, especially *Le Cézanne* in Craponne owned by Bruno and Annik who protected me from the overtly curious and allowed me to concentrate without being disturbed while discreetly refilling my glass with *un petit rosé.*